Jill

Jill

A BIOGRAPHY OF

THE FIRST LADY

Julie Pace

Darlene Superville

with Evelyn M. Duffy

Little, Brown and Company

New York   Boston   London

Little, Brown and Company
Hachette Book Group
1290 Avenue of the Americas, New York, NY 10104
littlebrown.com

First Edition: April 2022

Little, Brown and Company is a division of Hachette Book Group, Inc. The Little, Brown name and logo are trademarks of Hachette Book Group, Inc.

The publisher is not responsible for websites (or their content) that are not owned by the publisher.

The Hachette Speakers Bureau provides a wide range of authors for speaking events. To find out more, go to hachettespeakersbureau.com or call (866) 376-6591.

ISBN 9780316377508
LCCN 2021950785

Printing 1, 2022

LSC-C

Printed in the United States of America

To our parents: James and Diane Pace, and Leslie and Vidda Superville

Contents

Contents

Contents

Contents

There are no requirements of the job...You do what makes your heart sing.

—*Lady Bird Johnson on being first lady*

Authors' Note:

Dr. Jill Biden sat with the authors for three interviews in September 2021. We thank her for her time and candor. We interviewed many others, including family members, friends, and colleagues, both on background and on the record.

Jill

Introduction

As a teacher for more than thirty years, Dr. Jill Biden had long been accustomed to waking up in the dark—but this was something else entirely.

She heard the whistle of the 5:20 a.m. Northeast Regional train break the still air as it sped by her home in Wilmington, Delaware. The winter of 2017 felt especially cold and dark. After eight years at the highest levels of the US government, Joe and Jill Biden had left Washington behind. Donald Trump was now in the White House, and the nineteenth-century mansion on the grounds of the Naval Observatory that had served as the Bidens' home during Joe's two terms as vice president was occupied by the new second family, Mike and Karen Pence.

But Jill continued teaching at a community college just outside Washington that had become a second home for her, a place where she could channel her passion for education and escape the political pressure cooker.

Teaching English classes at Northern Virginia Community College—which everyone called NOVA—now required a train ride, the same commute her husband had made for thirty-six years to his job in the Senate. Amtrak had renamed the station in Wilmington after Joe Biden five years earlier in recognition of the thousands of hours he'd spent commuting.

Teaching was about the only thing that could draw Jill back to Washington at the time. It was never a city she considered home, despite her husband's profession. She and the couple's three children had always lived in Wilmington, part of a close-knit community of family and friends. Jill had embraced her role as second lady, but Washington was also filled with difficult memories, most recently the loss of her son Beau to cancer.

From Wilmington, Jill would take the hour and a half ride to Washington's Union Station and then request an Uber for the nine-mile drive across the Potomac River, a trip that wound through areas of DC that mixed the grand and the grimy, past the Jefferson and Air Force memorials, and around the Pentagon to NOVA's Alexandria, Virginia, campus. It was only a twenty-minute ride on a good day, but Washington traffic was always bad in the mornings. She did the whole thing in reverse to get home later in the day. Despite the commitment she felt to her students, many of them immigrants and the first in their families to attend any type of college, the long commute was beginning to wear on her.

Jill's time as second lady had brought her great joy and meaningful work. She helped lead President Obama's proposal for free community college—an ambitious plan that ultimately went nowhere in Congress—cofounded an organization to support military families called Joining Forces with First Lady Michelle Obama, and had successfully taught at NOVA for all eight years.

Recent heartbreak had left Jill and Joe battered. Beau died in 2015 at forty-six of an aggressive brain cancer, leaving behind a wife and two young children. After a lengthy period of indecision following Beau's death, Joe had decided not to run for president in 2016; Hillary Clinton had run instead, and lost to Trump. Their younger son, Hunter, who had long struggled with drugs and alcohol, now seemed to find his life disintegrating into hard drug use, long disappearances, and a bitter, public divorce.

Returning to a more private life, Jill had to relearn its rhythms, of driving, of walking into a store without an ever-present entourage of staff and Secret Service agents. She had to learn new tools, like Uber and Venmo, to maneuver through the world.

In the past, she would have found the fun in all of that. She'd always been a gleeful and lifelong learner. But Beau's loss hung heavy over her every move. She wasn't just moving on—she was moving on without her son.

"Life just felt different," she said, looking back on that time during an interview in 2021. "You just can't lose a child and say, 'Oh now we'll go on.'"

Jill often turned on the early TV news as she got ready in the morning. The new administration was like nothing she had ever seen. She tried not to dwell on Trump's swift demolition of so much that Obama and her husband had built. She knew that any new president, Republican or Democrat, would have changed things done by their predecessors. She could only hope that Trump wouldn't be as bad as many feared.

Even with Joe out of politics for the first time in his adult life, they found new ways to serve. They were both devoted to cancer research. Joe met with scientists and experts; Jill with families and caregivers. They worked on establishing the Biden Foundation, which would fund initiatives on causes that had long been dear to the Bidens' hearts, like preventing violence against women and expanding access to college.

She was teaching, speaking, and starting work on a book. It was, Jill felt, a full life.

And she still had NOVA. She adored her students and was deeply invested in their future. The diverse and international backgrounds of her students had opened her eyes.

"I saw this whole world at NOVA," she said. "I just couldn't go back."

So she made the early Amtrak train her alarm clock, knowing by the time she reached Washington, the gloom of night would give way to brisk morning light. Life, in its unrelenting way, continued on.

As quickly as Jill tried to settle back into life outside of politics, politics pulled her back in. Her husband launched his third, and perhaps least anticipated, presidential campaign, successfully unseating Trump in November 2020, in the midst of a global pandemic and deep partisan divides.

Dr. Jill Biden assumed the role of first lady, decades later than she originally envisioned.

She arrived hardened, and at times jaded, by the harsh realities of American politics and the personal tragedies her family has endured in the public eye. Yet she also stepped into the White House as a symbol of resilience and relatability—a woman fiercely protective of her family and her passions and ambitions.

By choosing to keep her teaching position at NOVA while Joe occupied the Oval Office, Jill became the first first lady in American history to continue her career while in the White House. She spends her weeks crisscrossing the country, grading papers while she flies, and urging Americans to get vaccinated against COVID-19, or comforting those whose lives have been upended by natural disasters. Then she returns to Washington to teach her twice-weekly writing classes, where her students often refer to her simply as Dr. B. Jill taught virtually during the pandemic and returned to the classroom, masked like her students, for the fall 2021 semester.

Elected to public office at twenty-nine, Joe has been a senator, vice president, and president through tumultuous, historic times. In this book, we set out to learn what those years looked like from Jill's perspective.

Since Joe has taken office, Jill—like many first ladies before her—largely steers clear of active politicking and the heightened partisanship that has led millions of Americans to wrongly believe that her husband was not legitimately elected. Yet in private, she bemoans the corrosive nature of modern American politics, which has repeatedly put her family in the crosshairs.

She is, above all, a fiercely protective wife, mother, and grandmother.

Jill published a memoir, *Where the Light Enters*, in 2019, after her time in the Obama administration, but ours is the first book to capture her in her own words while serving as first lady.

———

First ladies have been a source of fascination to the American public since the nation's founding. They have been both beloved and vilified, idolized and scrutinized. They hold no formal office and carry no official mandate from voters. In modern American politics, they are expected to have weighty policy priorities, yet also know how to stay on the right side of the imaginary line that separates them from their elected husbands.

"The first lady, at least in my research, has not been reflective all the time of what's going on in society," said Myra Gutin, a communications professor at Rider University who studies first ladies. "Sometimes they're much more reflective of the time in which they were born."

Jill brings childhood values forged in the 1950s and 1960s, the experience of coming of age in the 1970s, a political life amid the culture wars of the 1980s and 1990s, and a Blue Star mother's experience of the post-9/11 era. Her past informs her perspective on the present and her role as one of the world's most prominent women. Her future, however, is deeply uncertain, interwoven with America's heightened polarization and political uncertainty, and the legacy of her husband's presidency. The present gives her one of the most prominent platforms in the world.

Chapter 1

Free Spirit

The summer after her junior year of high school, Jill Tracy Jacobs begged her parents for permission to relocate from Willow Grove, Pennsylvania, to work at the Jersey shore for a few months. When she got the okay, she and four girlfriends rented a house together and spent the summer in Ocean City.

It was 1968, and Jill was balancing the joys of youth with planning for the future. "When we were growing up, my parents didn't give us a lot of money—because they didn't have a lot of money to give us," she said. "We weren't spoiled in any way. So I realized early on that my parents could pay for college, but I would have to pick up a lot of the expenses."

Jill got a job at a restaurant owned by one of her grandmother's relatives called Chris' Seafood, a dockside spot on the bay just off the Ninth Street Bridge, with a distinctive green fiberglass roof that had beach balls and American flags hanging from its rafters. The strong scent of fish caught fresh daily by the restaurant's fleet of boats was ever-present.

Ocean City in those days was a small town whose full-time residents numbered only a few thousand. Recent construction of the New Jersey Turnpike, the Garden State Parkway, and the Atlantic City Expressway made it easy for tourists from Philadelphia and beyond to visit for a day or weekend.

The town welcomed tourists but had long adopted conservative, family-oriented laws like a ban on all public alcohol consumption and blue laws that kept businesses closed on Sundays.

The Ocean City boardwalk boasted Shriver's candy shop with its distinctive salt water taffy, Mack & Manco Pizza, and the amusement park rides at Gillian's Wonderland Pier. Author Gay Talese, who grew up in Ocean City, said, "It was never a fancy place. It's determinedly middle-class and conservative."

Jill's summer days went by languidly, filled with trips to the beach and walks on the boardwalk. Chris' fed the staff dinner promptly at four p.m. "Then we'd waitress like till I guess nine thirty, ten. And then I'd go home, change my clothes, and like everybody else, we'd go out to a party somewhere."

Jill didn't have a bank account, so each night she'd come home to the rental house smelling of seafood and empty the cash out of the pockets of her blue apron into a bedroom drawer. She saved nearly all she made.

The pockets of that blue apron also gave her a place to stash food. Sometimes she'd save a lobster tail from being thrown out by tucking it away to eat later. Jill and her friends enjoyed their freedom and the easygoing nature of the shore—full of nice weather, fellow young people, and not much to do besides work, stroll up and down the boardwalk, and lay on the beach. "We dated the lifeguards. We'd date the guys who worked at the restaurants who were the cooks and flipped the burgers and made the sandwiches, and it was fun." Occasionally she went out with a Marine she met in Ocean City.

It was a life removed from many of the worries the country was wrestling with in 1968. Racial tensions, war protests, the counterculture, and the women's movement did not intrude.

A lot of the guys were surfers, including one Jill dated who made the sandwiches at Bob's Grill. Jill decided to learn how to surf, buying a white board with a big butterfly on it. The sport didn't come naturally to her, but the swells in Ocean City were the right size for a novice.

For Jill, it was also a summer that deepened her connection to the beach and the ocean. As a child, she'd run through the sand, her blond hair flying behind her. As an adult, the beach became a destination for celebrations with friends and family or quiet walks during moments of despair. "I have always had that vivid picture all my life of her sitting on the edge of the water and making sandcastles and collecting shells and running up and down and laughing," her aunt Barbara Jacobs Hopkins said.

Chapter 2

Childhood in Hammonton

Jill was born in Hammonton, New Jersey, on June 3, 1951, the first of Bonny Jean and Donald Jacobs's five daughters. The Jacobses moved just over the state line to Hatboro, Pennsylvania, when Jill was a child, settling into a two-bedroom house that would quickly become crowded. Jill shared a bedroom with younger sisters Jan and Bonny. Three beds lined one wall and each girl had a dresser of their own. Her father worked at Hatboro Federal Savings & Loan.

The Jacobs family was part of a postwar population boom in Hatboro. Job opportunities in aviation manufacturing and a nearby naval air station drew many residents to the area. Hatboro was connected by train to Philadelphia and developed into a small commercial hub for the neighboring communities.

In the summertime, kids would pour out of all the houses to play outside. "You'd wake up, you'd eat your bowl of cereal, you'd run out the door, and you wouldn't come home until the streetlights went on," she recalled.

Her childhood was "really beautiful, idyllic," Jill said. She characterized it as a cocoon-like *Leave It to Beaver* type of upbringing—she explored the woods, played with dolls, and voraciously read Nancy Drew and Bobbsey Twins books. Jill played Spring in the kindergarten play, joined the Brownies, and was later a Girl Scout. "One of the things that my parents created was a very safe and secure environment. I never really worried about anything as a child."

Jill walked to school or rode her bike. "There were lots of houses, lots of kids." Jill and her friends played at each other's houses and in the woods. They played with dolls and played kickball and kick the can. She was never bored, and rarely watched TV. "There was just something going on all the time."

A highlight of the year was Halloween, when the Jacobs family would pull out a big cardboard box filled with costumes—a time capsule of sorts from holidays past. There was a bee costume, a scarecrow, a gypsy. Jill and her sisters would head out with their Acme grocery store paper bags and trick-or-treat around their neighborhood until late at night.

Jill grew up surrounded by a sprawling, but tight-knit, extended family—grandparents, aunts and uncles, cousins—who all lived nearby in Hammonton, where her parents had grown up.

Hammonton was an affluent farming town of about ten thousand people. It was especially known for its blueberries, but also grew peaches, strawberries, tomatoes, and grapes, which were often used to make homemade wine in the cellars of the area's Italian families. The town had several clothing factories that produced high-end men's suits, ladies' coats, and raincoats for the military. Pharmaceutical labs manufactured and packaged pills on huge assembly lines. The population was mostly white, with periodic influxes of ethnic diversity through seasonal farmhands from Philadelphia and Puerto Rico.

Jill's mother was raised on the more attractive side of town, where there were big homes with manicured lawns. Her father grew up on the other side of the railroad tracks that divided the city, which Jill described as "not the nicest part." Hammonton's cultural divide between Catholics and Protestants was deeper than that marked by the tracks. Each July, the Catholic festival of the Lady of Mount Carmel drew more than sixty thousand Italians to Hammonton, where they processed through the streets with statues of Mary, the mother of Jesus, and other saints.

Jill's father, Donald Jacobs, came from a blue-collar, immigrant family and had parents who worked at a furniture store and did home-care nursing. Donald left for Navy service in World War II at seventeen. As a signalman, he used flags, semaphores, and signal lights to communicate between ships, and transmitted Morse code with shuttered searchlights.

When he returned, he joined the eight million World War II veterans who received education or job training through the GI Bill, using it to go to business school in Philadelphia.

Hammonton's Bellevue Avenue, about a third of a mile long, was lined with restaurants, shops, and ice cream parlors frequented by the teenagers who drove up and down the main drag. Seeing friends for pizza and vanilla floats was the thing to do. Godfrey's Rexall Drugstore stood at one end of it. When Donald returned to Hammonton to work as a bank teller, he'd frequently stop in at Godfrey's.

There he met Bonny Jean Godfrey, who worked the soda fountain. Her parents, Harold and Mabel Godfrey, owned the store; Harold was a pharmacist and Mabel, whom the family called Ma, was a teacher. Against her parents' wishes, Bonny Jean and Donald fell in love. "They weren't quite the Montagues and Capulets," Jill later wrote, but something like them.

Howard and Mabel Godfrey were an unusual couple for the time in that both had gone to college, and they wanted their daughter to as well. They forbade her to see Donald, believing he wasn't good enough for their daughter and didn't come from a wealthy enough family. But unknown to the Godfreys, Bonny Jean and Donald had been secretly married for a year, eloping to Elkton, Maryland, and returning to live apart, before having a second, more public wedding that their families attended. Jill was born more than a year into the young couple's second marriage.

Donald and Bonny Jean and their growing family stayed close with both sets of grandparents. But Jill grew up highly aware that her mother's mother, Ma Godfrey, had a certain ambivalence toward her as the oldest grandchild, the glue that held Bonny Jean and Donald's marriage together.

"My mother's mother realized that there was no way she was ever going to get my parents to separate," Jill said. "I had sealed the deal, my birth."

Jill always felt there was an edge in Ma's voice when they spoke. All the grandchildren talked back at times, but Jill noticed she was the only one who got a beating. "Ma wasn't a warm woman, not with any of us girls, but her lack of affection seemed most pronounced with me," Jill wrote. It was a bitter dynamic. "We all just ended up sidestepping her anger."

Ma Godfrey never came around; she always believed that Donald wasn't good enough for her daughter. For the rest of their lives, Jill's maternal grandparents never found out about the elopement. "We all knew," Jill recalled. "It was like a family secret that we knew, but we could not tell my mother's parents."

In the face of that adversity, Jill saw her parents' marriage as the model for real love. "Give me a love like theirs," she prayed. "Give me a family of my own."

———

While their secret elopement showed a daring side to Donald and Bonny Jean, their home life after marrying hewed to tradition. Donald was a banker who would return from work in the evenings, settle into his chair, and read the newspaper. Bonny Jean was a stay-at-home mom, forging a close bond with her five daughters.

Every day, Jill would arrive home from school, come in the front door, and yell to her mom that she was home. "I can maybe remember twice in my life" that she wasn't there, Jill recalled. "She wanted to be a mom, and she did a great job."

Jill and her sisters Bonny and Jan were close in age; twins Kim and Kelly arrived when Jill was already in high school. There were the occasional fights between Jill and her sisters, but none of them had a contentious relationship with their mom. "We were all so close to my mother, every one of us," Jill recalled. She once pranked her mother with this note as a child:

> Dear Mom,
> I don't want to hurt your feelings, but I hate you.
>
> > Love,
> > Jill

As a banker, Donald got off work right at five p.m. Some of Jill's earliest memories are of waiting at the end of her street for his car. When he got there, she'd climb on his lap and he'd let her drive down the street to the house.

"I have all those really good memories of my father," Jill said, but "fathers now are more involved with their kids' lives."

"Don't disturb Daddy," Jill's mother would tell her.

They would watch Phillies games together on the black-and-white Philco TV.

On Sundays, her father would often take Jill and her sisters to the memorial for Hammonton's World War II veterans, erected less than a year after she was born. The gray obelisk is carved with a likeness of an eternal flame and the insignia of the Army, Navy, Air Force, and Marines, and bears the names of men from Hammonton who fought in the war. Donald and his daughters would polish the bronze plaques filled with names of war veterans, including his own. "A constant source of inspiration to the living men and women of this community," read the memorial.

Later Jill recalled, "It was a small thing that he could do—a communion with his brothers in arms, a way of honoring the bond that they had with each other and the sacrifice they made together."

Donald was proud of his service as a Navy signalman in the South Pacific, and proud of his country. He always had a flag on the front lawn, and took the girls to parades. There was, Jill said, "a lot of patriotism growing up."

Jill's Aunt Barbara was fourteen years older than Jill, and loved spending time with her eldest niece. "She was kind of my little sidekick," Barbara recalled. "She spent a lot of her years sitting on my hip because I would just tote her around and be with her, be close to her, talk to her." They became more like sisters.

When Barbara was eighteen, she decided to take four-year-old Jill on a field trip in the new car her brother Donald had just helped her pick out. She took Jill out to the Pine Barrens and they walked around the ruins of Batsto Village—wandering through the grounds, smelling the magnolias, looking at the stream, and taking pictures of the collection of buildings built around an ironworks dating to the mid-1700s. Barbara investigated the cemetery's old headstones, but Jill wouldn't get close.

On the way home Barbara made a wrong turn and got a little lost. There were no cell phones, no way to call home to tell Jill's parents they would be late.

"We got home and Jill's dad really yelled at me. We were gone such a long time," Barbara recalled. "He was so worried....He was worried about this little girl. Her dad was overprotective, that's for sure."

It was Aunt Barbara who helped spark Jill's love of education and her desire to be a teacher. After Barbara became a teacher, she would bring a young Jill to her classroom for visits.

———

Education, it turns out, would also become a bridge between Jill and Ma Godfrey, who had been a teacher for fifty years. Despite her lack of warmth toward Jill, she brought her granddaughter to her school as a girl, showing her the one-room schoolhouse where children were educated across multiple grades—one row for first grade, one for second, one for third, and so on. Jill sometimes would get to ring the brass bell that called the students to class.

Many of Ma's students came from poor homes and Jill recalled every year her grandmother distributing coats, gloves, and scarves to students who needed them and pushed them to do their best. She particularly enjoyed reading to her students, pushing Jill as well to develop a fondness for books.

"That grandmother taught me my love of reading, I have to say," Jill recalled. "She would give me a subscription to book clubs, and the *Weekly Reader*, I mean, all of that. Scholastic." Some of her favorites were Nancy Drew, Mary Poppins, *Old Yeller*, and *The Incredible Journey*.

Jill, along with her sisters, also sometimes attended services with Ma Godfrey at her Presbyterian church. Her parents weren't religious, but Jill found comfort in the dark wood and stained glass, and was touched by the music. "I loved listening to Ma sing the hymns in her strong alto," Jill recalled.

Still, the relationship between Jill and her maternal grandmother never warmed, and Ma Godfrey never stopped making clear her disappointment with the marriage that led to Jill's birth.

"You know, Jill, you're not a Godfrey, you're a Jacobs," she would say.

It didn't help that Jill took after her father in both looks and temperament. She had his family's blond hair and blue eyes, and was built more like him than her mother. Her sisters looked more like her mother, brownhaired and brown-eyed.

Chapter 3

Double-Dinner Sundays

Jill's relationship with her father's parents was the opposite. As the eldest granddaughter, and perhaps to make up for the chill on the other side of the family, Jill received royal treatment in the Jacobses' home. Her grandmother "just was so warm and loving and welcoming," Jill recalled. Jill would arrive at the house and her grandmother would rush down the steps, throw her arms around her, and kiss her.

As Donald moved through the ranks of local banks, the Jacobs family settled in Willow Grove, Pennsylvania, a leafy, middle-class suburb north of Philadelphia. The area was famous for Willow Grove Park, an upscale amusement park that drew Philadelphians out to the suburb by trolley and bus. "Up there where life is a lark, you bet, it's Willow Grove Park. Not far from Phil-a-delph-i-a, they're happy and gay," went its well-known jingle.

Though the Jacobses' house wasn't huge, it did afford the family of seven more space. Jill, now in fifth grade, finally had her own bedroom. A stream ran behind the house and quickly became a regular play area for the Jacobs girls and their extended family. "I always took a change of clothes because I knew for sure, without fail, that my kids were going to go into that stream and get all wet," Barbara recalled.

On Sundays, Jill and her family would make the hour-long drive from Willow Grove to Hammonton for dueling family dinners, one right after the other.

"The grandmothers would compete against each other," Jill remembered. "We'd drive through all the row homes in Philadelphia, over the Tacony–Palmyra Bridge, down the Black Horse Pike, and so I would stay with my father at his parents' house, only me, and then my sisters would stay with my mother's parents." She never slept at her other grandparents' house.

In the morning, a buzzer in her paternal grandparents' kitchen would ring upstairs to wake Jill and her dad. Jill would go down to the kitchen and take in the scents of Italian bread and coffee. Her grandpop would sit at the table beside the toaster, dunking his toast in his coffee while her grandma made oatmeal. Jill would duck under the toaster cord to make her way to the table, where a cream donut and cantaloupe—her favorites—awaited. "I was treated special, like I was special," Jill recalled.

The house was small and a little shabby, but it felt like home. Her grandparents kept photographs of Donald in his Navy uniform all over the house, and he once gave Jill his sailor cap while they were there.

Her grandfather loved to fish off the Seven Bridges Road. "My grandfather would come home with this big catch of fish," Jill said. "I don't mean like three. I mean like twenty. And all the fish would be all over the kitchen counters, all over the little back porch, all over the railing, on the back porch, these black shiny skins of black fish." Her grandmother swore at her husband in Italian—the only Italian she knew was curse words—as he covered all the surfaces of their home with fish. "Maledetto!"

Her grandmother usually wore a housedress and an apron, and black shoes that laced up. Her knee was wired together—a relic of a car accident on an icy night in her twenties that had killed a friend of hers—but Jill remembers the beauty that still radiated from her. "She just had beautiful skin."

It was in that tiny kitchen, with the washing machine sandwiched next to the fridge, that Jill's Grandma Jacobs taught her how to cook. They would go shopping at the grocery store right across the street, which became Bagliani's Food Market in 1959, for all the things they'd need for the evening. Bagliani's remains to this day a quintessential Italian market with old-world staples and fresh produce. Grandma Jacobs's family was Dutch and German, but after marrying Dominic—whose family name was changed from Giacoppa when his grandfather emigrated from Italy—she'd learned to "cook Italian like a champ," her daughter Barbara recalled.

She made her own noodles, "phenomenal chicken soup," and canned vegetables from her large garden.

There would be flour strewn all over the little kitchen table. "We'd be rolling out the dough for pasta and cutting it," Jill remembers. "And then she'd have the racks where we would put the noodles and the noodles would be drying. She'd be cooking braciole," a flat steak made with chopped-up boiled eggs, parsley, salt and pepper, and bread crumbs. "And then you roll it up and you put the toothpicks in and then string to tie it," and bake the rolled-up mixture in the oven with tomato sauce.

Braciole, meatballs, tomato sauce, handmade noodles — Grandmom Jacobs made it all, and she let Jill be a part of it.

"I could still picture Jill in the kitchen with my mom, laughing," Barbara said. "And I remember her rolling the pasta, cutting it up for the chicken soup."

The whole family would finally sit down to the meal together. "My mother would put out a feast for all of us to eat and laugh and talk, and it was a very warm and happy get-together," Barbara said.

After eating with the Jacobses, Jill's family would immediately head over to Ma Godfrey's house for a second dinner. The Godfreys' house, in contrast, was well-appointed and immaculate, with a perfect lawn and rose garden.

Ma Godfrey drew on her English Scottish heritage for Sunday dinner, serving roast beef with gravy, mashed potatoes, green beans, and homemade coleslaw, followed by cake for dessert. Dinner was always served on Lenox china with the good silverware.

The double dinners made for hectic, full Sundays, and usually ended in a stomachache for all the kids.

Chapter 4

Leader of the Pack

Jill's family tradition at Christmas was to make Christmas Eve the big night. After a pasta dinner and bedtime for the kids, her parents would decorate the tree and then wake Jill and her sisters at one or two in the morning.

"Santa's been here, Santa's been here," her parents would say.

Jill and her sisters rushed down the stairs and opened their gifts. Their exhausted parents soon headed off to sleep, and "we would pretend we were going to bed. But once they got in bed, I would wake up my sisters and we would go down and we would play with our toys like at three and four and five in the morning," Jill said.

Christmas Day was spent with their grandparents. Her grandmom Jacobs's house always had a small tree and stockings up. "No matter what else was in it, we always got the orange" in the toe of the stocking, she recalled, in remembrance of her grandparents' experiences in the Depression, when fruit was scarce.

Christmas, like Sundays, came with the two grandmothers fighting their battles through the preparation of two full, separate dinners. An Italian feast at the Jacobses' was followed by an American one at the Godfreys'.

Politics played little role in the Jacobses' family life. Donald and Bonny Jean were Republicans, but they rarely talked about politics with their daughters.

"I wasn't political, really, or I didn't really pay attention to politics that much," Jill said. "I wasn't really wrapped up in the current events. You know, I was typically leading my own life."

Still, there were moments that burst through.

Jill was twelve years old on November 22, 1963, when President John F. Kennedy was shot and killed by Lee Harvey Oswald as his motorcade left downtown Dallas.

"I'm pretty sure it was a Friday," she recalled correctly, nearly sixty years later. "I think I was in eighth grade. They called us all into the gym in our middle school and told us the news."

The entire school gathered silently in the gymnasium. It was only a year past the anxiety of the Cuban Missile Crisis, when reconnaissance photos revealed that the Soviets had been installing nuclear missiles in Cuba—missiles that could kill millions of Americans within minutes—and President Kennedy scrambled military forces for a potential invasion. The students sat in shock, "and then they dismissed us all to go home on the buses."

"Transfixed" by the live TV news broadcast during the following days, Jill and her family watched live as Jack Ruby shot Lee Harvey Oswald in the Dallas police station two days later.

"I can just remember watching the coverage over the next couple of days and seeing a lot of people crying," Jill recalled. "It really was shocking, I think, to the country. And I think anybody, all Americans felt it, you know, the heaviness and the grief and the sorrow" over Kennedy.

———————

As Jill navigated childhood in the classroom and the neighborhood, she was a bright, kind, and determined child, her aunt Barbara recalled. "When she got on a subject that she wanted to do, she was a leader of the pack."

Jill and her sisters would fight, of course. "Wrestling would break out, and it would last until I sat on Jan to subdue her or said something mean enough to shut her up," she wrote of her younger sister. Once she chased one of her sisters with a fireplace poker. "I wouldn't have actually stabbed her with it, but she didn't know that."

As the oldest, though, she was protective of her sisters, and they looked up to her. "She took care of me," Jill's sister Bonny said later. "She was there if I needed her. As she got older, I watched everything she did—she put on makeup and when she would leave I'd try her makeup on."

In 1964, a boy named Drew repeatedly threw worms at Bonny, then nine years old and shy. Jill went to Drew's house—"on a mission," she remembered—and banged on the door until he answered. "Don't you ever throw worms at my sister again!" she yelled, and punched him in the face.

She ran home and told her father. "Daddy! I just punched a kid for throwing worms at Bonny!"

"Good for you, Jilly-bean!" he said. "That's the way to look out for your sister."

Jill wrote, "In 1964, not every father would be thrilled that his thirteen-year-old—his daughter, no less—had gotten into a fistfight, but my father beamed with pride."

By the time high school came around, Jill was still defining herself academically but always found social groups to join, including the school's cheerleading squad.

"Yo, yo," she once began a cheer at the Jacobses' house, showing her grandfather what she had learned, going through the whole cheer routine for him.

Barbara recalled, "I can remember my parents, of course, interested in every word she ever spoke.... Years and years after that little scene that was in the living room with her cheering, my father would go around the house and do a two-step and quote this cheer and laugh and smile.... He'd bring Jill right back into the room again, you know, walking around cheering and quoting her."

Jill's parents, both from Protestant families who'd grown up in a heavily Catholic area, considered themselves "agnostic realists" and didn't attend a church. Yet Jill found herself drawn to religion as a teenager. During her sophomore year of high school, Jill started attending services at the Presbyterian church down the road from her parents' house. Eventually she took membership classes and was confirmed at age sixteen. She was touched that her mother attended the service.

"Sitting in the candlelight, listening to the doxology, taking the bread and wine—I was a part of something greater than myself," Jill wrote. "And when I prayed, I felt truly connected to God."

Jill hid cigarettes, an ashtray, and dirty books under her bed. "I cut school once in a while," she recalled. "I wasn't the perfect, you know, A-student, but I did okay."

Sometimes she'd sneak out of the house late at night to meet up with her friend Susan. Together they'd cross the Pennsylvania Turnpike on foot and climb the chain-link fence to swim in a nearby members-only pool in the early hours. "Even now, I can't believe we did this—two young girls, out alone at three a.m., darting across multiple lanes of highway traffic," Jill wrote.

She was fifteen when her father found her cigarettes. He smoked, too, and didn't want her to take up the habit. As punishment, he made Jill smoke three cigars in quick succession. "You're going to smoke these, and I want you to inhale them," she remembered her father saying. With her lungs burning, she finished the cigars, ran upstairs to vomit, and spent the evening angry at her father. She refused to come down for dinner.

Jill kept smoking for years, quitting only after she went to college "and realized I didn't have anything to prove by doing it."

Her mother, who was thirty-five, had become pregnant with the twins, Kim and Kelly. Jill, repulsed by the realization that her parents were still sexually active, recalled her mother's pregnancy with a teenager's cruelty:

> I can picture her so clearly, standing in the kitchen, dressed in what might as well be a tent, with the veins in her legs blue and swollen. She seemed enormous, and I was mortified by her. I tried to steer my friends away from her.

Even so, she and her mother were close while Jill was a teen. "My sisters and I always felt like we could tell her anything, and we did," she wrote. "Mom knew when I had my first boyfriend, she knew when other kids in the class started smoking marijuana (or grass, as we all called it back then), she knew when one of the girls at school got pregnant. There was nothing I was afraid to share."

———————

Upper Moreland High School in Willow Grove was close enough for Jill to walk to, but her best friend's brother usually picked her up in his car. "And of course, we were always late for school and, you know, we'd go running out the door late," she recalled.

Jill was popular, running with a close-knit group of girlfriends and dating boys throughout. Friday nights were for football games and Saturday was date night.

"I would say I usually had a boyfriend," she recalled in an interview, with a laugh. The boys Jill dated tended to get along with her father, who was protective but enjoyed engaging with them. They'd come over for a date with her and end up spending time with Donald, who had wanted a son and wound up with five daughters. "It's like, 'C'mon, guys, you know the movie starts at eight,'" Jill recalled. "But they all loved my dad."

Jill liked her high school classes, but she acknowledged not being the best student. She studied French and history, but struggled with math. Her passion was English. She forged a particularly close bond with a senior year writing teacher, Mrs. Helwig. "She was so tough, and that made me want to do better," Jill recalled.

In 1969, when Jill was eighteen, she returned to the shore to work for a second time the summer after graduation.

During her last month there she doubled up, working her waitressing job at Chris' until nine thirty or ten at night and then another shift at a diner from midnight until eight a.m. She was trying to save money, and it worked.

"I would go home, put on my bikini, and take my towel, and I'd sleep all day on the beach," she recalled. "Unless it rained, I did it every day. We all did. All the girls did. I had a really dark tan that summer, mostly on my back from sleeping on the beach—I actually have pictures of that which are funny, that I've seen. But that was our summer."

That summer, she met and started seriously dating a college football player named Bill Stevenson.

Chapter 5

Classes, Marriage, and Rock 'n' Roll

Following her high school graduation, Jill chose the university path. While the pursuit of higher education was not always a given for women of the time, Jill's decision to go was a surprise to none, especially her father.

In her autobiography, Jill recalls the day she told her dad that she wanted to go to college. Rather than questioning her decision, he simply asked, "Which one?"

These moments were not unusual between Jill and her father. His expectations of her had always been high, sometimes unfairly, she thought, but they were expectations rooted in admiration for her natural abilities. Donald Jacobs knew his eldest daughter was destined for a future much larger than that of a housewife.

In 1969, when Jill and her best friend were applying to different schools, they both got into Brandywine Junior College, which later merged with Widener University. They both accepted Brandywine's offer, and decided they would room together.

But after only a few weeks on campus, it became clear to Jill that Brandywine wasn't a good fit. Nor was her decision to major in fashion merchandising. She'd picked the subject area thinking it would put her on the path to a glamorous career, not expecting the heavy load of economics classes that studying fashion merchandising would entail.

"I said to my parents after a month, maybe two months there, I said, 'You know, I don't really like this. I don't, I'm not really getting anything out of it. It's not what I expected.' And they said, 'Okay, come home.'"

Rather than dwelling on Jill's decision to leave Brandywine, her parents encouraged her to apply to Temple or another of the many reputable schools in or near Philadelphia.

———————

Bill lived in Newark, Delaware, and played football for the University of Delaware, so Jill applied and was provisionally admitted for the spring semester. "They said, let's see how you do in these courses that you're taking. And then if you do well, which I did, we'll admit you. And so that's how I ended up at Delaware."

The year was 1969—Jill was busy finding her academic footing and her personal love story in Delaware; elsewhere, Apollo 11 landed on the moon, the Manson murders sent shockwaves through suburbs across the nation, and birth control changed free love. For some, the assassination of Robert Kennedy gave the sense that all was falling apart; for others, Woodstock showcased that peace and love could put it back together again.

By the late 1960s, the conflict in Vietnam had been a part of American life for more than a decade, and feelings of discontent ran deep within the US and around the world. Thousands of young Americans watched their friends, boyfriends, husbands, and brothers deploy to Asia, while President Richard Nixon spoke of "peace with honor." By the time the conflict ultimately ended several years later, nearly sixty thousand US soldiers had been killed. So stiff was opposition to the war—and Nixon's continuation of it—that on November 15, 1969, as many as half a million protesters peacefully marched through the streets of Washington, demanding the withdrawal of US troops from Vietnam.

"I suddenly saw the cracks in our society up close," Jill wrote in her memoir. "My friends and I sat glued to the television coverage every night. We were the first generation to watch a faraway war unfold on the evening news."

The night of December 1, 1969, mere weeks after the antiwar march on Washington, the draft lottery was broadcast live. That evening, Jill gathered with friends in front of a television in Newark, Delaware, to watch the lottery balls, each with a date inside, be plucked and read by suited bureaucrats. One man she knew drew number 042; other friends drew numbers even lower.

"I can remember so clearly the night that they picked those draft numbers," Jill said. "I can remember all the guys gathering around, it was the TV in my apartment, our apartment, picking the draft numbers. I mean, it was really a tense time and everybody was so worried about being drafted."

On May 4, 1970, Jill heard the names of the students who were killed or wounded when members of the National Guard, called up by the governor, opened fire on students peacefully protesting on the campus of Kent State University in Ohio. Her friend Scott Mackenzie, who had grown up near Hatboro, was shot walking home from class. The bullet barely missed his spine and caused lasting nerve damage in his face. His jaw was wired shut through his monthslong recovery.

That was as close to home as the war reached for Jill. There were occasional rumors about boys she'd known in Willow Grove being shot down in helicopters in the war, but they were often unconfirmed.

"I had been raised to believe in the basic goodness of our country," Jill wrote, "but all I could see on the nightly news was callousness for life."

When she turned twenty-one—the minimum voting age at the time—Jill registered as a Republican. She wasn't into politics, but wanted to vote.

"My parents were Republicans and so I didn't really know the difference between Democrats and Republicans," she said.

———

Jill, eighteen, and her boyfriend, Bill Stevenson, twenty-one, soon decided to tie the knot.

"My parents didn't object; in fact, my parents loved him," she writes. "And most importantly, I thought I had found a love like my parents', a partnership built on loyalty and devotion. For a moment, we were happy. I had found my Prince Charming, and I was sure it would last forever."

Jill thought it was wonderful they were going to the same school. She and her new husband took classes together and she began creating a home for the couple in an apartment just off campus. But it was jarring to suddenly go from being a student to being a wife.

College would become a haven for Jill. She pursued an English degree and relished her studies. But Bill decided college wasn't for him. He dropped out to open a music venue.

The Stone Balloon, a rock and roll bar that was a hit with the local university crowd, was an occasional stop for major musicians—Bruce Springsteen, Chubby Checker, Tiny Tim, Pat Benatar, Robert Palmer, Hall & Oates, David Crosby, and Blood, Sweat & Tears among them.

"Students and local residents packed the bar six nights a week," reported *The Review*, the University of Delaware's student newspaper. Stevenson had purchased the old tavern and added multiple bars, a patio, a room with a stage, and a loading dock for bands. "As the Balloon's popularity increased, so did the quality of the bands. It became almost a symbiotic relationship, with the bands popularizing the bar and the bar getting out the name of the bands."

The young couple fell into a routine: Bill would work nights at the bar while Jill went to class during the day and studied at night. At ten or eleven, she'd join him at the bar.

"I loved the classes I took," Jill recalled, but "all my friends were friends from the bar. I didn't have outside friends that were in my world, really."

Chapter 6

Senator of a New Generation

While Jill and Bill Stevenson were building their lives, young Joe Biden, an attorney and councilman for New Castle County, was busy charting his path toward Washington. Still in his twenties, Joe was pitching himself to voters as a capable young leader, in touch with the evolving issues of the time. He labeled his challenger, Republican incumbent Cale Boggs, as being too old and out of touch. But the odds were stacked against Joe. Only eighteen percent of Delawareans knew who he was.

The campaign didn't have money for television, but they designed high-quality print, newspaper, and billboard ads. Joe had a good voice for radio, too.

One ad run by Biden read, "Cale Boggs' generation dreamed of conquering polio. Joe Biden's generation dreams of conquering heroin." Another read, "To Cale Boggs, an unfair tax was the 1948 poll tax. To Joe Biden, an unfair tax is the 1972 income tax."

Rather than a nasty campaign, Norm Lockman, reporting for the *Wilmington News Journal*, described Joe's approach toward Boggs as more pragmatic than anything: "Dear old dad may have been right for his time—and I love him—but things are different now."

From economic issues to the changing environmental needs of the coastal state, Joe and the voters of Delaware agreed that it was time for new blood. To save money on postage, Joe relied on large groups of young enthusiasts to hand-deliver his campaign material door-to-door.

Joe cast himself as a new type of leader in a state that typically valued middle-of-the-road politics. Delaware in the 1970s was changing—and in such a small state, everyone was witness to the change. The DuPont family, owners of the chemical giant, were Delaware aristocrats with enormous clout in state politics. DuPont employees had once been the engine of downtown Wilmington, but many residents had left for the suburbs. The city was hollowed out by economic loss and events such as the riots that took place following Dr. Martin Luther King's April 1968 assassination in Memphis, Tennessee. In what was widely viewed as an overreaction by the governor, the National Guard had occupied Wilmington for nine months. The city fell into a downturn and saw massive increases in drug arrests for cocaine and heroin possession; poverty took hold of the city.

Amid the depressed job market, Joe called for economic stability and addressed issues overlooked by older generations of Delaware politicians, such as protecting the beaches and coastal waters. Young voters in the state were particularly drawn to what was seen at the time as Biden's progressive platform, including his early environmentalism.

Jill's husband, Bill Stevenson, was one of those young people, excited about the prospect of a senator from their generation. Jill's dining room was stacked with Biden campaign literature for Bill to distribute. She eventually read through them—but that was the extent of her interest. "I didn't decide to become involved in the campaign or anything like that," she said.

In what was considered a major upset, at only twenty-nine years old— still too young to officially join the upper chamber of Congress—Biden came away victorious, winning the election by 3,162 votes, as the second-youngest US senator elected in the twentieth century.

"I remember I was in college and I remember I voted for Joe, thank God, you know, even though he was a Democrat," Jill said in a 2021 interview.

Biden's campaign had been a family affair. His wife, Neilia, was active, speaking at events and working with campaign volunteers. The couple had three young children—sons Beau and Hunter and daughter Naomi, nicknamed Amy, who was eighteen months old at the time of the election.

On election night, the Biden campaign held a celebration at Wilmington's elegant Hotel Du Pont. Joe's sister, Valerie, had taken a chance on booking the ballroom, the customary site of the Republican victory party, earlier in the year.

Bill wanted to go to the party to celebrate his state's newly elected senator. He needed to convince his wife to join him, so he promised her dinner at a restaurant across the street that she loved. She acquiesced.

Once there, Jill was shocked at how electric the evening was. The ballroom was packed with people. She also remembers being taken with the Biden family, especially Joe's wife, Neilia.

"She had an easy, natural beauty that made her look almost out of place in the frantic crowd," Jill recalled. "Even surrounded by strangers vying for attention, she seemed calm, with a warm, genuine smile. From across the room, you could see how happy she was—happy, and incredibly proud."

Jill made her way over to shake Neilia's hand.

"Congratulations," she said.

"I didn't know much about her, but in that instant, I thought about how picturesque their family was—the handsome young senator, trying to better the world; his beautiful, loving wife, representing their family, always there to cheer him on; and three adorable kids. Here they were, with the world at their feet, taking on the political establishment and *winning*," Jill wrote.

Then Jill and Bill went to dinner—gone by the time Joe gave his acceptance speech.

On December 18, Joe was in Washington interviewing potential staffers and organizing his new team on Capitol Hill while Neilia took Beau, Hunter, and Amy to pick out a Christmas tree.

On their way home, Neilia pulled away from a stop sign and was struck by a tractor trailer. Her station wagon was sent spinning 150 feet backward down an embankment, where it struck a group of trees, finally coming to rest.

Joe's brother Jimmy got a call from a friend in the state police. Neilia had been in an accident with the kids. Soon after, the news broke on the radio.

Jesus! Joe's going to find out, Jimmy thought. He immediately dialed Joe's office in DC with a message to come home and head straight to the hospital.

Joe left immediately for Memorial Division Hospital in Delaware.

"They flew us to Wilmington, but I didn't know anything for sure until I got to the hospital," Joe wrote in his memoir. "All the way up, I kept telling myself that everything was going to be okay, that I was letting my imagination run away with me, but the minute I got to the hospital and saw Jimmy's face, I knew the worst had happened.

"Beau, Hunt, and Naomi had been in the car with Neilia when the accident happened. Neilia had been killed and so had our baby daughter. The boys were both alive, but Beau had a lot of broken bones and Hunt had injuries. The doctors couldn't rule out permanent damage. I could not speak, only felt this hollow core grow in my chest, like I was going to be sucked inside a black hole."

Neilia was only thirty years old, and Amy, eighteen months.

The future that had looked so promising for Joe was thrown into uncertainty.

President Nixon called Joe at the hospital the next day. On the phone with Joe, Nixon urged him to think "as you must, in terms of the future, because you have the great fortune of being young...You can remember that she was there when you won a great victory, and you enjoyed it together. And now, I'm sure that she'll be watching you from now on. Good luck to you."

Joe also credits an early friend in the chamber, Majority Leader Mike Mansfield, who convinced him that in spite of all he was going through, it was futile to throw away the Senate.

———

"I can remember the night that Neilia was killed," Jill said. "I remember I was on my way to take a final exam."

The news came over the car radio. Jill turned off her ignition, sat in her car, and said a prayer.

"It's sort of odd," she reflected in an interview forty-nine years later.

"The things that are weaved through one another, you know? The things that happen."

Joe was eventually sworn in, in a ceremony that took place in the chapel of the Delaware Division of the Wilmington Medical Center, with Beau attending in his hospital bed, still in traction. Hunter, released a few days earlier, looked on as well. "We had a number of plans, Neilia and I, for the swearing-in day," Joe said. "My children were to have been with us that day. I felt I should be sworn in with my children today."

Neilia's father held the Bible while Joe took his oath. Joe swallowed hard and stared fixedly through moist eyes during the brief ceremony.

"I hope to be a good senator," Joe said. "If a conflict develops in six months or so between being a good senator and good father, I will contact [the governor]. They can always get another senator, but my boys can't get another father."

Joe decided that he would commute to his daily duties in DC from his home in Wilmington, and be home every evening with Beau and Hunt. He found tremendous support at home, with his sister, Val, who immediately moved in to help care for the boys, as well as in Washington with sympathetic new colleagues, but he struggled personally to get back on track.

In his book *Promises to Keep*, Joe described how fraught his life had become. "Christmas passed with the boys in the hospital, and I began to feel my anger. When the boys were asleep or when Val or Mom was taking a turn at their bedside, I'd bust out of the hospital and go walking the nearby streets. Jimmy would go with me, and I'd steer him wordlessly down into the darkest and seediest neighborhoods I could find. I liked to go at night when I thought there was a better chance of finding a fight. I was always looking for a fight. I had not known I was capable of such rage. I knew I had been cheated out of a future, but I felt I'd been cheated of a past, too."

Chapter 7

A Date with the Young Senator

While Joe was mourning and starting his life as a senator, Jill's marriage to Bill Stevenson was quickly fading.

"I tried to make the relationship work. I thought I could will our marriage back to life," she wrote. "But I had to separate what I thought my family should be from the reality of what this relationship was. Before long, I began to see that the breaks were beyond repair. I wouldn't settle for a counterfeit love. Like a broken spell, the truth of the reality struck me suddenly; I was going to get divorced."

The divorce was not widely reported and made few appearances in the public record. In Delaware, court records for divorces are not generally available to the public. At one point in a 2021 interview, Jill spoke of Stevenson with a slight edge in her voice and didn't elaborate on their relationship.

In the fall of 1974, Jill moved out of their home in Newark, Delaware, and relocated to Chadds Ford, Pennsylvania, where she rented a one-bedroom town house, about twenty minutes from campus. Feeling that their separation indicated personal failure in an era where divorce wasn't nearly as common as today, Jill—a college junior—took a year away from school to slowly put the pieces of her life back together. "Things were a little too rough, too emotional," she later said about juggling college and going through a divorce. "But I knew I would finish. I was determined."

Their divorce would be finalized in May 1975. Later, *The Review* reported, "after a turbulent court case, Stevenson walked away only paying [Jill] less than half what she had wanted, not including the half-ownership she sought of the bar." Years afterward, the *Wilmington News Journal* reported that Stevenson was sentenced to four years in jail for writing bad checks in 1985 and convicted on a federal bank fraud charge in 1986. He served probation and paid fines for both crimes. Stevenson declined to comment for this book.

When Jill returned to school as a senior, she focused on her studies and dated casually, with low expectations. Jill was an English major, not an education major, but she began to think it would be smart to do student teaching to qualify her to teach school.

She began working with older students at a special school on campus for kids with reading problems. She was able to share with them the joy she found in books, and the work piqued her interest in becoming a reading specialist. "It was then that I knew that I'd found my calling," she later said.

On March 7, 1975, Joe's brother Frank picked him up at the Wilmington airport. As the two exited the terminal, they passed posters run by the local New Castle County Parks and Recreation Department. Featured in the ads, bringing added attention to the landscapes, was fair-haired Jill.

Jill, wearing a tank top that emphasized her toned biceps, gazed directly into the camera and at the viewer. Her look was intense but welcoming; she seemed about to share a thought or crack a joke.

"She was blond and gorgeous," Joe wrote in his memoir. "I couldn't imagine who was looking at trees with her in the photograph."

That's exactly what photographer Tom Stiltz was going for when he asked his friend Jill to model for the shots. "People aren't going to look at a picture of a tree and a pond," Stiltz had said. "Will you stand in the photo?"

"Look, Frankie," Joe said. "That's the kind of girl I'd like to date." What followed next was the first of a succession of surprises. "Well, why don't you, then? I know her," Frank told his brother. "You'll like her, Joe," he said. "She doesn't like politics."

Frank Biden and Jill had been acquaintances from the University of Delaware. By the next day, Frank had Jill's number for Joe, who called Jill that evening.

"How did you get this number?" was the first thing Jill said. She had changed her phone number when she split with Stevenson.

"My brother Frank gave it to me," Joe said. "I just got back into town and was wondering—are you free tonight?"

Much to Joe's surprise, given his public persona as one of the nation's most eligible bachelors, Jill said no. She already had a date.

"Well, I'm only in town for one day. Do you think you could break it?"

"Call me back in an hour," she said.

She was inclined to accept the offer from the young senator she had already found herself impressed with from a distance. And unbeknownst to the senator, the two had met briefly once before.

She waited for Joe's return call.

"I broke my date," she told Joe.

"Great," he said. "I'll pick you up at seven."

"I never expected to be attracted to Joe," Jill said in 2021. She imagined they'd have little in common, and she went on that first date out of curiosity. "I mean, I didn't even know what a senator did, quite honestly."

Suddenly straying from her past life of yellow Chevy Camaros and rock and roll bars, Jill remembers pondering "what one might wear on a date with a senator," she wrote. "I imagined something smart and tailored, probably pearls and a skirt. Well, I wasn't wearing that."

Jill, in emerald slacks, a flowered blouse, and wedges, met Joe at seven p.m. on the dot. He was thirty-one years old, and wearing what Jill remembers as a perfect suit and leather loafers.

My god, what have I gotten myself into? she thought. *Oh well, it's only a date.*

Keen to enjoy their evening without the peering eyes of the Delaware press, Joe and Jill drove to Philadelphia for dinner and a movie. The French film, *A Man and a Woman*, was about a relationship that forms in the shadow of lost spouses. Dinner was at a place down a set of stairs on Chestnut Street, a main road in Philadelphia lined with restaurants and dotted with historic landmarks. Dinner had a casual tone. "Despite his appearance and dress, he was laid-back and funny," Jill wrote. "We talked for a few hours, there in the booth, and I was surprised by how easy and comfortable it felt."

On Joe's part, he was relieved. "Jill showed no interest in politics. She didn't ask a single thing about my career, about Washington, about the famous people I'd met. I didn't want to talk about that stuff anyway. So we talked about family and mutual friends in Delaware. We talked about books and real life."

Dropping her off at home, Joe wasted no time. "Any chance you're free tomorrow night?" he asked Jill. "Yes," she said. "I am." With that and a handshake, the two parted ways.

"I was so stunned," she recalled. He wasn't pushy, and didn't try to come inside to have a drink and extend the evening. "He was different, and he sort of took me off guard, I guess," she said. Jill remembers calling her mother at one a.m. to tell her, "Mom, I've finally met a real gentleman."

"That sort of sealed the deal," she said later.

By the end of the second date, Joe was smitten, and even asked Jill to stop seeing other people—something she wasn't yet ready to do. Not to mention, her divorce was not yet finalized.

Joe understood, at least at first. "She'd married young, was separated, and in the process of getting divorced," he wrote. "Jill liked her life as a single woman; she was looking forward to starting her first teaching job in the fall; and most of all she did not want to be involved with somebody in politics, let alone a United States senator. We should just think of this as fun."

Jill later said she thought his request to be exclusive was "a little bold, but he seemed to have some logical reason for it." As a senator, or a father—or both—he probably shouldn't have been seen as "someone who was one of many people I was dating."

In spite of their mismatched enthusiasm, the two once again discussed when they could see each other next, what with Joe's busy schedule in Washington. Flipping through his calendar to find a time, he told her the following evening was his last chance for the foreseeable future.

"Three dates, three nights in a row?" Jill wrote. "*Buddy*, I thought, *you just blew your cover.*"

Chapter 8

"Groundedness" Paired with Charisma

Jill was student teaching while Joe juggled the roles of senator and committed single father. He was considering buying a house in Wilmington for what he hoped would be a growing family, and was looking toward the future.

Joe was also beginning to think about running for reelection to his second Senate term. Even in the 1970s, when campaign seasons were shorter and the cost of running for office less expensive, ambitious politicians needed to plan well ahead for their next move. Joe credited Jill with his ability to think toward the future. Dating her had given him a normal life again, and "for the first time the Senate seemed fun."

Joe took Jill to see the big house he planned to purchase on Montchan Drive in Wilmington. He also wanted her to meet his family, especially his boys, and his sister, Val. Joe was moving fast, and Jill's tendency was to hold back.

Jill knew Joe's brother Frank through school, she had also met his brother Jimmy, but the looming introduction to Val made her nervous. Val was more than a sister. She was one of her brother's closest confidants, and one of his key political advisers, having managed his Senate campaign. Her opinion, Jill knew, could make or break her standing in Joe's life.

Jill put off her introductory meeting with Val four or five times. Finally she gave in, agreeing not only to meet Joe's sister, but also his sons, Beau and Hunter. She went over to Joe's home on North Star Road—an old colonial farmhouse with a large porch and a barn out back—where she found Val and her boyfriend, Jack, hard at work, helping Joe finish painting the walls before he put it up for sale. Val and the boys were eager to meet her.

Jill was nervous, but everyone was kind and warm. It wasn't a test. Jill was struck by Val's sense of humor and the boys roughhousing in the yard. It was a successful introduction, but a bit overwhelming for Jill. After an hour of conversation and jokes over tuna sandwiches, Joe and Jill conjured up an excuse to depart.

As their relationship grew, Jill began spending more time at Joe's family home. She became more at ease around the house, and Beau and Hunter took an immediate liking to her. "They were like puppies who always wanted to snuggle up and climb in my lap," she wrote. "They were constantly touching and connected to each other and to Joe as well, as if, at any moment, one of them could be gone."

Even as she grew more comfortable with Joe and his family, Jill had her reservations. Her first marriage had fallen apart. Simply getting married again was a risk. But marriage to Joe would bring both the scrutiny of being a politician's wife and the responsibility of raising two young boys who had recently lost their mother.

One day, standing in Joe's kitchen around nine a.m., Jill heard the door open. Joe had already departed earlier that morning for Washington, and the boys had caught the bus for school. It was Joe's mother, a towering figure in her son's life and a member of the family Jill had yet to meet.

"I've been wanting to talk to you," Jean Biden, whom the family called Mom-Mom, said.

Jill had heard stories about Joe's mother. She was said to be a kind woman who placed love for her kids and grandchildren above all else, but Jill had found her intimidating so far.

"I don't know where this is going between you and Joe, but I want to thank you," Jill remembers Jean saying.

"For what?" Jill asked, stunned at how quickly the interaction veered from her worst assumptions.

"For making my son believe he could love again," Jean said.

At only twenty-four years old, divorced, and falling for a political star in the making, Jill appreciated having earned the support of Joe's family. But she was nervous about introducing Joe to her own. It was the first serious relationship she'd had since her divorce, and there was the additional complexity of Beau and Hunter.

Jill told her aunt Barbara she was dating a man with two young kids.

"Is it serious?" Barbara asked.

"Well, I'm not ready to be a mother," Jill said, "but I adore those boys."

A few months into their relationship, though, Jill realized it was time. She invited Joe and the boys to her parents' twenty-fifth anniversary party, which took place at her paternal grandparents' backyard in Hammonton, New Jersey.

Jill, Joe, Beau, and Hunter all drove together, but Jill asked to be dropped off for some initial time alone with her family, so Joe and the boys took off to get some pizza. She visited with her family for a while, and told them who she had invited as her guests. Everyone was thrilled, especially Jill's Grandmom Jacobs.

Barbara recalled, "My mom came running down the steps, threw her arms up in the air and said to Joe, 'Welcome. I love you, and I'm a Democrat, too.'" She proudly announced, "I worked for President Roosevelt on the WPA."

Led in by their new friend, Joe and the boys found a comfortable form of chaos in the backyard: family members chasing each other around, people laughing loudly, kids playing in the garden and around the tomato plants. "It felt like home," Joe wrote. After a bear hug from Jill's Grandpop, it was certain that Joe and the two youngest Bidens were warmly welcomed.

Barbara was eager to see where the relationship would go. She saw that Jill was great with the boys, and all the kids played ball together. There was a lot of laughter and happiness. "And Joe ate a lot of that pasta," she remembered.

"Her father was a reliable man," Joe wrote, "and he prized reliability in other men. He liked me because I wanted to take care of his daughter even when she made it clear she didn't need to be taken care of."

"My family seemed to adore him, and he was sure they'd be on his side when he asked me to marry him," Jill wrote. "Even if I was confused at the time about what I wanted, he could see how important family was to me, and he knew I would want it again, eventually."

Don't get your hopes up, Jill warned her family; it might not last.

———————

As the next year passed, it wasn't just the relationship between Joe and Jill that grew. Jill began spending more time with Beau and Hunter, and over time, found herself taking on more and more responsibility for them.

Jill became their "moral support," Barbara recalled. "She automatically took to those boys. She loved them. She truly loved them."

The three started spending time together when Joe was occupied with work. She'd help by making dinner at Joe's house, would shuttle the boys back and forth from school, or simply hang around with them in the evening, passing time while they waited for their dad to arrive home. They began to form their own relationship that wasn't dependent on the fondness that Jill and Joe shared for each other.

Jill found Hunter to be a kindred spirit. He was full of life, but at times reserved. He'd snuggle up with Jill as a means of showing the love that he would at other times have trouble expressing. Beau was the opposite, but no less loving. He was similar to his father—gregarious and a gifted orator—and as the oldest child, helped conduct things with his sense of responsibility.

"When I say that I fell in love with the boys before I fell in love with Joe, it is the truth," she said.

While she was uncertain about the prospect of a second marriage so early in life, especially when considering a relationship that came with so many appendages—politics, children, lost love—she adapted to the new sense of purpose that the boys brought to her life.

The love and stability that Jill provided was exactly what the Biden family needed. While she worked alongside Joe to raise the boys, Jill channeled the influences of her parents—strong and stoic—allowing her to grow into adulthood.

"I saw my mother cry only one time, at my dad's funeral. She didn't even cry when her own parents died. I saw that stoicism as strength—and that strength was what I wanted for myself more than anything," Jill wrote. "I worked hard to live up to that with the kids, always fighting to keep control of myself, especially in times of hardship and adversity."

What Jill refers to as her groundedness, paired with Joe's charisma, made them a formidable pair. Eventually, the compatibility and enjoyment they shared became a force of its own.

"She could talk with anyone. Not that she believed everyone. No, she believed what she believed. She had backbone. She was private—Joe liked that, her cool way of hiding the girl inside, and old hurts...he could see that. She had that way of looking at you, to make sure you meant what she thought was so funny...and then that quick shy smile, half-doubting—she could sniff out bullshit. She'd tell him, too—especially when it was his bullshit—she'd tell him straight. Very soft of manner was Jill, but smart: she knew who she liked," wrote Biden chronicler Richard Ben Cramer.

"After the disappointment of my divorce, I never wanted to feel so out of control of my heart again," Jill wrote. "But in the months that Joe and I were dating, that desire ran up against a new reality: I was falling in love."

In the fall of 1975, when they'd been dating for around nine months, the foursome started one of the family's longest-running traditions: Thanksgiving on Nantucket island in Massachusetts. Joe considered it a form of diplomacy: Jill's parents had wanted the group to join them, Joe's parents wanted the same, and even Neilia's parents, still very involved in the lives of their grandchildren, invited the four of them to join them in upstate New York for the holiday. Rather than choosing one group and offending the rest, Joe and Jill packed up the car and the boys and headed to Nantucket, a place neither of them had ever been to, but would end up calling them back for decades.

"Over the years, I've been asked what decisions helped form our family. But they were so rarely made overtly—our lives just began to follow a natural rhythm. We didn't speak of it, but there was a driving force behind it all: We were becoming whole again—Joe and the boys, and me as well," Jill wrote in her autobiography.

They drove up in Joe's Jeep Wagoneer with the boys and a German shepherd in the back seat. Jill had prepared for the long trip by stockpiling catalogs; when Beau and Hunter began to act up, she gave them to the boys. They spent the next few hours compiling Christmas lists for Santa.

Take your time and get it right, Jill assured them. There's no rush.

Joe, in the driver's seat, saw Jill proving herself as a resourceful caregiver.

On the island, they wandered through the handful of open shops and watched the town light the Christmas tree. They even toyed with buying a small saltbox-style beach house, but the asking price was too high. On the front porch a sign read "Forever Wild," and Joe, Jill, Beau, and Hunter had their picture taken beneath it.

Chapter 9

Tying the Knot

Joe's first marriage proposal arrived without frills in 1976.

"I want us to get married," he said. Jill wasn't caught off guard; she already knew Joe wanted to marry her. She also knew she wasn't ready to make that commitment.

Joe told her that he and the boys had discussed the prospect, but not at his behest. Beau and Hunter had decided on their own that since they came with their dad as a package deal, "we" should marry Jill. After the boys approached Joe about the idea one morning, it was settled—everyone loved Jill, and it was up to Joe to formally bring her into the fold.

The second proposal came a few months after the first. Once again, Jill said no. In spite of two dodged proposals, she wasn't scared off, nor was Joe deterred. While Jill's lack of certainty in her ability to love again had faded, her worry about being in the political spotlight began to grow. She didn't go to his political events, and as a couple they stayed out of the public eye.

She liked living with a degree of privacy, and she was in the first year of her teaching career. She'd started at St. Mark's, a private Catholic high school on a suburban campus in New Castle County with a good academic reputation, where she taught English to ninth and tenth graders. She very much enjoyed it, and didn't want to give it up. She'd also begun attending West Chester University to get her master of education with a specialty in reading.

Marcelle Leahy, the wife of Democratic senator Pat Leahy of Vermont, remembered Joe bringing Jill to Senate events while they were still dating. The Senate then was like a family, she said, "and bringing a date to something is like introducing someone to the family." Jill's presence sent a clear signal: this is not a casual date. "Joe was smitten with her from the very beginning."

Joe proposed a third time, and a fourth. Jill refused to be swayed. After two years together, her reasons continued to shift. Jill knew that Joe didn't expect her to withdraw from her own aspirations to simply take up his, or become a housewife. She had also had time to fully recover from her divorce, finding new love in Joe and security in her work. The last hurdle was the boys.

"They were so easy to love," she said. "They were such great kids and so warm. So that's why when Joe kept saying, 'Will you marry me? Will you marry me?' I really had to make sure it was going to work, because I could not break their hearts if it didn't work," Jill said.

"They had endured the loss of one mother already, and I couldn't risk having them lose another. It was them against the world. And they were asking me to join that sacred circle," she wrote. "They trusted me to step into their lives and give them the love and devotion that had been stolen from them. They weren't afraid that I wouldn't measure up. But I was."

"One of the things I loved most about Jill—aside from the simple fact that every time I saw her my heart skipped a beat—was her practicality," Joe wrote. "She was beautiful, sure, humble, and confident, and she had a rock-ribbed strength. Jill was never going to let you see her down, and she had no time for excuses. I always trusted that she'd carry her share of any burden, and with grace. But above all, Jill wasn't going to allow herself to be swept away."

As Joe and Jill's relationship evolved, so did Joe's political career. In February of 1977, Joe was assigned to the Senate Judiciary Committee along with his seat on the Foreign Relations Committee. "Even in this committee post, which he had aggressively sought out, Biden could be heard at times grumbling at his lot," wrote biographer Jules Witcover. "To a *Wilmington Journal* columnist he complained of getting unsatisfactory assignments... and being trapped as an independent between committee factions.

'They have conservatives, they have liberals, and they have Biden,' he lamented."

Joe was likewise "occupied with cosponsoring and helping to write the Foreign Intelligence Surveillance Act," or FISA, and "had a full plate for a first-term senator and widower with small children to whom he rushed home in Delaware nearly every night."

At some point, Joe's brothers took Jill to dinner. She later recalled that Jimmy and Frank Biden "told me it was a dream of this family that Joe would be president, and did I have any problem with that? I guess I thought it would go away."

Jill listened, taking it all in. "I heard all the discussions, and why he should." She saw the rationale for running. "Everybody thought he could be president."

Joe hadn't minded being patient for Jill to settle into their relationship, but he worried about his boys. They were getting used to having a new mother figure in their life and he needed to protect them if she wasn't committed for the long haul. So in the spring of 1977, Joe stopped by Jill's apartment on his way to South Africa on Senate business to give her an ultimatum.

"Look," Jill remembers him saying. "I've been as patient as I know how to be, but this has got my Irish up. Either you decide to marry me, or that's it—I'm out. I'm not asking again. I'm too much in love with you to just be friends." By the end of his trip, Joe wanted an answer.

Joe returned to the US ten days later and went straight from the airport to see Jill. He was stern, and made no time for small talk about the trip. He refused to even step into the apartment beyond the foyer.

"I could see that he didn't want to lose me, but he would walk away for his boys," she wrote. "But even in the tension of that small entryway, I could feel his love, and I knew it was forever, unconditional. I knew that he and the boys had my heart, and we were too intertwined now to protect ourselves from each other."

"This is it," Joe said. "I'm not going to ask you again. I have two boys here. I love you, but my responsibility is to them. This [courtship has been] going on; I want a family." While he'd been abroad, he told her, he decided not to run for the Senate again if she agreed to marry him.

Jill told him she didn't think he meant it. As proof, he picked up the phone and said he was calling the *Wilmington News Journal.*

There was a brief dial tone, then, "Jill had her finger on the phone cradle," Joe wrote in his memoir. "She'd cut off the call."

"If I denied your dream," he recalls her saying, "I would not be marrying the man I fell in love with."

Jill said yes.

"Oh, Jill, don't worry," she later recalled him saying. "Your life will never change."

"He did say that," she marveled in 2021, sitting in her office in the East Wing of the White House. "He did say those words."

Chapter 10

Becoming a Mom

In June 1977, Jill and Joe decided to get married in New York. They wanted to quietly tie the knot in a place where they weren't known, which had ruled out Wilmington or DC.

"I remember Joe being so excited before they were going to get married," Marcelle Leahy recalled. He told everyone the story of how Beau and Hunt had asked him to marry Jill. "Joe just loved telling that story. And that was when we learned that they were getting married."

Earlier, Jill and Joe had taken the train up to New York to fill out their paperwork for a marriage license at the city clerk's office in the Bronx. "To my relief, no one seemed to be taking any notice of us," Jill wrote in her autobiography. "After about fifteen minutes, we heard a loud voice calling, 'Bidden!...BIDDEN!' I burst out laughing, turning to Joe. 'Well, it looks like our secret is still safe!'"

Joe had watched Jill grow nervous in the lead-up to the wedding, but on June 17, she stood at the altar in a white eyelet dress.

The ceremony was family only. Of course, family, for the Bidens and the Jacobses, meant a crowd of almost forty people.

The chapel they had chosen at the United Nations had become known as a space for hosting interfaith, cross-culture, and second weddings. It was a perfect fit for the Bidens. Tucked behind a large, swirling piece of modernist art paired with stained glass dedicated to the search for peace, the sanctuary seemed far away from the bustle of Manhattan traffic and the line of world flags at the UN across the street.

The Jesuit priest began the ceremony. In an unplanned moment, Beau, eight, and Hunter, seven, left their pew and silently joined Joe and Jill at the altar. "They just instinctively understood that this was a marriage of the four of us," Jill recalled. "These precious little boys knew the obvious better than anyone else." She felt the entire family got married.

Biden's office sent a press release after the fact. "Sen. Joseph R. Biden Jr. has married Jill Tracy Jacobs in a private ceremony in New York," The Associated Press reported. Joe's father called the wedding "a very private affair."

After a reception lunch at the Sign of the Dove, the Bidens stayed in New York for a honeymoon with the boys. The family rounded out the day with a Broadway show—*Annie*—and hamburgers.

"We took the honeymoon suite, part of it, Hunt and I, and left them the other room," Beau remembered. "We were all together and we've been together ever since."

"That night my life felt back together again," Joe recalled in his autobiography.

A month later, in another nontraditional arrangement, Joe sat alone for an interview to talk about his new wife. "I don't want to get her into the political thing. Jill married me, my boys and the entire state of Delaware, you know. She's entitled to a little privacy," Biden told a reporter. He gave the paper a photo and a rundown of Jill's education, her teaching work, her volunteer work at the Child Abuse Center, and her hobbies of learning piano and tending plants.

But a week later the paper ran a second article reporting that Jill was a divorcée, and Joe had left that detail out of his interview. "I thought the fact Jill was married before had no relevance," Joe told the reporter. "There were no children. I thought all that was common knowledge in Wilmington."

Jill had been teaching for a year by the time they got married, but afterward she stepped away from work for a few years.

"I really felt it was important that I establish myself as the boys' mother," she said. "Even though we had been almost family already for two years, I just felt that it was important for them to see me as their mom." Joe's mother and sister, Val, had done a tremendous job raising the boys, but Jill wanted to give them the secure feeling her own mother staying home had given her during her childhood. She wanted them to be able to feel whole again.

She helped out with Hot Dog Day, when the mothers would cook hot dogs and deliver them around the school to the kids, and took an active role in their school. Beau and Hunter did "every sport," she recalled. She listed them: football, soccer, tennis, lacrosse, baseball. "Oh, they didn't swim." Although they were only a year and a day apart, it was often enough of an age difference to land them on different teams, with different practice and game schedules. "So I was always carpooling and sitting on one field or another," she said. "I spent a lot of time on fields."

After growing up in a home of five girls, living with two sons came with surprises.

The boys were always outside; they came home covered in mud all the time and brought home snakes. A week or two after they got married, Beau asked Jill, "Aren't you going to do the wash?"

"Well, you know, I wash once a week," Jill said.

"No, you're supposed to wash every day," Beau said.

With Joe away all day working, Jill did what she dubbed "mom things." She loved to cook, and would plan out meals for the week. She baked cookies and cakes and pies, even facetiously making a "baked good of the day." She made their home comfortable for Beau's and Hunter's friends and the neighborhood kids. They would come over for dinner, and in the summer they would all come over and swim in the pool.

Jill found Beau to be "a mini-Joe," but with a sense of humor much like hers. The two of them loved to tease Joe. He wouldn't always take it from Jill, but he would from Beau. And with Joe often home late or out at evening events at the Hotel Du Pont, "Beau sort of took on a role of the man of the house. He was very protective of me," Jill said.

Hunter was quieter. He could draw, he loved art, and he was a good writer.

One morning, a couple months after Jill and Joe got married, Beau and Hunter ran outside for the school bus. They came to kiss Jill goodbye.

"Goodbye, Mom," they said. It was the first time they had referred to her in that way.

"I didn't say a word," Jill recalled. "We didn't recognize it. It just happened. And from then on, I was Mom."

Chapter 11

Into the Public Arena

Joe's first Senate reelection campaign demanded Jill's participation.

"It was a little overwhelming," she said, the first time that Joe took her to a campaign event. A picnic at Archmere Academy, Joe's high school alma mater, was one of Jill's first political appearances as Joe's wife. She was unprepared for the throngs of people. "I felt like I was being pulled and tugged every which way, literally." Everyone wanted to talk to her:

Oh, meet my sister.

Do you know so-and-so?

Oh, did you meet this person?

I'm from Sussex!

"I can remember going home, going up into the bedroom and just shutting the door," Jill said. "I mean I just had to breathe. It was just so overwhelming for me."

But then she started to travel the state and campaign in earnest. "I would go to every senior center and have lunch with seniors," she said. "I would go to coffees. I'd go to the state fair."

Joe's sister and campaign manager, Val, became Jill's mentor, helping her practice her public remarks and patiently explaining various political organizations and key people she needed to get to know.

Jill was more at ease in smaller settings, where she felt like she could relate better to people.

She slowly started to get to know Joe's colleagues in the Senate and their spouses. "They loved Joe and they wanted him to be happy," she recalled. "I was just welcomed into the Senate."

Three or four times a year, the sitting senators and their spouses would get together for dinner. The tables were a mix of Democrats and Republicans. "These were done to foster good relationships between the senators regardless of party," Marcelle Leahy recalled. Jill began to forge friendships that would last for decades.

———

Joe's electoral chances in the upcoming Senate race were bolstered by a guest appearance by President Jimmy Carter at a pair of Wilmington fundraisers in February 1978.

The first, a dinner in the glittering Gold Ballroom at the Hotel Du Pont, was formal but at Carter's request did not require black-tie dress. Racks of lamb, seafood, and American wines were served beneath ceiling bas-reliefs of Helen of Troy, Cleopatra, and other famous women. Guests paid upward of a thousand dollars to take photos with Joe and the president, and Jill helped work the crowds as they navigated the ballroom.

Following the dinner, Joe and President Carter attended an additional stop at the Padua Academy, a more accessible event. A thousand or so attendees, many of whom had been supporters of Joe's since his initial run for the Senate, paid thirty-five dollars to support his reelection bid, have a drink, and dance with fellow Delaware Democrats.

The evening was a necessary exercise in party unity. Although Joe had been the first senator to support Carter's 1976 run for president, he had recently been critical of the administration. "They got to Washington and didn't know how Washington worked," he'd said. "The president is learning, but not fast enough." Carter, for his part, paid Joe the backhanded compliment that he was "independent almost to a fault."

Carter spent only sixty-four minutes with the Bidens that evening, but his visit helped Joe's campaign bring in more than sixty thousand dollars.

As the campaign year wore on, and political tensions across Delaware began to heighten, demands on Jill began to shift away from hostess duties. Joe's rivalry with James H. Baxter, the Republican challenger, started to push her closer to the public arena.

Baxter attacked Biden as a "no-show" senator, running an ad claiming, "Biden misses 502 Senate votes." Baxter's main message to the public was that Joe, instead of representing Delawareans in Washington, was out wasting taxpayer dollars traveling on frivolous business trips. In truth, Joe had a typical attendance record for a senator.

Joe played into his opponent's hands by missing an event sponsored by the Hadassah Women's Zionist Organization that Baxter and other Delaware officials attended. Jill, Beau, and Hunter attended.

Baxter once again returned to his mockeries of "no-show Joe." Ironically, Joe's absence was due to a ten p.m. vote in DC on a bill that he had cosponsored. This time Baxter was criticizing him for *not* missing a vote.

Jill stood in as his protector.

"I just cannot let this go by," she told the gathering. "I just can't let you go out that door thinking that Joe just sloughs off down in Washington! Joe is a smart man and he knows which votes are important…If he misses a vote because it's an amendment to an amendment, he's made a good decision on that!"

Jill increasingly found herself in the local spotlight in the usual ways for a Senate spouse. She headed up Operation Reindeer, an event put on by the Mental Health Association that provided small gifts for the thousands of patients throughout the Delaware state mental health treatment system. And she signed autographs for people who bought copies of a cookbook that included a recipe for Jill Biden's Chocolate Cake that benefited the Wilmington Hadassah.

After being married to Joe for more than a year, Jill was still registered as a Republican. Once the local papers found out, she told them that she planned on changing her party registration to Democrat. But she missed the deadline, meaning that if she wanted to vote in the Senate primary, it would have to be in the Republican contest, where her choice would be to help Joe's main rival, James Baxter, or Baxter's primary challenger, James Veneman. She voted, but would not tell Joe, the kids, or the press who she voted for.

On Election Day, Joe secured his Senate seat for a second time. He won with more than 93,000 votes to Baxter's 66,479.

In the spring of 1978, Joe met a young lawyer, Mark Gitenstein, at a Senate hearing on the Foreign Intelligence Surveillance Act (FISA) of 1978. Gitenstein detailed the work on intelligence overreaches by US government agencies that he had done for Minnesota senator Walter Mondale as counsel to the US Senate Select Committee on Intelligence.

Joe was impressed with Gitenstein's command of the issue and invited him to speak privately.

Gitenstein thought Biden wanted to talk about the FISA issues at hand and concentrated on convincing Biden about what should go in the FISA statute. Following a period of civil rights abuses, and the classifying of citizens such as Martin Luther King Jr. as potential threats against the state, FISA and the Foreign Intelligence Surveillance Court were meant to be positive steps toward institutionalizing channels through which intelligence could be collected.

But Joe talked more broadly, asking questions and running Gitenstein through his paces. Eventually Gitenstein realized Joe was interviewing him for a job. Biden invited Gitenstein to dinner in the Senate dining room with his chief of staff, Ted Kaufman, Jill, and the boys. Gitenstein found the Bidens—particularly Jill—delightful.

"It was out of that evening that I came away saying, 'You know what? I like this guy, and I like the way he treats his kids,'" Gitenstein said.

In those early years, sometimes Gitenstein would travel with Joe and Jill on official trips, and while Joe certainly wielded his own charisma in the right settings, it was Jill who brought the jokes and could cut a rug.

John McCain, the Arizona Republican who would later be elected to the US Senate and run for president in 2000 and 2008, was still in the Navy as a captain and acted as Biden's Navy liaison on a trip to the Mediterranean. Joe would later tell a story about returning from dinner with the prime minister of Greece and finding Jill and McCain dancing on a concrete table in a taverna on an Athens beach. McCain danced with "a red bandanna clenched in his teeth," wrote author Robert Timberg.

Jill eventually returned to teaching part-time. "They needed reading specialists in the state of Delaware, because Delaware was going through 'deseg,'" Jill recalled.

School segregation had deep roots in Delaware. A local court case known as *Gebhart v. Belton* had been folded into the collection of cases that made up *Brown v. Board of Education,* ultimately leading to the 1954 Supreme Court decision that determined "separate educational facilities are inherently unequal."

Delaware public schools were forced to desegregate, with varying degrees of success. Schools in Wilmington became predominantly Black, while the surrounding suburban schools remained de facto white. Eventually, in 1978, *Evans v. Buchanan*—a case centered around Wilmington's eleven school districts—mandated a plan for Black students in the city to be bused to white suburban schools, while white suburban students would be bused into the city.

Busing was opposed by whites who supported de facto segregation, and by some Black residents who saw it as changing the fabric of their communities and adding unnecessary logistical hurdles to their children's education. In response to his constituents, Joe began voicing his opposition to busing in 1974, arguing in part that housing integration was a better area of focus to address inequality. Over the next four years, he put forward numerous proposals to limit federal and judicial authority on busing mandates.

"They wanted reading specialists in a lot of the schools," Jill recalled. After a short time at Concord High School, she began working at Claymont High School as a reading specialist even though she would not finish her master's degree until 1981. Ironically, Claymont had been the first school in the state to integrate, but the school board would later permanently close it in 1990 because of the school's "racial imbalance."

Through her role in the public school system, Jill saw firsthand the rapidly shifting situation. "They were desperate" for specialists, she said, to assist the new Black students who had come from underfunded schools and were behind in their reading skills.

Jill taught in the mornings, which let her keep many of the family's life rhythms the same. She was still there to pick the boys up from school, waiting in the carpool line with the other parents each afternoon.

But Joe's presence in the Senate kept her in the public eye. Although Jill registered for her graduate courses under Jacobs, her maiden name, people recognized her.

"The country didn't know her," Joe's chief of staff, Ted Kaufman, later said, "but obviously every single person in Delaware knew her."

Chapter 12

Ashley

On another trip—this one on Air Force Two with Vice President Walter Mondale in 1980—Jill, Joe, and Mark Gitenstein were traveling with Republican Senate minority leader Howard Baker and a number of influential Democrats. Baker told the group about his experiences earlier that year, when he'd been forced out of the Republican presidential primary by candidate Ronald Reagan.

The plane was comfortable, with big first-class seats that let passengers rock back. Everyone was exhausted and Jill wanted to get some rest, but Joe and Gitenstein couldn't sleep on the plane and stayed up talking.

"Tell Mark about how you're going to be president one day," Jill told Joe. "You want to talk, tell him how you're going to be president one day."

Jill may have been teasing him, but the notion that Biden might run for president someday had been floating around Democratic circles. He was young and ambitious and starting to build the type of résumé that would position him to make a run.

Biden was quoted saying, "If I were serious [about a presidential race] I'd have to devote two full years to running flat out...It's difficult to be the kind of father I want to be and go flat out for two years."

The national mood at the moment was not favorable for Democrats. Ronald Reagan won the general election in a landslide over Carter in 1980, and the Republicans took the Senate.

Though his party remained in the minority, Joe moved up to become the ranking Democrat on the Judiciary Committee. He traveled extensively in his work on the Foreign Relations Committee, and Jill often traveled with him.

During a congressional delegation trip to Paris during this time, Senator Pat Leahy found a café within walking distance of their hotel. After dining together, they walked over to the Eiffel Tower. It was late, and the tower was lit up beautifully. Jill and Joe posed in front of the tower, and Pat, a hobbyist photographer, took their picture.

The next day, Jill found Marcelle. "Tell Patrick not to tell Joe he has a picture," she said. "I want to surprise him with something. When you get the picture, give it to me. Don't tell Joe you have it."

Back in Washington, Pat told Joe, "Something was wrong with my camera, and none of the pictures came out. Joe, I'm so sorry."

Pat managed to get the photo to Jill, and she had it put in a frame that read, "You Light Up My Life."

———————

Jill was initially opposed to the idea of having more children, already content and in love with Beau and Hunter, who always referred to her as "mom," never "stepmom." But she eventually decided she wanted to have a child with Joe.

"There were so many reasons not to have a baby—but as time went on, they seemed less and less important. I felt a growing desire to fill that space that had opened up. I didn't tell Joe for several months, but eventually, I couldn't keep it to myself," Jill wrote in her autobiography.

It was during a date in Philadelphia that Jill broached the topic of having a third child. Joe was surprised in the moment, he wasn't sure, but it didn't take him long to come around. Jill had been warned by her doctor that it may take a while for her to conceive, but a mere month later, Jill was pregnant. As a means of ensuring that Beau and Hunter felt like they were looped in, and secure about Jill's unwavering love for them, she told them the news even before she told Joe.

"I think I might be pregnant," she explained, "But I don't want to tell Dad yet. Let's find out together."

In what Jill described as a "spy mission" to the drugstore, they built up the excitement together. The boys waited eagerly in the car while she went in for a pregnancy test, wrapped up in a scarf and sunglasses to avoid curious eyes.

With the news confirmed, Jill asked the boys if they wanted to tell Joe. "Dad! We're having a baby!" Jill recalled them yelling.

Jill completed her master's degree in education in 1981, just weeks before the baby was due.

Early in the morning on June 8, Jill went into labor and woke up Joe.

"Go back to sleep," the father of three told her. He knew it could be hours before they needed to go to the hospital.

Unable to sleep, Jill decided to get up and do her hair. "What can I say? It was the '80s, and I didn't want to show up to one of the biggest moments of my life looking frazzled," she wrote in her memoir. "As far as I could see, there was no reason not to look nice in the delivery room."

She was also worried about Beau and Hunter. "I remembered how traumatic I found my mother's entire pregnancy, and how long those images had stuck with me."

By the time the family showed up to the emergency room, Jill's shoes were squeaking; her water had broken in the car. As they navigated the hospital entrance, Joe's celebrity competed with Jill's real-time needs—a memory that is funnier to her now than it was at the time. While nurses were tending to handsome, famous Joe, who was feeling a bit woozy, Jill gave birth to six-pound, eight-ounce Ashley Blazer Biden.

Joe and Jill had let the boys pick her name. They adored their new baby sister. "We brought her home together, and each of us knew our family was complete," she wrote.

Ashley "lit up my dad's life," Beau later said.

Joe gave a major speech at the New Jersey Democratic Convention in 1983, stoking calls for him to run for president, but he and Jill weren't ready.

His campaign gurus egged him into signing the paperwork for the New Hampshire primary, but Joe insisted the papers stay with his sister, Val. He didn't intend to file them, but if he changed his mind she could take them up to New Hampshire to turn them in.

That December, shortly before the filing deadline, Joe and Jill went on a vacation. One of the campaign gurus, Pat Caddell, contacted Joe at the airport just before the plane took off to try to convince him to run. According to Caddell, Joe said he would—but later called back and said he'd changed his mind again.

"Jill and I had a serious talk on the flight," Joe wrote. "What if, unlikely as it was, I did win?"

After the plane touched down, he called Val. "Don't file that thing," he told her. "I'm not running."

During her time away from teaching, while Ashley was a baby, Jill began to take an active role in the Senate Wives Club. Technically named the Senate Ladies Red Cross Unit and sometimes known as the Ladies of the Senate, the club dated to World War I. "Members of the group were all wives of current US senators, and eventually wives of former senators as well as a few female senators joined the group," according to the Senate Historical Office. They did charity work, sponsored Red Cross blood drives and CPR lessons, and held a weekly luncheon.

"It's a good way for the spouses to develop friendships and give one another support, because there's only the potential for a hundred of us," Marcelle Leahy said. "And so we're in a rather unique position."

Jill was able to go down to Washington on Tuesdays for the lunches with baby Ashley in tow. In the spirit of the club's Red Cross connection, the spouses really did roll bandages before lunching. Politics was always left at the door, with Republican and Democratic women forging warm relationships with each other.

Marcelle worked as a registered nurse at what was then Arlington Hospital in Northern Virginia. She recalled Jill being unable to attend daytime events for spouses after she resumed teaching. Few spouses of senators had their own careers at the time, and most senators would move their families to the DC area rather than commute to their home states all the time.

She and Jill hit it off and became friends. "She greets everybody with equal warmth and interest," Marcelle said. "There's no one else in the room when she's talking to you. She's clearly interested in you."

After a few years away from work, Jill found a long-term babysitter and returned to teaching. Her first job back was as a history and English teacher at the Rockford Center, a psychiatric hospital that had opened in the 1970s as a private sanatorium and had recently begun operating a dedicated inpatient, fourteen-bed program for adolescents. The center brought in state-certified teachers like Jill for the three hours of compulsory school the patients attended each morning. The press at the time described the patients as "seriously disturbed young people" between the ages of thirteen and eighteen.

Jill taught students with a range of mental health issues, from depression to anorexia to drug addiction. She recalled her time there as "one of the most intensely difficult jobs I've ever had," writing in her memoir, "when I trudged home at the end of the day, I knew I'd made a difference in their lives—at least some of them."

Chapter 13

First Run

By the mid-1980s, the calls for Biden to run for president were mounting. Weekends in Delaware became consumed by meetings at the Biden home where a dozen advisers debated the pros and cons of running and brainstormed what a campaign might look like.

Jill took part in some of the discussions, but rarely gave her opinion in front of the group. She waited until afterward to discuss her views with him privately. Joe used his Senate travels as a test run for how his family might adapt to life on the campaign trail.

"I'm taking my family out and letting them get a taste of what it would be like" to run, Joe said. "If I decide to go for it, we're going to have to handle it as a family." Ashley was still very small. "Can we do this without Jill becoming a single parent?" Joe said. "That question is not answered yet."

Joe wove family issues into his stump speech, saying cynics believed "that having reached the conservative age of mortgage payments, pediatricians' bills, and saving for our children's education, that we are ripe for Republican picking. But they've misjudged us."

Democrats took back the Senate in the 1986 midterms, making Joe chairman of the Judiciary Committee. Now Joe "had to ask himself whether he could undertake the rigors of a presidential campaign while taking on his new legislative responsibilities, which would include confrontations with the Republican administration over more high judicial appointments."

"I think I can do both," Joe told an AP reporter.

Around this time, the Bidens sold their house, although they stayed in the neighborhood and downsized. Beau was heading off to college, with Hunter a year behind him. Ashley was still a little girl.

Ashley later told biographer Jules Witcover, "I just always remember Dad being present. He was present every morning, I talked to him two times a day by phone, he was always home at night, most of the nights, to catch dinner and to tuck us into bed. He was around on the weekends. I think Dad was around more than some of my friends' fathers who lived two blocks away....He had a rule that no matter where he was, no matter what he was doing, if us kids called, that was it. You got him out of the meeting."

One year Joe was going to miss his own birthday, stuck in Washington for a Senate vote. Ashley had made him a cake, and was upset he wouldn't be home in time to celebrate. Joe arranged to slip out between votes to catch an evening train to Wilmington.

"I got off the train. My wife, Jill, was standing there, and my daughter had the cake, candle lit," Joe recalled. "I blew them out. Gave me a kiss. Walked across and got on the southbound" train back to Washington.

Joe began traveling to New Hampshire and Iowa on the weekends, thinking about how best to fundraise, and meeting with party leaders. He "reasoned with" Jill that "there was no harm in taking these early steps."

On the way back from a Christmas trip to Hawaii, Joe and Jill got stuck in the plane on the tarmac for hours. They'd stayed with friends and done a little fundraising over the holidays. Now they were quiet, and Jill was staring out the window.

She sighed—the sound of "concentrated sadness," wrote Cramer.

"What?" Joe asked.

"Nothing," she said. "Just...it's never going to be the same—is it?"

"Don't you want to run?" Joe asked.

It wasn't that, Jill said. "It's just...everything's so perfect now."

As the intention to run took shape in January 1987, Joe's advisers met with him. "This was the big leagues," Cramer wrote of their advice. "They'd try to kill him, and Joe would have to watch every move." Anything he'd said, anything he'd done, in politics, with women, in his real estate deals—"it's all going to come out."

Late at night—starting around one in the morning—Joe took them through everything. "The debts—he went through his finances whole, the mortgages, the credit cards. He was into Visa, Amex for thousands." His life with Neilia, and the women he'd dated between his marriages.

He told them about Jill's first marriage—"not the greatest guy in the world."

At two a.m. or even a bit later, Joe brought Jill downstairs "to tell the guys about her inventory."

Joe's campaign staff "took Jill for a political infant, or a problem to be circumvented. But Jill Biden was a woman of realistic judgment: she'd been around politics for a decade now, and she had good eyes."

After a ski trip that was meant to include significant family time but turned into yet another chance for political gladhanding and media appearances, Jill sat with Joe's trip director, Ruth Berry, on the plane while Joe slept.

Ruth had worked in the Carter White House. Jill asked her about being first lady. What could I do? she asked. What would I have to do?

Anything you choose to do, Ruth told her. There are a hundred ways to help Joe, and Jill could work on "education, family services, better day care"—her own issues and things that mattered to her.

"That's when Joe woke up," Cramer wrote, "and the only part he heard was Ruth telling Jill how she could work on those issues. And he jerked into instant fury. He was not in this goddamn thing to have his family bossed around. His jaw started working and his teeth clenched in that killer grin. No one was going to tell his wife what to do!"

"Honey, don't listen to anyone," Joe said. "You just do what you're comfortable with."

Turning to Ruth, he said, "Goddamnit! Don't you ever tell Jill what she's got to do."

Cramer wrote that "later, in the bathroom, Jill told Ruth, 'When he gets like that, just ignore him. He just gets that way, sometimes.'"

———

One day in their bedroom, after a meeting with the campaign staff and while they prepared for the first public event of their day, Joe told Jill, "I don't want to do this." Their private life was too good. Once the announcement was made, they couldn't turn back.

"You have to do this now," she told him, sitting at her makeup table, without the slightest hesitation. "You have too many people's lives on hold."

"He decided to run, or we decided to run," Jill recalled. "I don't remember the exact moment—I don't think there was an exact moment where we said, 'We'll run.' It just sort of took over."

Chapter 14

Learning the Campaign Trail

On June 9, 1987, Joe formally announced his bid to become the Democratic nominee for president of the United States.

Joe launched his campaign with a message of national unity in a speech at the train station in Wilmington, where his sentiment hit especially close to home.

In the 1960s, the construction of I-95 through some of Wilmington's most stable communities had led to a significant decrease in population size and rising crime rates. Construction of the interstate destroyed homes, churches, and businesses in the middle of town and segregated Wilmington, dividing the once walkable city in two. In the years that followed, much of the city's industry contracted or relocated out of state, leaving dozens of hazardous industrial sites in its wake. By the time Biden launched his campaign, the divided and impoverished city had been shrinking for decades.

After his speech, everyone—Joe, Jill, their kids, Joe's parents and siblings and other relatives—boarded a campaign train to Washington while a high school band played "It's a Small World After All"—as "the small-state candidate" set out to take the presidency.

As Joe planned his first try for the Oval Office, it meant a great deal more would be demanded of Jill. Over the preceding decades, the atmosphere for political spouses had changed rapidly, with subdued political roles by former first ladies giving way to a new era of savvy, influential spouses.

The modern understanding of the role of first lady arguably originates with Eleanor Roosevelt. She held press conferences, traveled on speaking tours, wrote a daily newspaper column from the White House, and gave a keynote speech at the convention nominating President Franklin Roosevelt for his third term.

The next great evolution of the role of first lady came with Jacqueline Kennedy, who in 1962 gave Americans a televised tour of the White House following the restoration and renovation she had overseen. By harnessing the relatively new medium of television, the first lady was able to extend the hospitality of the White House to Americans who would never visit it in person, room by majestic room. The tour was widely watched and had broad bipartisan appeal.

Following John F. Kennedy's assassination and Johnson's swearing in as president, Claudia "Lady Bird" Johnson took up advocacy for environmental issues. She actively lobbied Congress for the passage of the Highway Beautification Act, which limited the sprawl of billboards and litter along the nation's highways. "She was more responsible for it" than Johnson himself, said Anita McBride, former chief of staff to Laura Bush and now director of the First Ladies Initiative at American University. "She called members. Don't forget, she was a spouse of the Hill. She knew them all. So she was very involved." Johnson had been a longtime senator and had served as Senate majority leader. Lady Bird was also the first presidential spouse to be involved directly in policy planning and the first to have a staff director and a press secretary, according to the Miller Center at the University of Virginia.

Although Lady Bird considered campaigning unseemly and unladylike, McBride said, she campaigned on Lyndon's behalf "at great personal peril and threat" in the 1964 campaign. The first lady embarked on a four-day whistle-stop train tour through the South dubbed the Lady Bird Special, traveling from Washington, DC, to New Orleans. "Before it was over, she would make 47 speeches, shake hands with more than 1,000 Democratic leaders, and speak before more than 200,000 people," wrote historian Meredith Hindley. She campaigned on civil rights, urging even those southern voters outraged at the recent passage of the Civil Rights Act to vote for Johnson and acknowledge the law of the land.

Lady Bird turned out to be a courageous campaigner and effective public speaker who loved people, McBride said. "First lady followers and historians really do point to that as an incredible example of courage and value in a presidential campaign."

After Lady Bird, the role of the first lady became much more involved, and being able to take the president's message to the public was not uncommon. Some spouses, like Pat Nixon, who was the first first lady to speak at a convention since Eleanor Roosevelt, were widely more popular than their commander-in-chief husbands. But there remained no set expectation that they would participate in campaigns and advocate for the administration's priorities. It was welcomed and accepted, but far from requisite.

"None of what the first lady does, what a spouse does, should be in a vacuum," McBride said. "It should be part of the plan, part of the strategy. It should be adding value, not detracting. It shouldn't be off-message."

By 1987, it was clear that future first ladies were expected to add to their husbands' campaigns, rather than merely stand by to support it; but in a country where positions of authority are not formally conveyed through marriage, the position remained a challenge to fill. "The American public does still get a little uncomfortable when you cross the line," McBride said. "We don't want them to waste the time there, but we don't want them to exploit it."

The 1987 spouses that Jill was being compared to were highly accomplished. Elizabeth Dole was a graduate of Harvard Law School, served in both the Nixon and Reagan administrations, and was acting secretary of transportation in 1987; Hillary Rodham Clinton, a graduate of Yale Law School, had made a name for herself working on education reform in Arkansas; Kitty Dukakis had chartered her own successful business career and headed the Massachusetts task force on homelessness; Jeanne Simon was an Illinois state legislator and author; Hattie Babbitt was a well-respected trial lawyer; and Elise du Pont, yet another attorney, had served as a foreign aid officer under the Reagan administration.

Jill, in contrast, was a schoolteacher making a reported income of $3,255 to Joe's $93,572. Teaching represented a significantly more blue-collar career than the other campaign spouses.

It made for a different political image, too. In a column headlined "New

Breed of Political Wives Poses Challenges for the Press—and Voters,"
David Broder outlined the credentials and backgrounds of the various
campaign spouses. Of Jill, he wrote, "Jill Biden, wife of Sen. Joe Biden,
D-Del., another possible presidential candidate, teaches adolescents at the
Rockford Center, a home for severely retarded people."

Once the 1988 field began to take shape, speculation about the would-be
first lady became a considerable part of the national discourse, with voters
speaking more openly about the ways in which spouses could influence
their husband's administration. Voters were being forced to acknowledge
that a future first lady may know just as much about a particular topic as her
husband, and command an influence over decisions that directly affected
national and international affairs.

Regardless of how individual voters interpreted the role of first lady, one
certainty was clear: The lives of political spouses were becoming scrutinized as they had never been. And while Jill had gradually taken a more
active role in Joe's political life in recent years, the race for president was a
whole new world.

Just slightly more than two weeks after Joe had announced his candidacy,
he and Jill were flying to Los Angeles to fundraise when they got the news
that Supreme Court justice Lewis F. Powell Jr., seventy-nine, was going to
retire.

President Ronald Reagan would nominate his replacement, and as
chairman of the Judiciary Committee, Joe would oversee the confirmation
hearing. Word came soon after that Reagan intended to nominate Robert
Bork. Justice Powell had been nominated by Nixon but proved to be, as Joe
would later put it, "essentially the finger in the dam holding back the
Supreme Court from ratifying the [Reagan] conservative social agenda."
Bork, Biden decided, needed to be defeated.

Robert Bork was already a controversial figure in American politics. In
1973, he was serving as solicitor general for the Department of Justice when
the Saturday Night Massacre took place. When President Nixon called on

acting attorney general Elliot Richardson to fire special prosecutor Archibald Cox, Richardson resigned. Next in line, deputy AG William Ruckelshaus, also refused and resigned. It then fell to third-in-command, Robert Bork, to fire Cox, which he willingly did. The fallout from the firings was swift and, ten days later, the impeachment proceedings against Nixon began. It was ultimately determined that Bork's dismissal of Cox was unlawful.

Still, Bork served as solicitor general for another four years, making a name for himself as a provocative and effective conservative voice, arguing cases such as *Milliken v. Bradley*, where he represented the state of Michigan against the NAACP on the topic of school desegregation. He also argued against voter protections and against civil rights decisions, and favored Southern states' authority to levy a poll tax.

He went on to serve on the DC Court of Appeals, where he wrote a number of high-profile, controversial opinions. His nomination for the Supreme Court drew outcry from civil rights leaders across the country.

Joe met with constitutional scholars and learned as much as possible about Bork's judicial record. "The more I knew about the judge, the more strongly I felt that it was necessary to keep him off the Court," Joe wrote.

With so much riding on the Bork hearing, Joe knew he needed to stay in Washington to prepare for the confirmation fight despite the protests of his Iowa campaign staff, who wanted their candidate on the ground in the early caucus state. Joe "responded to concerns about his presidential campaign by saying he had told his campaign staff that he would sacrifice the whole presidential effort if necessary to see the nomination and hearings through."

Joe proposed a compromise. If he couldn't be in Iowa as often as the campaign wanted, the Biden family would fill the void. He persuaded Jill, who had the summer off from school, to be his surrogate in Iowa. Val, his sister, was out there constantly as well.

"Up to now, Jill was going along with my dream," Joe wrote. "I had always told her she wouldn't have to do anything she didn't want to, and I knew she wanted no part of going out on the road to campaign on her own. But now I was asking her to do just that. And she agreed."

———————

Christine Vilsack, a teacher who would go on to be first lady of Iowa when her husband, Tom, served as governor from 1999 to 2007, recalled the first time she heard of Jill. She was reading the *Des Moines Register* and saw that Senator Joe Biden, one of the presidential candidates, was married to a teacher and was encouraging young people to get involved in public service.

"I think I found somebody I can support in the Iowa caucus," she told Tom. "His name's Joe Biden. He's from Delaware."

"Oh, that's kind of who I want to support, too," he said.

The couple got involved with the Biden campaign and held an event for Biden at their home in Mount Pleasant. It was the start of a decades-long political friendship between the Bidens and the Vilsacks, one that underscores the loyalty Joe and Jill have to many of their earliest political backers.

Biden leaned heavily into his youth during the campaign, casting himself as the representative of a younger generation pushing for change. In one campaign video, Joe appealed directly to younger voters. He argued that if they didn't get involved in politics and public service, they would pay the price of being governed by people less qualified than them. Christine took it around the state and played it for high school students.

For Jill, the presidential campaign was also the first time she began working closely with her own political staff. It reflected the higher stakes of presidential politics and the greater scrutiny of her role on the campaign trail.

Cathy Russell, then a law student serving as a volunteer on the presidential campaign, traveled with Jill in the early stages of it. Jill was kind and forgiving of a rookie scheduling mistake that caused them to miss a flight.

"My first impression of her was that she was just a super nice person," Russell recalled. They held small-group events in people's living rooms. Jill was nervous, but her sincerity came through, and people connected with her.

"Just talk to them," Russell urged her. "They're not looking to you to be a policy expert." They wanted to see Joe through the eyes of his spouse.

Voters in Iowa were responding well to Biden and his wife. But the campaign was taking a toll on the young mom, who spent the summer shuttling between Wilmington and Iowa, balancing her role as a campaign surrogate and a mom. Though Beau and Hunter were more independent at that point, Ashley was just six years old. And even when Jill was back in Delaware, there were days of follow-up notes to write to the people she'd met and preparation for her next trip.

"I can remember that summer, my God," Jill recalled. "I can remember so clearly that I always wished I had one day to just go to a hotel and sleep. Because as soon as I got home, it was like, Mommy, Mommy, do this, do that."

But the strain was worth it. Jill believed there was real support and momentum building in Iowa for Joe's candidacy.

"I saw the response in Iowa," she recalled. "I totally believed he would win. I just believed. He is such a good man."

Chapter 15

Career, Goals, and Pranks

On July 26, six out of seven Democratic potential first ladies, including Jill, participated in a forum at Drake University in Des Moines, Iowa. In front of dozens of reporters and TV crews, the women would directly communicate what they hoped to contribute if their husbands were to win the White House.

The cameras caught Jill looking daunted—blinking, smiling, clearing her throat. She told a German film crew she felt "just a little" nervous. But the rules worked in her favor. It was a forum, not a debate; each woman spoke for five minutes, and there were no questions allowed.

"As a mother, my children are my first priority," Jill said. "As first lady, America's children will be my first concern." It was also an opportunity for Jill to showcase her passion for education and her experience in the area. "I want a school system that does not have to teach remedial reading to twelfth graders," Jill said. "I want an America that is one hundred percent literate."

She also made clear to voters that she would maintain her independent career if her husband were to win the White House. "It's my profession," she said, "and I don't think Joe would expect me to give it up."

It was something of a radical position—no first lady had ever held a paying job while her husband occupied the Oval Office. But times were changing; a USA Today–Gannett News Service poll in 1987 found that almost seventy percent of Americans supported the idea of the first lady pursuing her own career while her husband held the presidency.

The spouses' event was the first of its kind, and it drew attention from around the globe. Joe, briefly in Iowa and keen to support his wife, had sat in the audience. He was the only candidate to attend. "Hey, where she comes is where I go," Joe said.

When a reporter asked Jill if she appreciated having Joe there to watch the event, she gave an unabashed yes, highlighting her years behind the scenes. "I've supported him for ten years. And now he's supporting me." Jill told another reporter, "People want to see a team in the White House."

"Hey! You were great!" Joe said as Jill joined him after the event. "I'm letting you do all the speaking from now on."

"Never," Jill said. "Never."

Columnist Roger Simon concluded, "I think he just wanted to be with his wife on a day that was important to her. Which is not a bad thing to know about a guy who wants to run the country."

———

While Joe remained largely holed up with his staff in Bethany Beach, Delaware, to study briefing books on Bork's record, breaking away only for rare campaign needs, Jill continued to campaign on his behalf in Iowa through August.

Volunteer staffer Cathy Russell booked Jill's room under her name. At one hotel, they roomed next door to each other. She heard Jill's phone ring, and Jill answered.

Then Russell's phone rang. It was Tom Donilon, back in DC advising Joe on the Bork hearings. Russell and Donilon had been dating while she worked on the campaign. Until now, it had been a secret.

Donilon had called the hotel and asked for Russell's room, but the hotel had put him through to Jill's.

"I thought it was you," Donilon said later to Cathy. "And I said something slightly embarrassing."

Jill had simply replied, "Tom, this is Jill. Cathy's in the room next door." Russell was mortified.

When they saw each other the next morning, Jill looked at Cathy.

"Do you have anything you want to say to me?" she asked.

"No," Cathy said.

"Okay, fine," Jill said.

That was all they said about it until much later when Joe found out Donilon and Russell were dating. Jill said, "Oh, Joe, how did you not know that?"

In Iowa Jill spoke directly to working women about the struggles to balance motherhood and family life with careers—a balancing act she was living in real time. Her advocacy for increased support for education came naturally, as well, rooted in her own classroom experiences, but also paired perfectly with the campaign's platform.

The Biden campaign made the case that the American family was modernizing, and that the government could be there to offer significant support for this transition. The campaign used its events in Iowa to model the type of policies Joe would push for on the national level if elected. It began offering free childcare at campaign events, and promised that if Joe won, White House staffers would continue to have the same childcare support—a novel promise at the time.

On one of Jill's trips to Iowa, she met with Christine Vilsack and five or six others at a restaurant in Ames to discuss the creation of the Teachers for Biden group. The members agreed to travel on behalf of the campaign, and Jill, as teachers and educators.

In August, Jill met in an 1870s one-room schoolhouse with seventy Iowan teachers who had organized to support Joe's nomination. Christine's young children were there, too, carrying baskets of apples and presenting them to Jill. The event would be Christine's first television appearance, and she had to make a speech. Like Jill, she was terrified; she couldn't sleep at all the night before. "That was the beginning of the relationship," she recalled. Jill was respectful, empathic, and a listener. There was immediate trust between them.

The teachers' support gave Jill a chance to publicize Joe's goals to improve teachers' salaries, modernize educational basics by adding computer science to the likes of math and English, and hold high school seniors accountable for a semester of community service.

In Iowa, a state with more than thirty thousand teachers, Biden became a name brand for educational reform early in the race, due in large part to Jill's bona fides. She would carry this same commitment to Joe's campaign as she toured the country on his behalf, talking to crowds.

Jill also sought to balance the stress of the campaign and her hectic schedule with what would become a signature of her years on the road—pranks.

"Traveling with her was kind of an adventure," Cathy Russell recalled. "You never really knew what she was going to do."

For one thing, they looked a little alike. Not identical, by any means, but they both had blond hair and blue eyes and stood at about the same height. Jill played this to her full prankster advantage.

In a hotel lobby, walking up to two men they had a scheduled meeting with, Jill introduced herself.

"Hi, I'm Cathy Russell," Jill said. "This is Jill Biden."

Oh, for the love of God, Jill, Russell remembers thinking. She didn't know what to do, and wound up playing along for several minutes.

Chapter 16

"You've Got to Quit"

In his campaign speeches, Joe had begun frequently quoting material from a speech given by UK Labour MP Neil Kinnock, who was locked in a race against Margaret Thatcher, Great Britain's "Iron Lady," for the position of prime minister in 1987. Kinnock, who was of Welsh descent, was the son of a miner and a nurse. He had a history with workers' rights and education.

Kinnock's speech resonated with Joe, even though it was directed at another nation across the Atlantic:

> Why am I the first Kinnock in a thousand generations to be able to get to university? Why is Glenys [his wife] the first woman in her family in a thousand generations to be able to get to university? Is it because all of our predecessors were thick? Did they lack talent? Those people who could sing, and play, and recite, and write poetry, those people who could make wonderful, beautiful things with their hands? Those people who could dream dreams, see visions? Why didn't they get it? Was it because they were weak? Those people who could work eight hours underground and then come up and play football? Weak? Those women who could survive eleven child-bearings? Were they weak? Anybody really think they didn't get what we have because they didn't have the talent, or the strength, or the endurance, or the commitment? Of course not. It was because there was no platform upon which they could stand.

Joe had arrived in Iowa for the State Fair Debate—a can't-miss event for presidential candidates, where contenders are judged as much on their policy proposals as their affinity for greasy fair food—preoccupied with the looming Bork hearings.

"The debate went fine, and when I got to my close, I just did Kinnock's platform thing," Joe later wrote of the event. "But it was a limited time so I rushed...I ran through the piece whole, from memory...the power of the sentiment was hard to miss."

As it often did, the speech resonated with the silent crowd before him. Joe even recalled one woman in the front row standing in tears as she listened to the message. While the delivery was good, one of Joe's aides noticed that he had failed to mention Kinnock's name before leaving the stage. In the past, Joe had diligently credited Kinnock from the podium, but this time, he forgot.

"All I had to say was, 'Like Kinnock,' and I didn't," Joe reflected. "It was my fault, nobody else's fault."

To those who were aware of the mistake, there were mixed feelings about what would, or should, come next. Reporters from major news organizations had heard him use the speech before, always naming Kinnock when he did.

"I followed him for three days and every time he used it, he gave Kinnock credit," Jack Farrell of the *Boston Globe* said. "It was awful hard for me to criticize him for not using it once in Iowa."

It would take twenty days before the gaffe began to generate national attention. Stories popped in both the *New York Times* and the *Des Moines Register*, raising doubts about Biden at a critical moment both for the campaign and his Senate career. The Bork hearings would begin in just days.

Jill was angry. She "wanted to take some starch out of the Reagan administration," Joe wrote. "She was convinced the White House had played a part."

The momentum Jill had seen building earlier that summer quickly started to fade. "I just really felt that he was going to do this until the speech," she recalled. After the Iowa State Fair, "the whole thing blew up."

In the aftermath of the Kinnock revelation, journalists and rival campaigns began to scrutinize all of Joe's previous speeches. If Joe had used one unattributed quote, he may have used more.

Earlier that year, Joe delivered remarks in California that pulled directly from a speech Robert Kennedy had given a decade earlier, but once again, the context was sticky. Biden's aides said they had written the speech for Joe. There was no question that the campaign had been wrong in using it how they did, aides said, but they insisted Joe was not responsible for the mishap. While Joe did what he could to step up and assume responsibility, the press also found that he had used language that hewed closely to a 1976 Hubert Humphrey speech in Iowa in 1985 and Nevada in 1986.

The allegations were damaging to Biden and his presidential prospects. But the timing also presented larger problems for the Democratic Party on the eve of the Bork hearings. A Judiciary Committee chairman tainted by scandal was hardly what the party needed as it fought to keep Bork off the high court.

"Our basic game plan went like this," Ted Kaufman said, "break out in Iowa, do well in New Hampshire. The Bork nomination was going to be the opportunity for Americans to see Joe Biden for the first time, to really think about him as a president." Now all that was in jeopardy.

The next bombshell fell on the Biden camp when another article ran in the *New York Times*, stating that while in law school, Joe had failed to cite material he used from an article in the *Fordham Law Review* in a paper on legal methods — academic plagiarism.

"I've done some dumb things, and I'll do some dumb things again," Joe said in a press conference. "I'm in this race to stay. I'm in this race to win. And here I come."

Biden initially was determined to stay in the race. Jill, too, was committed, believing fiercely that her husband was the best-qualified candidate in the field. Beau and Hunter were also on board with continuing the campaign, the whole Biden family having started to let themselves imagine what life in the White House might be like.

But by the end of September, it was becoming more apparent that the hole might be too deep to emerge from.

"The floodgate had opened. It was like the red tide was rolling. And all the time I was having to get up every morning, bang the gavel, know what

I'm talking about with Bork, keep my committee in a posture I thought it should adopt," Joe said.

The incessant calls and questions from reporters about Joe's past began to weigh heavy on everyone, especially Jill.

"It was tough. I mean, it was really tough. It was a tough time," Jill said. "I felt that the press was threatening Joe." They seemed to be saying if he didn't get out of the race, they would "do this or that." She was offended Joe was being attacked for his integrity, which she saw as his greatest strength.

Beau and Hunter felt it, too. "They had had such hopes for their dad," Jill said. "They wanted him to be president. They thought he was going to be president. I mean, they admired him. And then to be publicly disgraced, I mean, it was tough on all of us."

Both Joe's presidential ambitions and his stewardship of the Judiciary Committee at a critical juncture were thrown into a state of uncertainty. It seemed impossible that he could continue on both tracks.

His first attempt at penance was to offer to step down as Judiciary chair, allowing Democrats to slot another lawmaker into the high-profile role during the Bork hearings. But with the confirmation fight looming and little time for another senator to get up to speed, members from both parties backed his leadership and ability to press on.

Their confidence in Biden's Judiciary leadership was validated from the start of the hearings, which unfolded smoothly, despite the high stakes and heated political atmosphere. Democrats were particularly buoyed by Biden's ability to hold his own in one-on-one exchanges with Bork, demonstrating his competent understanding of the law.

But the media remained relentlessly focused on Biden's past mistakes. Solid leadership of the Senate hearings seemed unlikely to be enough to change the national narrative surrounding his faltering presidential campaign.

Joe, along with Jill, their children, his sister, Val, brothers Jimmy and Frank, his mother, Jean, and other family members, discussed his withdrawal from the race. A handful of close political advisers also huddled with Joe at his house in Wilmington to make the final decision. Both Biden's family and his political team agreed that if he left the race on his own terms with grace and humility, he had the best chance of rebuilding his brand for future contests.

Joe's chief of staff, Ted Kaufman, told him, "There's only one way to stop the sharks, and that's to pull out. Then we can catch our breath, win the Bork fight, and come back into this thing sometime later."

Joe's mother echoed the same thought when Joe asked her directly.

"I think it's time to get out," she said.

The two people it appeared hardest on were Beau and Hunter. Still teenagers, they hadn't yet shaken the idyllic view that the American people should be able to understand their father as the same person they knew him to be—an honest and caring man who placed honor above all else.

"If I let the story drag on so long that it compromised my ability to help stop Bork, that would be a mistake I'd have trouble living with," Joe later wrote.

Jill shared that view. After the final meeting with advisers in Wilmington, she was the last one her husband consulted before the ultimate decision to drop out.

"You've got to quit" and beat Bork, Jill said.

"I felt that with everything I had," she recalled in an interview.

Chapter 17

Bork Hearings

On September 24, during a break in the Bork proceedings, Joe called a press conference to make a statement about suspending his presidential campaign. Jill had gone with him to Washington and recalled standing in the back with Mark Gitenstein.

"Hello, everybody. You know my wife, Jill," he began. "Although it's awfully clear to me what choice I have to make, I have to tell you honestly I do it with incredible reluctance—it makes me angry...I'm angry with myself for having been put in this position...I have made mistakes...Now the exaggerated shadow of those mistakes has begun to obscure the essence of my candidacy and the essence of Joe Biden."

He made clear that he still harbored presidential ambitions. "There will be other opportunities. There will be other battles in other places at other times, and I'll be there. But there may not be other opportunities for me to influence President Reagan's choice for the Supreme Court."

"I thought he was strong," Jill remembered. "He didn't falter in the speech."

Leaving the press conference, she grabbed Joe's arm and looked into his blue eyes. It was a moment that reflected how far she had come in her own political evolution, how closely she understood the importance of the next moves her husband would make to his political future and the future of their family.

As Joe remembered, she uttered "something that sounded like profanity. Jill didn't often use profanity, but she wanted my full attention. She wanted me to understand doing my best wasn't good enough now: 'You have to win this thing!'"

Joe went straight from announcing the end of his campaign back to the hearing room to continue presiding over the Bork confirmation. He looked up and saw Jill walk in and stand against the back wall. She rarely attended Senate hearings, even high-profile ones, but in this moment, when her husband needed her support, she made sure she was there.

Senator Alan Simpson—a Republican from Wyoming and an advocate of Bork, and therefore Joe's opponent in this moment—saw Jill enter, too. "Nothing else matters, man," he said to Joe. "Nothing else matters."

Jill blew Joe a kiss and mouthed *I love you* across the hearing room.

Once Jill was home and everything was over, she shut the door to her bedroom tight and cried. When Joe's mother heard how upset she was over the phone, she came over to comfort her daughter-in-law.

"I called Mom-Mom and I just broke down," Jill said. "She just came and held me—which, when you think about it, you think of her strength. Because here it's her son, and she comes and holds me."

The day after the announcement, Joe, Jill, and Val flew to Iowa and New Hampshire to thank his supporters and wind down his campaign.

Despite the fact that the controversy surrounding Biden had been swirling for weeks, the end of the campaign felt abrupt to some of his most loyal supporters in the early caucus states.

"We had established Teachers for Biden, we were getting ready to start it up," Christine Vilsack recalled. "Then the campaign was over."

While Joe was able to ease the sting of dropping out by channeling his energies into the Bork hearings, Jill took longer to move on. Everywhere she went in Delaware—work, school events for Ashley, even trips to Janssen's, her regular grocery store—people greeted her sympathetically. She despised the feeling of being pitied.

Others in Delaware, who had become invested in the prospect of a home state senator making it to the White House, sought out Jill for comfort of their own. At one of the lowest points of her time as a political spouse so far, she found herself having to console others about the end of her husband's campaign.

"It just felt so prickly," she said.

After weeks of hearings, the moment finally had come for the full Senate to decide Bork's fate. The vote was set for October 23, 1987, and as the Senate clerk called the roll it became increasingly clear that Bork would be denied a seat on the nation's highest court. He failed his confirmation by a vote of 58–42, the largest vote a Supreme Court nominee had ever lost by, with Joe responsible for securing *No* votes from key Senate members.

"He needed to be vindicated," Jill said later about Joe. "It was about Bork, it was about Bork's politics, but it was also about Joe."

Following Bork's rejection by the Senate, Reagan nominated Anthony Kennedy for the Supreme Court seat. Months later on, February 3, 1988, Kennedy was confirmed unanimously, 97–0.

It was a period of vindication for Biden, a validation of his decision to forgo the campaign to focus on the Bork hearings. Kennedy's confirmation helped set the high court on a more moderate path and Biden burnished his reputation as a skilled and effective Senate leader.

Gitenstein felt they'd done something good for the country. "We got a whole generation of decent jurisprudence because of that fight," he later said.

But if Joe was back on solid ground, his wife was struggling, still not able to move past the frenzy that had derailed her husband's presidential campaign and damaged his reputation.

"After being such a rock," Joe wrote, "Jill was having a hard time." The reporters, the helicopters, the frenzy—"she considered the whole thing menacing and so sad."

Late at night after the kids were in bed, Jill would soak in the tub and Joe would come in to sit on a stool beside her.

"It's hard to smile," Jill said.

"I know," Joe said. "Things will get better."

Chapter 18

Holding Hands Through All

The Bidens would soon try to settle into a new routine. It was January 1988, and instead of campaigning in Iowa and other early-voting states, Jill was starting a new position teaching English at Claymont High School. Life was quiet again. They refocused on raising their children and improving their home in Delaware, and Joe dug back into his work on the Senate Foreign Relations Committee.

"It was getting back to normal," Jill recalled.

Joe went on a two-week trip to discuss the Intermediate-Range Nuclear Forces Treaty with European leaders and NATO. While overseas, he briefly met with Neil Kinnock, the British lawmaker whose words he had recited on the campaign trail. They laughed about the events of the campaign, but it was still too close to home for Joe.

Jill knew Joe had been ignoring his health for months. The forty-five-year-old had multiple headaches a day on the campaign trail and carried a bottle of Tylenol with him. He sometimes took ten a day. They'd all assumed it was stress from the competing demands of the campaign and the Bork hearings. "I just kept thinking it was pressure," Jill recalled.

One day, when Joe was back in the US and lifting weights in the Senate gym, he felt a sharp pain in his neck that got worse that night. His right side was numb and his legs were heavy. He wondered if he'd had a heart attack but didn't want to scare Jill; he told her he thought he'd pulled a muscle. A doctor told him he'd likely pinched a nerve during his workout.

Joe got a neck brace and went on a swing of speeches through Scranton, Pennsylvania, New York, and Connecticut.

If anything, he seemed to want to work harder. He delivered a foreign policy speech on February 12 at the University of Rochester, then spent ninety minutes answering questions. An aide gave Joe a signal to stop, but he kept going. After another hour, the audience microphones were turned off, but rather than Joe taking the hint, he simply got down off the stage so he could better hear what they were asking. After four hours, Joe's team packed up their stuff and waited by the door. Joe simply moved to stand there with them while he fielded more questions.

His head was bothering him, but he simply chalked it up to the long day and a lack of sustenance.

"Hey! You think we can still get a pizza?" he asked his team. But nothing was open, and Joe went back to his hotel room.

He keeled over at the foot of his bed. Five hours later, he woke up alone and on the floor.

The next morning, he was nauseated and struggled to carry his briefcase. He flew to Philadelphia and returned to his home, where he told his aides to just let him sleep.

"Bullshit," his brother Jimmy said. "Get a doctor."

Jimmy called Jill's school with word that her husband was ill.

At Claymont High School, Jill saw the principal and a colleague standing at her classroom door, motioning for her to come over.

"You've got to go home," they said. "We got a phone call, and Joe's sick."

Jill rushed home in the car. She found him in bed. "His color was just— he was gray," she recalled.

Jill and Jimmy took Joe to Saint Francis Hospital in Wilmington. An initial CAT scan showed nothing.

While they waited for a spinal tap, Jill went home to get things settled with the kids. Beau was off at college, a freshman at the University of Pennsylvania. But Hunter was still living at home, and Ashley would be coming home on the bus. It was near the end of the school day.

"I had kids coming home from school," Jill remembered. "I couldn't have them come home to an empty house and wonder where the heck everybody was."

She rushed home and lined up a babysitter for Ashley, but she couldn't find Hunter anywhere. He and his girlfriend had decided to go out to dinner without telling anyone.

"I had Joe's staff calling every restaurant in Wilmington, literally trying to find Hunter," Jill recalled.

Jill returned to Saint Francis an hour later, but the situation had changed dramatically during her short absence.

She walked down the hallway to Joe's room, where a nurse sat at a table outside the door doing charts.

"Wait, wait, wait," the nurse said. "Don't go in there."

"What do you mean, 'don't go in there'?" Jill asked. "My husband's in there."

"I know, I know," the nurse said. "But they're giving him last rites."

"What? He's not gonna die," Jill said.

She rushed into the hospital room and found a priest administering the Catholic sacrament reserved for patients facing death, grave illness, or a life-threatening operation.

"Get out! Get out!" she shouted. "My husband is not going to die."

In her memoir she wrote, "I yell so rarely that the sound of my voice surprised me almost as much as it did the priest."

The priest "got up and out he went," she recalled.

The spinal tap had found blood in Joe's spinal fluid, which indicated an aneurysm. If he was to live, he'd need immediate surgery.

"That just changed life in an instant," Jill recalled.

Suddenly Joe's whole family flooded into the hospital. How do we find the best doctors? She remembered all the phone calls.

Jimmy lined up the chief of neurosurgery at Walter Reed Army Medical Center in Washington, where Joe, as a senator, was entitled to care. But there was no safe way to fly Joe there; if there were any complications due to atmospheric pressure, it could kill him.

The weather conditions were bad, too—it was snowing, and getting worse. But they had no choice. They would have to drive one hundred miles south to the hospital.

Jill rode in the ambulance with Joe. Beau rode with the state police escort, and other family members packed into cars for the journey.

Jill cracked wise as they loaded Joe into the back of the ambulance. "Well, you've really ruined Valentine's Day," she said. "If you die, I'm moving to North Carolina. I'm done with this winter business." It roused a smile out of Joe.

They crossed the Delaware state line in a blizzard, and signals got crossed with the Maryland police who were supposed to guide the way. Eventually the Biden convoy was forced to stop on the side of the road and radio for support.

"Why are we stopped?" Jill asked. "Why are we stopped?"

After a few minutes, Jill was fed up with waiting. She pounded on the wall from the back of the ambulance.

"Move!" Jill yelled. "Dammit, move this ambulance!"

Dr. Eugene George, who was a top surgeon at Walter Reed, was overseeing Joe's care, but still wasn't good enough for Jimmy. He started calling around to find the best surgeons in the world, going so far as to prepare for a jet to pick up a team in New York.

Dr. George informed Jimmy that even if the team could arrive later that afternoon, there simply wasn't time to spare. He explained to the family that each passing moment was a threat to Joe. Surgery was needed before the aneurysm popped. Joe's chances of survival were okay, the doctor said, but there was a high likelihood that he may walk away with any number of impairments.

Val, Jimmy, and Jean Biden all talked over the next move in the room the hospital gave them. Jill sat almost in a trance, watching them argue.

"Wait a minute, this is *my* husband," Jill finally said. "*I* make the decisions."

The room was quiet for a moment. Then Jean said, "She's right. This is her decision, not yours."

Later Jill wrote, "In that moment, I truly felt I was a Biden. And I belonged at that table, making decisions that would affect us all."

The medical staff explained the procedure and the odds to Joe. He understood the risks as well as any non-doctor could have, and then asked to see his family one by one.

"It wasn't like the movies—there wasn't big stuff he had to fix," Cramer wrote. They knew he loved them, and he knew they would take care of each other without being told. "But he wanted them to know what he'd found out fifteen years before: they would go on."

"I guarantee you," Joe told the boys, "every single time you have a problem, when you got a tough decision to make, you look: I'll be there with you. Every time."

"Jill was so strong," Joe wrote later. "She hadn't shown a hint of panic through the entire ordeal....I had an overwhelming sense of sadness. Ashley was only six years old...Jill would have to tell my daughter I wasn't coming home again. Beau and Hunter might be losing a second parent. Hunter wasn't even out of high school yet."

Then they wheeled him in for surgery. Jill held his hand until they reached the door of the operating room.

The family sat around waiting. It was "like an Irish wake...except there was no body," Cramer wrote. Food was picked up, and old stories and jokes began to circulate.

Chapter 19

A Second Chance

After many hours of surgery, Dr. George emerged. He told the Bidens they could not have waited any longer. As soon as they cut into Joe's skull, the aneurysm burst.

The surgery went well, but Joe faced a long road ahead. The risks to his health remained high and it was unclear what the lasting damage would be.

The mere sight of Joe after surgery, hooked up to machines and tubes, caused Jill's knees to buckle when she walked into his room in the intensive care unit.

"Jilly, is that you?" he asked. "Am I alive?"

"It's me," she said. "I'm here. You're alive."

The doctors let Jill take Beau and Hunter into Joe's ICU room, but no other family members were allowed. The decision stung Jill, who by now understood how deep the Biden family bonds ran and how hurtful it would be to his parents to not be allowed to see their son in that moment.

"Those moments stick with you," she said later. "I thought, how could they say [that] to his mother and his father after he almost died? We didn't know whether he was going to live. They told us he may not come through this, and then to say, you know, no, you can't see your child?"

She teared up and her voice broke at the memory. "Sorry, it's just emotional moments," she said, apologizing.

Jill, as she often did in difficult moments, forced herself to compartmentalize. She tucked away her fears and focused on providing support and reassurance to her children. She still thought of Beau and Hunter as the children she'd fallen in love with ten years before. "I had two little boys that were just scared to death for their dad."

Jill sat with Joe in the ICU as he wiggled his toes and ran simple mental math. His speech was unharmed.

She also found a silver lining in the decision months earlier to end Joe's presidential campaign.

"Honestly, I believe this with every fiber of my being," Jill said, "that if he had stayed on the campaign trail, he would have died." Joe, she believed, never would have gone to the hospital if he'd still been running. "Not that I thought it was meant to happen, but I saw what would have happened had he not gotten out."

Joe wasn't fully out of the woods yet. Before the surgery, the doctors had found a smaller, second aneurysm on the other side of Joe's brain. It was more stable, but it presented a serious risk and would need to be operated on soon.

Joe was hospitalized for ten days. Jill stayed at Walter Reed for as long as she could, in a room right next to Joe's. The family's babysitter stayed at their home with the kids.

Eventually, though, Claymont High School, where Jill had just started working, called her. They were sympathetic to what the family had been through, but they also made clear that as a new employee, she didn't have enough leave time banked to be missing work.

She realized they had probably already pushed things further than they should have. "It was my contract, and they couldn't give me special treatment," she said. "Eventually it was like, 'Hey, you have a job here.'"

So Jill resumed teaching. Some days she would drive the hundred miles down to Walter Reed after school, visit Joe, and drive back. Sometimes someone gave her a ride there and back. When she couldn't go, Jean or Jimmy or Val went. "Everybody pitched in and took days, took turns," Jill said. "It was a long haul," but they got through it.

Despite the difficulties, returning to the classroom—which had long been a sanctuary for Jill, a place where she could escape outside troubles or distractions—was cathartic. "I could walk into that classroom, and I had to be present," Jill recalled. "I couldn't think about what was going on."

Soon after he was released, Joe had to go back to Walter Reed even sooner than planned to deal with a blood clot in his lung.

When he was discharged that time, Joe spoke to the press gathered outside Walter Reed. "I've asked you all to come today," he joked, "because I've decided to announce that I am reentering the race for president."

Joe went home again to recuperate and rest up to be strong enough for the second aneurysm surgery. Jill made a strict rule: no phone calls. President Reagan tried to call, twice; she said thank you, but wouldn't put him through to Joe. "The world kept spinning without my help, Jill assured me," Joe wrote.

After the second surgery, in May, Joe stayed at Walter Reed for close to a month. This surgery was planned and not as traumatic for everyone around Joe. "They knew what they were doing and they knew that he would easily come through it," Jill recalled.

Even as he recuperated, Joe's physical appearance was jarring to those who came to visit him, expecting to see the young, vibrant senator who had been a rising star in Democratic politics. He had a large scar on his head and his hair was still growing back. He was frail and took time to regain the weight he'd lost. He eased back into daily life, starting to drive again and playing golf. Senator Ted Kennedy came up for a visit. Other colleagues were in touch.

Joe and Jill had had a lot of time to think.

"The biggest thing it changed," Joe said, "was, prior to that, I used to think that every meeting, every opportunity, was critical, and I realized that there aren't that many things that are important, that are actually critical. It really gave me a different perspective." Instead of the driving sense of urgency he might have expected, it gave him a "quiet resolve."

"When you almost die," Val said later, "you look at life with a different perspective." She told Joe, "You've got a second chance here. Make it good."

It wasn't until fall—roughly eight months after the initial aneurysm—that Joe began to get his energy back. After her summer break, Jill returned to the classroom. Joe was ready to head back to Washington.

His first day back in the Senate began like so many days before, boarding an Amtrak train in Wilmington, bound for Washington's Union Station. Rail employees greeted him that morning with balloons and signs welcoming him back.

Chapter 20

Like Mother, Like Daughter

With Joe's health back, the family settled into a good rhythm in the 1990s. Jill stayed involved in a lot of the kids' activities despite teaching full time. She served as the head of the prom committee and helped in the cafeteria. She was a regular at Hunter's games and added Ashley's—lacrosse and field hockey.

"I leave school, go sit in the bleachers, grade papers," Jill recalled, describing this time.

Outside of teaching, exercise was a major part of her life—a way to clear her mind and work out frustrations with her kids, particularly in their teenage years.

After the flurry of the late 1980s—the failed presidential campaign, the Bork hearings, Joe's health scares—this was a quieter, more manageable period for Jill. She was more comfortable and experienced in her role as a Senate spouse, but didn't let obligations overwhelm her. She sometimes attended political events in the evenings in Delaware if they fit the family's schedule, but didn't make regular trips to Washington. That was where her husband worked—but their life was in Wilmington. "It was a full life, but not an overwhelming life," Jill said.

Still, the reality was that politics was a part of the Biden family's life. Unlike Jill's father, who'd left his bank job promptly at the end of each working day, Joe's Senate schedule could be demanding. There were obligations for the family, a familiar routine of political events and parades, and the knowledge that they were subject to scrutiny, even in a small state where everyone seemed to have a connection to the Bidens.

Being a senator, Jill felt, was more of a lifestyle than a job, one that pulled in the entire family. "It's something you live," she said. "You live it twenty-four hours a day."

Jill was certain this made their family stronger. "We knew the highs were so high and the lows were so low, and all you have, really, is one another. And it's a shared experience, so you know someone else's pain."

Jill found it was especially hard on her as a mother not to be able to shelter the kids from the negative aspects of Joe's career. She knew people were saying rude or mean things to them.

She and Joe would keep tabs and talk about it: So-and-so said this to Hunter. This is what was said at the bus stop. "I guess that's the hardest part of being a parent," Jill said.

But there were also advantages to being raised as the child of a senator.

Ashley was eight or nine years old when she became upset about the staggering number of dolphins that were getting caught in tuna nets—an estimated one hundred thousand dolphins were killed annually. Ashley was active in a movement of schoolchildren who mounted a letter-writing campaign and tuna sandwich boycott in protest. Unlike other kids, she had a powerful connection she could leverage: her father. "I would come prepared with research and posters and talk about how we needed to save the dolphins," Ashley has said.

Her father rewarded her efforts with a trip to Congress. Representative Barbara Boxer had introduced a bill in the House that required canners to label tuna that is caught by nets that ensnare dolphins, and she took Ashley onto the floor to help convince the congressmen. Joe then sponsored a similar bill in the Senate.

"Ashley was an activist to save the dolphins," Boxer recalled. "I get a call from Joe and he says, 'Barbara, I got to carry your bill in the Senate because Ashley's going to kill me.'"

The 1990 Dolphin Protection Consumer Information Act became law and prompted several US tuna canners to announce they would no longer buy or sell tuna captured along with dolphins.

"I loved it and never forgot it," Boxer, who later was elected to the Senate, said of Ashley's youth activism. "I don't know that Jill pushed it, but I have a hunch. I have thought it was Jill and Ashley versus Joe. 'You better do this.' And he did it for the family."

Around the same time, Ashley wrote an essay saying she "wanted to help abused women" when she grew up. Joe had been trying to pass the Violence Against Women Act for years, and the issue was something they talked about at home a lot.

Throughout the 1990s, Joe held hearings on domestic abuse, sex crimes, and hate crimes against women. The Violence Against Women Act was passed under President Bill Clinton in 1994 as part of the overall Violent Crime Control and Law Enforcement Act—which Joe dubbed the Biden Crime Bill—that called for one hundred thousand new police officers.

Years later, Jill would tout Biden's work on the Violence Against Women Act as a signature accomplishment, one that revealed him to be a champion of women. But at the time he was working on the legislation, she was skeptical, not necessarily seeing the need for the bill.

"The first discussion I had with Jill about the legislation was an eye-opener," Joe wrote. He told her about the bill while she was getting ready for work. "After a long silence she said, 'Why are you doing that? We don't need protection.'"

Sometime later, they had argued about where she should park while attending night classes for one of her two master's degrees, as there'd been reports of a rapist on campus. Why not park in front of the main building, which was well lit? Joe asked as she was about to pull away.

"There's no parking there," she said.

"Just park there, and we'll pay the damn ticket," Joe said.

Jill, angry, started to drive away. Joe chased after the car.

"Dammit, Jill, slow up," he said. "Promise me you'll park out front. What's the matter with you?"

"What's the matter with me?" she asked. "I really resent it. I know you're right, but as a man you don't have to do that, and I resent it."

In the 1990s, as more women were elected to the Senate, the Senate Wives Club changed its name to Senate Spouses. Jill recalled being present when the name changed. "There was a vote," she remembered, "and the first vote didn't pass."

Though she wasn't a regular presence in Washington, Jill had forged some close relationships with some of the Senate spouses, including Marcelle Leahy, wife of Vermont senator Patrick Leahy, and Florida senator Bill Nelson's wife, Grace—both Democrats—as well as Catherine Stevens, the wife of the long-serving Alaska Republican Ted Stevens. "At that time, I could have called anybody, any other spouse in the Senate and said, 'Hey, I need you to do X,'" she recalled, "and they would have shown up." No one would have wondered why she was asking or whether there was some ulterior motive. "It was just that kind of camaraderie."

Jill also developed her own relationships with some of the lawmakers who served alongside her husband, particularly some of the trailblazing women who were being elected to Congress in increasing numbers.

Barbara Boxer, who represented California first in the House and then in the Senate, recalled getting to know Jill through Senate family gatherings and retreats. Though Jill had long been a part of Joe's life by this point, the tragic elements of his life still made his relationship with her stand out to his colleagues.

"We all knew that, and we all knew the importance of Jill," Boxer said.

A new hurdle emerged in Jill's life during these years: her relationship with Ashley, now a challenging teenager.

Jill's relationship with Ashley was much different from the one she'd had as a teenager with her mother. As Ashley got older, it grew trying. "Girls are a little bit, you know, with their mom," Jill said delicately in an interview. "Sometimes a little more challenging."

They fought a lot, and it frustrated Jill. Ashley was strong-willed—"which is a good thing, in my opinion," Jill added—and rebellious. "With Ashley, I also saw the relationship I had with my father played back to me like a song stuck on repeat," Jill wrote in her autobiography.

"That's how I became a runner," she said. "Honestly, I kept my sneakers by the door. And if I didn't want to fight about something, on would go those sneaks, and out the door I'd go. And that's how I kept my calm balance."

She became more disciplined about her running after she and Joe were asked to participate in a Race for the Cure—the signature event of Susan G. Komen, the largest breast cancer organization in the country. "After sounding the horn, we ran to get out of everyone's way," Jill told *Runner's World* in a 2010 interview. "I got so winded."

She started with short races, and kept increasing her distances until she "got the bug."

Jill had always loved exercise, and running gave her a chance to have alone time, work on her health, and make physical and mental space from daily life.

Chapter 21

Intensity of the Time

In July 1991, President George H. W. Bush nominated Clarence Thomas to replace retiring Supreme Court justice Thurgood Marshall, a liberal, a passionate civil rights advocate, and the first Black person to become an associate justice of the Supreme Court. Thomas was a conservative Black jurist with only a year as a federal judge.

As chairman of the Senate Judiciary Committee, Joe was responsible for leading Thomas's confirmation hearing.

Law professor Anita Hill alleged to FBI agents during a secret, two-day inquiry that Thomas had made unwanted sexual advances and lewd remarks to her when she worked for him at the Equal Employment Opportunity Commission ten years earlier. The Judiciary Committee had sent Thomas's nomination to the full Senate despite knowing about the allegations, and the Senate was poised to vote to confirm Thomas for the Supreme Court.

Public anger erupted after Hill's allegations leaked to the press. "What disturbs me as much as the allegations themselves is that the Senate appears not to take the charge of sexual harassment seriously," Senator Barbara Mikulski, a Democrat from Maryland, said. She was the only female senator at the time.

A group of seven women Democrats in the House, including Barbara Boxer, marched to the Capitol to argue for a delayed vote to allow for additional testimony from Hill.

"This isn't pleasant, and it isn't happy, and it isn't pretty. Neither is sexual harassment," Boxer said. "To respect women in this society means you give these charges your attention."

The Senate agreed to delay Thomas's confirmation vote.

"This is not a trial, this is not a courtroom. There will be no formal verdict of guilt or innocence," Joe said in the televised hearing. The Associated Press at the time dubbed it "daytime television like none before."

Jill watched Hill's testimony unfold on television along with the rest of the country.

Hill, soft-spoken and deliberate in a bright blue suit, sat before an all-male Senate panel and recounted a series of episodes in which she said Thomas asked her for dates, bragged of his sexual prowess, and told her—in the face of her obvious discomfort and objections—of X-rated movies of women engaging in sex acts with animals. Hill said she told him, more than once, that she didn't want to go out with him and didn't want to talk about the sexual matters he raised. She said she feared for her career, felt helpless, and didn't want to burn professional bridges.

"Everybody was glued to their TV," Jill recalled. She believed Hill.

Thomas said he would answer questions about the harassment allegation but nothing else because "I will not provide the rope for my own lynching." He testified under oath that "I cannot imagine anything that I said or did to Anita Hill that could have been mistaken for sexual harassment."

On September 27, 1991, a motion in the Senate Judiciary Committee to send Thomas's nomination to the full Senate with a favorable recommendation failed 7–7. Later in the day, the committee voted to send the nomination to the full Senate without a recommendation.

On October 15, the Senate confirmed Thomas to the court with a 52–48 vote.

The makeup of the committee—all white and all male—fed perceptions that a bunch of older men were interrogating a woman about a topic that bewildered them or, at best, made them uncomfortable. The Republicans on the panel aggressively sought to undermine Hill's credibility, accusing her of lying under oath. On the Democratic side, senators were criticized for being weak in their defense of Hill and their questioning of Thomas.

Joe, as chairman, struggled with how to preside over the hearing, the likes of which had never been seen in a court confirmation fight. "He resented its tawdry nature and did not realize the implications until years later," recalled Charles Geyh, who was then an informal Biden adviser.

Jill recalled that during the hearings, Joe would come home at night and get right back on the telephone. "There were so many people calling and trying to figure out what was going on," she said. She felt the intensity of the time. "It felt like a swirl. There was so much going on, and so much preparation. So I was sort of outside looking in."

Decades later, as he mulled a third presidential bid at a time of heightened awareness about the sexual harassment of women, Joe lamented the role he played in undermining Hill's credibility. "I regret I couldn't come up with a way to give her the kind of hearing she deserved," he said in New York in March 2019 at the Biden Courage Awards, an event honoring those who have worked to combat sexual assault on college campuses. He said he should have protected Anita Hill from what he called "character assassination." He argued the experience had prompted him to invite women senators to join the Judiciary Committee in subsequent years.

The FBI did investigate Hill's allegations and witnesses corroborating her story testified on her behalf. But the committee in 1991 refused to hear from other women, independent of Hill, whose accounts of Thomas's behavior toward them were similar to what Hill had described.

Jill tried not to engage Joe about the hearings while they were going on. "I didn't pepper him with questions," she said, adding that she needed to be a "safe space" for him. Instead, she'd tell him Hunter won his game, and that he should've seen the basket, or the home run, or whatever it was. "Who else would he have if I didn't play that role?"

Still, Jill found moments to weigh in, always privately and discreetly. It was his career, not hers, so she tried to stop short of giving direct advice on how to vote or navigate a tricky issue.

In a larger sense, she said, "I still had my own life. And Joe would leave every day and go to this world." In their private life, Joe had none of the impulsive temper he was known for in the Senate and his presidential campaign. "He has more of a calm to him than an eruptedness," she said, and didn't really show stress. "He's pretty even keeled. He wasn't coming home ranting and raving. He was thinking through how to handle things."

Chapter 22

Running Ahead

In 1993, Jill was working at Brandywine High School in Wilmington when one of her colleagues left for a position at Delaware Technical Community College.

A few weeks later, Jill's friend called and urged her to consider a similar career move. Del Tech, which served some fourteen thousand students across four campuses, was Delaware's only community college. Students who earned an associate degree there could transfer their credits to four-year universities around the state.

"You've got to come by," the coworker said. "I promise you, you would love it."

"I wasn't sure," Jill wrote in her autobiography. "I liked my classes at Brandywine High School, and the notion of making the leap to teaching adults in college was intimidating. Still, the idea of no longer having to serve on cafeteria duty *was* enticing."

Just as her colleague had predicted, Jill was taken with the scene at Del Tech. Community college students had a gritty determination that Jill admired. Most students came from backgrounds that sent them into the world with limited resources and, sometimes, limited expectations. Many were first-generation higher education students, and being enrolled in college was an important shift for their entire families. Some students were older, juggling other jobs and children at home, while others were back for a second chance at college.

"Working with community college students was unlike anything I'd done up to that point. I got to know my students in a way I hadn't in past settings. When we talked about literature, they had life experiences to share. They brought diverse perspectives to our studies—of travels and jobs and families and challenges they had overcome. And they wanted to be there—*really* wanted to be there," she wrote. "They cared about education in a way that people who have never had to fight just to be in class, who have never skipped dinner so they could save up for tuition, just couldn't understand. It was such an honor to be the person to walk them through their studies, to give them the key that would unlock something life-changing."

Jill also found companionship in her fellow faculty. Mary Doody was at Del Tech when Jill was hired, and they would later become close friends. When she interviewed for the job, Jill looked very professional in a white blouse and navy jacket but was visibly nervous.

"Everybody knew she was Senator Biden's wife, and it struck me that she was nervous," Doody said. She found Jill warm and authentic. "She would never ever be a person who just assumed that she would get a job because she was Jill Biden."

Nerves aside, Doody could tell Jill would have a great presence in the classroom. With two master's degrees, she was certainly qualified. "You could just tell, like when teachers meet teachers, they can just tell if they're good teachers, and she had that kind of presence," Doody said.

The relationship Jill formed with her students was not limited to her formal lesson plans. Teaching in a community college setting, she found, often meant helping students navigate life at large.

Jill understood the direct link between not having to worry if you could afford gas to drive to class, or how you were going to feed your children next week, and being able to focus on your studies. Some challenges, like juggling adult learning at night while working at raising children, Jill knew about from personal experience. She began to look for ways to ease these burdens so her students could focus on school.

Jill brought food items to class for those who needed them, and she set up a box at the front of the room that served as a community food pantry—if students had the means to contribute something, they would, and if other students needed something, they could take it.

Jill always found ways to add fun into the mix. "This one time—I never did figure out how she did it," Doody said, "and of course she never fessed up to it. She put a fifty-pound pumpkin on my office chair and drew a face on it and had gotten a cigarette from somebody and stuck it in the pumpkin's mouth. And this pumpkin was so huge, I had to ask the custodial staff to come and remove it from my office."

Another time, Doody remembers finding a Post-it Note from Jill with a lock of hair taped to it and the words: "I pulled my hair out last class."

Jill and Joe invited the Del Tech English Department to their Christmas party during her first year teaching there. When the party was over, Mary Doody recalled Joe escorting her and a friend as they left.

"I hate Jill," the friend said to Joe.

"Why?" Joe asked.

"Because there's nothing about her that I don't like."

Doody had to agree. No one was perfect, but "she looks great. She is kind, she is generous. She is exactly the person you see." She was authentic and grounded, and both fun and funny. "She's a really good person to have as a friend."

In the early 1990s, Jill's friends started getting sick. Four were battling breast cancer, including one who died.

Blessed with resources and connections, Jill began to consider what she could do to help.

"As an educator, my first thought was what I could do?" she said. "I mean, I'm not a medical person, but what could I do as an educator."

The result was the Biden Breast Health Initiative, one of the nation's first breast health programs aimed at educating young women. The slogan of the organization was "to empower young women through awareness and education to assume responsibility for their overall well-being with a strong emphasis on breast health."

Focused mainly on sixteen- to eighteen-year-olds, the initiative was built around the ethos that teaching kids about their health was a great way to help them prepare for adulthood, and that they would share what they learned with their friends and other people.

Sherry Dorsey Walker, a former film producer, and now a Democratic member of the Delaware House of Representatives, worked with Jill on BBHI. When Jill contacted her, Dorsey Walker was twenty years old and had had what turned out to be benign tumors surgically removed.

"I was seventeen when I had my first breast surgery. So, when other students, when their mothers were taking them to look for prom gowns, my mother was literally looking for an oncologist," she said.

Dorsey Walker could connect with students in a unique way, since she had been through the trauma of surgery as she applied to college and scholarships and celebrated the end of high school with her friends. It gave her audience an easy frame of reference to understand.

"The best part of it was going into the high school and educating students about breast health. And the students would go home and tell their parents about it. So, through the work that we did with BBHI, we must have saved hundreds of lives because the Word tells us 'when a child will lead them,' and it was literally the children who were encouraging their mothers and fathers to get mammograms," she said.

In the early days of the initiative, everyone on staff lectured on a rotating schedule, including Jill, who was hands-on the entire time. "She never missed a meeting. Never missed a meeting. She actually went out and taught the classes, too," Dorsey Walker said.

Dorsey Walker said she considers Jill a mentor—both for the guidance she offered as the leader of BBHI and for the personal connections the senator's wife formed with so many others she interacted with.

"Being in the presence of Jill Biden, you feel like you're in the presence of someone who truly loves and cares for you as a human being," Dorsey Walker said. "Take away the politics, take away the voting and all of that. Jill just cares for humanity. And that was the beauty of being on BBHI with her, to see how she cares."

Jill continued working on her running, improving her time, and taking out her frustrations with her teenage daughter on the pavement. In 1998, at forty-seven, she completed the Marine Corps Marathon. The popular marathon's route wound around the monuments and neighborhoods of

Washington, DC, and Arlington, Virginia. She followed a strict training regimen and set her sights on crossing the finish line in four hours and thirty minutes. Seeing her family at a few points along the route, and feeding off the excitement of the race, Jill nailed her time, finishing in 4:30:32.

"I was ecstatic. I have to say it was one of the highlights of my life," Jill later told *Runner's World* magazine. "I tell you, at the end of that race, I felt like I could run five more miles. My adrenaline was through the roof."

Chapter 23

Fateful Day

It wasn't Jill's style—or, she felt, her role—to regularly advise Joe on policy matters. But when she felt strongly about an issue, she made it clear.

In the late 1990s, Joe was pushing President Bill Clinton to add American troops to the NATO air strikes under way in Kosovo, where a brutal war between separatist ethnic Albanian rebels and Serb forces was underway.

Joe returned from a trip to Macedonia late at night and got quietly into bed, but Jill was still awake and waiting for him in the dark.

"Welcome home," she said. "Are you sure you're right? Because if you're wrong, a lot of boys are going to die."

"C'mon, Jill, that's unfair," Joe said.

"No, it's not. Not if you're the one convincing the president to do this," she said.

The war ended after the seventy-eight-day NATO air campaign drove Serb troops out and a peacekeeping force moved in. Jill's concern was an early sign of her connection to military families, whose challenges would become one of her signature policy focuses in the future.

Jill was at Del Tech, getting ready for class, on September 11, 2001, when she saw TV reports that a plane had crashed into the World Trade Center. She reached Joe, en route to Washington on Amtrak, on his cell phone.

Mid-sentence, she cried, "Oh my God. Oh my God. Oh my God." She was staring at the TV in the teachers' lounge, watching in real time. "Another plane—the other tower!"

Jill went to class, shaken. So were her students and colleagues.

When his train arrived at Washington's Union Station, Joe could see "a brown haze of smoke hanging in the otherwise crystal-clear sky beyond the Capitol dome" where another plane had struck the Pentagon. Someone told him Congress had been evacuated—another plane was on its way.

Joe tried to make it to the Senate chamber anyway. "I thought it was awfully important that the Senate be in session," he said later. "That people see us. That they could turn on their TV and see where we were."

"Senator, you've got to get out of here," a Capitol police officer yelled. "Another hijacked plane, eighteen minutes out, heading our way."

Joe's cell phone rang again. This time it was Ashley calling in a panic. "Get out of there," she implored him. "Daddy, you have to leave Washington right now!" she said, crying. "They're going to do something in Washington."

"This is the safest place to be," Joe said.

After word spread that a plane presumably on its way to attack the Capitol had crashed in Pennsylvania, Joe was interviewed on television. "Nothing has fundamentally altered this government," he said. "We should be calm and cool and collected about going about our business as a nation. Terrorism wins when, in fact, they alter our civil liberties or shut down our institutions. We have to demonstrate neither of those things have happened."

Back in Delaware, Jill ended class and drove to visit her sister Bonny, a flight attendant. Bonny knew some of the crew on United Flight 93, the plane that went down in Pennsylvania.

Joe spent hours talking to his colleagues, staffers, reporters, and even tourists on the streets about what had happened before getting a ride back to Wilmington with a Pennsylvania congressman.

A few days later, Joe gave a speech to students at the University of Delaware in Newark. "Don't make these guys bigger than they are," he said of the 9/11 terrorists. "They did a horrible thing and got lucky, but they are not some great juggernaut. Put it in perspective. Don't let yourself get carried away. It will not, cannot, must not change our way of life."

He heard their concerns about the coming war. "You are worried about a war, all this talk of war," he said. "But this is not a war in the traditional, conventional sense. You won't see a return of the draft."

Chapter 24

Lightning Strike

In 2003, Joe began contemplating his next White House run. The impact of America's military involvement in Iraq and Afghanistan was proving to be uncertain at best, and no clearly defined parameters had been drawn to define the "war on terror." As chairman of the Senate Foreign Relations Committee, Joe was in a position to push back on US approaches in the Middle East, even though he had voted to authorize the wars himself.

Jill noticed the drumbeat pick up, too, with more and more people urging her husband to jump into the 2004 campaign to try to prevent President George W. Bush from winning a second term. "There were always so many people trying to get Joe to run," Jill said. It didn't matter what event they went to or who was there. Everyone urged him, "You've got to run again. You've got to try again. Always. It was constant."

But this was one of those moments when Jill had made her personal views abundantly clear to her husband. "He knew that I wasn't in favor of his running."

His press secretary, Larry Rasky, later said Joe had "worked very hard to rebuild his reputation of being thought of as the kind of person he thought of himself, as an honorable and substantive senator. By 2004 he had all that back." Running, Rasky said, would put that at risk, and "Jill was against him taking all that risk."

But Joe had grown increasingly frustrated with the Bush administration's leadership and wanted to at least consider his options.

Biden met with Mark Gitenstein at the Bidens' house in Delaware to discuss the prospect of building a campaign. They were joined by longtime Biden adviser Ron Klain on speakerphone. Klain and Gitenstein told Joe that even though his good friend John Kerry, also a senator, was planning on running for the Democratic presidential nomination, some party leaders thought Joe could go head-to-head with President Bush in the general election.

While the meeting unfolded, Jill decided to remove herself entirely, "fuming" out by the pool. Jill was less involved in Joe's political life at the time, focusing on her doctoral studies and childrearing, but it certainly didn't stop her from having an opinion. Jill was angry about the meeting, and angry that it was happening, of all places, in her living room.

"All these men — and they were mostly men — coming to our home," Jill recalled. "You know, 'you've got to run, you've got to run.' I wanted no part of it." It wasn't the right time, she felt. And the memories of 1987 had never gone away. "I didn't even know whether I wanted Joe to ever do it again. I mean, I had been so burned."

As she made a pass through the house, Joe called out to her. Ron was making good arguments, he said, and Mark had plans for the messaging.

Moments later, she returned with a two-letter message of her own. "As I walked through the kitchen, a Sharpie caught my eye," she wrote in her autobiography. "I drew *NO* on my stomach in big letters, and marched through the room in my bikini. Needless to say, they got the message."

Joe and Gitenstein did, at any rate. Klain, still eagerly engaged on speakerphone and unaware of what had just transpired in the room, kept brainstorming away.

"I don't understand it," a bewildered Klain said later when Gitenstein called to explain. "The conversation was going so great and all of a sudden, it just stopped."

Joe's 2004 campaign was over before it even started.

———

On a Sunday in August 2004, Joe was picked up at six a.m. to appear on *Meet the Press*, while Jill, home alone with the cat, slept in. An early-morning summer storm that led to flooding across two states and left hundreds without power had caused many lightning strikes in the area. When she heard "a tremendous *boom*" at 8:16, Jill looked out the windows to see whether a nearby tree had been hit but saw nothing alarming.

She turned into the kitchen and found it filled with smoke. She grabbed the fire extinguisher, but "no matter where I looked, I couldn't find the flames. All around me was black smoke, billowing, seemingly coming from the vents in the ceiling—and I realized with horror that the fire had to be *inside* the walls."

The direct lightning strike to the house had left the phone dead. In her bathrobe, she ran to a neighbor's house to call 911 and her son Beau. By that time, Joe was already being interviewed by Tim Russert, "so there was no point in trying to get in touch with him. It would have to be a terrible surprise whenever he was done."

Jill ran back to the house, yelling for their cat. "Daisy! Daisy!"

She tried three times to get back inside but couldn't—too much smoke.

The third time she opened the door, the cat bolted out of the house and ran away into the woods. Daisy hid there for three days before returning home.

The fire was ultimately contained to the kitchen, but smoke filled the house. "I stood watching the smoke roil out of my house—out every window, every chimney, every doorway," she recalled. "The rain was pouring down as I stood in the driveway, watching our home be consumed by flames."

The fire department and Beau arrived. Someone from the Women's Auxiliary put a yellow slicker over her. The fire brigade made quick work of the job, and the flames were put out in about twenty minutes.

A firefighter approached them. "Mrs. Biden! Do you remember me? It's Harry!" Jill immediately recognized the man; he had been a former student of hers. "For a brief moment I laughed at the absurdity of this reunion and felt a tinge of pride that he'd gone on to follow his dream of becoming a firefighter," she recalled.

Joe got there two hours later to comfort his wife and assess the damage. "Look at it this way," he said. "Now we can fix all the things we didn't like when it was built."

Even with the house on fire, Jill wrote, "he was the Tigger to my Eeyore."

Joe later joked to a group of firefighters and EMTs that after lightning struck his home and destroyed "a significant portion of it," he was grateful that they'd first made sure Jill was safe and then "you got my second-best love out of the house: my '67 Corvette."

Joe had loved the green four-speed 1967 Corvette Stingray since his father had given it to him and his late wife, Neilia, as a wedding gift. "So thank you all. So I owe you. When I say I owe you, I mean I owe you."

Chapter 25

Right for the Time

Jill and Joe watched the 2004 election results at home. John Kerry had talked about making Joe his secretary of state if he won.

When the results weren't looking good, Jill went to bed. Joe stayed up, hoping Kerry would win. He wound up staying in front of the TV all night. "I felt terrible for John, but I also felt really worried for the country," Joe wrote.

Joe was still in front of the TV when Jill came downstairs the next morning.

"What happened?" she asked.

"It's over," Joe said. "We lost."

Jill stood in the doorway, visibly shaken and upset.

"I knew she couldn't believe the country had elected George Bush again," Joe wrote, but he thought there was more to it. "Had John Kerry won the election, it would have closed off the question of my running for president of the United States. And I think it upset her that the question was back on the table."

Joe felt he "didn't dare" bring up the subject of running again over their Thanksgiving trip to Nantucket.

"I looked at Jill and remembered that day so long ago in the U.N. chapel when she was a nervous young bride who had given me back my life," he wrote. "Whatever happened from here on out, Jill and I had accomplished all the big things, and we'd done it together."

Jill's views on her husband's presidential ambitions had indeed begun to change. She, too, was jaded by the Bush administration and the war. Beau had joined the Delaware Army National Guard in 2003, and though he hadn't yet deployed to a combat zone, it loomed as a possibility.

On the ferry on the way home from Nantucket, Jill conferred privately with Beau and Hunter.

"Look what Bush is doing to this country," she said. "Look at this war we're into. Dad's the only one who can change things."

The family began to talk more about the prospect of Joe running in 2008.

"I was so against the war," Jill recalled. "'Joe, you have got to end this war, and you're the only who can do it.'"

This time, the 1987 campaign felt like the source of lessons learned rather than an open wound. Jill felt less naive. She knew Joe would be attacked—unfairly at times. "I went in more eyes wide open, and knew how bad things could get," she said.

Beau, Hunter, and Ashley believed in Joe and encouraged him. "Things sort of evolve," Jill said. "They just sort of naturally evolve; maybe at dinner one night we start talking, but it doesn't go anywhere. It's just, a seed is planted."

In December, the Bidens gathered at the house in Delaware to celebrate their eldest granddaughter Naomi's birthday.

"We're having a family meeting tomorrow morning in the library," Jill told Joe after they'd cleaned the kitchen and gone up to bed. "We need to talk to you about something."

"Then, as is her way," he wrote, "she rolled over and went to sleep." He assumed the meeting would be for the family to ask him not to run for president.

The next day, Jill gathered the kids, Val, and longtime Biden political adviser Ted Kaufman in the library. Joe sat beside the fireplace to hear them out.

"We've been meeting," Jill said. "I want you to run this time. It's up to you, but we'll support it."

"Why?" Joe asked, after a moment.

"We think you can unite the country," Jill said. "We think you're the best person to pull the country together."

Later she said, "I feel like I was the one who encouraged him to run."

"Jill was aboard," Rasky said. "She really felt now that Joe was right for the job, not just a good candidate, and right for the time."

In March 2005, two months after Bush's second inaugural, the Bidens and their political advisers gathered in Wilmington. "We were inexorably moving toward running in 2008," Rasky said.

In June, Joe announced he intended to run in 2008—three years away. "I know I'm supposed to be more coy with you," he said on *Face the Nation*. "But if, in fact, I think that I have a clear shot at winning the nomination by this November or December, then I'm going to seek the nomination."

Chapter 26

Dr. Biden

In 2007, Jill completed work on her doctor of education in educational leadership at the University of Delaware.

She published her dissertation under the name Jill Jacobs-Biden and wouldn't let Joe in the room while she defended it to avoid coloring anyone's perception of her work. She dedicated her dissertation to her father, Donald Jacobs, who had died of cancer in 1999, "for always believing in me."

Jill's academic research focused on community college retention rates. Her dissertation was a zoomed-out view that began with the history of community college in America, as a means of understanding where it was headed, and how it could be improved.

Community college as we know it today first emerged as a means of meeting local needs during the Great Depression. Following World War II and the GI Bill, enrollment in two-year programs boomed; veterans pursued vocational training along with academic instruction. Community colleges continued to adapt over the following decades, keeping as broad an admissions policy as possible. To that end, it's important that community colleges know how to meet people where they are at the very beginning, to support their higher education journey.

A central focus in Jill's dissertation was Del Tech, which offered a variety of remedial reading and writing courses to help students find their academic footing. As students from diverse economic backgrounds and of different ages entered the college setting, the school needed to serve those who lacked access to advanced medical services or had undiagnosed or untreated learning disabilities, or lacked the social, mental, or emotional stability to keep their grades up and otherwise function well in an academic setting.

Beyond the nuanced challenges that Jill highlighted, there were also, of course, more typical struggles like trying to complete schoolwork while holding one or more jobs, raising a family, or facing a lack of reliable transportation.

In the community college world, the term "stop out" often applies more frequently than "drop out." Rather than permanently leave school, students' already limited capacity for academics becomes more limited, and they may not return. Del Tech retained students at the national average—about sixty-six percent—but after a period of roughly six years, Jill reported, only one in five students wound up completing their course of studies.

Effective remedies, Jill found, could be simple. The first year in college was critically important and pairing new students with mentors was a great way to build community and impart key advice. English tutoring for ESL students helped to bridge the communication gap. Clubs and academic centers for after-hours support allowed students to seek their own help where they saw fit.

"The holistic approach—academic, social, psychological and physical—is the optimum goal in addressing students' needs and ensuring the path to success," Jill wrote.

When Jill got home she saw Joe had put signs along the driveway saying "Dr. and Senator Biden live here." He also later handed her her doctorate on the stage at Delaware.

"I'll never forget when she got her doctorate, Joe talking with all of us at the Senate," Marcelle Leahy recalled. Joe told everyone, 'Oh, my wife's a doctor. Just think, it's Dr. Biden.' He was more thrilled than she was, I think."

"The role I have always felt most at home in is Dr. Biden," Jill wrote in her memoir.

Chapter 27

Boots on the Ground

The prospect of an incumbent-free field and Republican George W. Bush's dismal approval ratings made the 2008 campaign tempting for many of the Democratic Party's biggest stars. Experienced lawmakers and governors threw their hats in the ring, along with rising stars like Senators Barack Obama and John Edwards. Then there was the looming presence of former first lady and senator Hillary Clinton, who was expected to be a fundraising juggernaut.

Joe and Hillary had worked closely together in the Senate, and Jill had gotten to know both Clintons during the eight years they spent in the White House. But the relationship between the two couples wasn't particularly close at the time, and Jill didn't see Hillary as an unstoppable force in the race. She believed deeply that Joe could win, particularly if the race focused on foreign policy.

As a senator, he had served as chairman of the Foreign Relations Committee and was a member of the Subcommittee on European Affairs and the Senate NATO Observer Group. He was a long-standing advocate of international nuclear nonproliferation, and he had met with more than 150 world leaders.

"You've got to believe, or else you just get out," she said. "It's not for the faint of heart."

Twenty years after Biden's first presidential run, Jill also was a more experienced and savvy political spouse. She spent nearly every day of the campaign in briefings, making calls to potential supporters or donors, and campaigning for her husband in Iowa, crisscrossing much of the same territory as in the 1987 Democratic primary.

She hoped the results would be different this time around.

But there were new and uncomfortable dynamics to contend with, including colleagues and friends who were now competitors.

Tom Vilsack and his wife, Christine, for example, had been among Biden's most loyal supporters in Iowa during the 1987 race, and the couples had remained friends.

Joe's 1987 Iowa message—that voters who don't get involved may pay the price of being governed by people less qualified than themselves—had inspired Tom to run for office. He ran first for mayor of the town of Mount Pleasant, then governor of Iowa. He'd become a popular national figure for Democrats, and instead of backing his friend Biden in the 2008 race, Vilsack was seeking the Democratic nomination for himself.

Biden found himself struggling with verbal gaffes once again, this time over comments he made about Obama, the popular US senator from Illinois who was vying to become the nation's first Black president. On the day Biden was scheduled to launch his campaign, he was quoted in the *New York Observer* praising Obama as "the first mainstream African American who is articulate and bright and clean and a nice-looking guy."

The large field of candidates meant a larger group of political spouses were also crisscrossing Iowa. For Jill Biden, there were familiar faces, like Christine Vilsack, and new faces, like Michelle Obama.

Jill and Michelle didn't know each other well at all. While their husbands were colleagues in the Senate, Jill taught in Delaware and Michelle worked in Chicago and was raising two young girls, so there were few opportunities to chat.

But the campaign pushed Jill and Michelle together, often in forced and uncomfortable settings. At the primary debates, for example, organizers always sat the spouses together—a tradition Jill loathed.

"When somebody says something about your spouse and you just want to scream at them, *'What did you say'?* you just have to sit there demurely," Jill said.

But she and Michelle chatted and made small talk. "I like your shoes," Jill remembers Michelle whispering to her.

"Jill's authenticity at once disarms and connects," Michelle later said.

Despite the awkwardness that could come from campaign life, Jill was more comfortable on the trail in 2008, more confident in her own role and opinions.

Christine Vilsack remembered seeing Jill at a soup supper in Ames, Iowa, and thinking as she watched her longtime friend interact with voters, "She's still the same person I remember when I met her for the first time."

Christine said that by 2008, Jill had found a sweet spot as a political spouse. "Some of them don't want to be involved at all, and some of them actually run their spouse's campaign. And she's neither of those."

Jill also stuck to the issues she knew and cared about. Even with the Iraq War at the center of the campaign, Jill wasn't likely to show up on the trail armed with a foreign policy speech. But she spoke with knowledge and warmth about education. "Education is something that people can understand," Christine observed. Nearly everyone's lives were touched by or involved in education in some way, and nearly everyone had an opinion on it. Listening to Jill talk about education was something they could connect with and not feel stupid or uninformed about. "I think that people gravitated toward her," Christine said. "And that's what I saw on the campaign."

But voters didn't gravitate toward Joe. His campaign never gained traction and he was quickly overshadowed by Obama and Clinton, as well as another young, dynamic candidate, North Carolina senator John Edwards. Biden was often little more than an afterthought.

When the Iowa caucus results were tabulated, Biden had secured just one percent of the vote. There was no path ahead—and even if there was, there was no fundraising money left to keep him on it. He quickly ended his campaign.

———

On the flight home, Jill was largely at peace. Certainly there were elements of the race she'd been unhappy with, and things she felt disillusioned about. There were people who had made promises, who had said they would show up to support Joe, then ended up in somebody else's corner. "There's just so much that you have to absorb, and keep that smile on your face, and go on," she said.

But it was much easier to move on this time. "That didn't sting the way '87 did," she said. She'd been through it all before, and despite her whole-hearted belief that Joe could win, she felt she'd been more realistic about the way it could go.

On the way back to Delaware, "I was full of resolve about the things I wanted to do," she said. She'd met amazing military families on the campaign trail, and she wanted to work to help them. Blue Star families—so-called for the flags bearing blue stars that mothers put in their windows during World War I—were those with a family member serving in a period of hostilities. The blue stars were replaced with gold stars if the service member died.

On the flight home, she told Joe she wanted to help military families.

Two weeks later, she was meeting at the local Borders bookstore with a contact at Delaware Boots on the Ground, an organization that supports military families and helps them find services.

Boots on the Ground was small, with maybe thirty members, and focused on supporting those who fell through the cracks of the USO, Veterans of Foreign Wars, and other military support organizations.

"I want to be part of this organization," she said. "What can I do to help military families? What can I do to help the National Guard?"

Jill chaired fundraising events and published op-eds to raise awareness and support. "Defending our nation should not just be left to the sacrifices of a few, but the commitment of us all," she wrote in the *Wilmington News Journal*. "After all they are doing for us, it is the least we can, and must, do for them. This is our sacred obligation."

She raised the group's profile, bringing the Biden family's name and fundraising connections, and participated in more direct appeals, like grocery-store fundraisers.

"When she came to us initially, we thought she was just going to lend us her name," Boots on the Ground cofounder Shirley Brooks said. "But it turns out that she was a volunteer who got down into the trenches with us to fundraise."

The *Philadelphia Inquirer* reported, "Before Jill Biden, the organization had only $1,500. After one week of fund-raising, the group had more than $30,000."

Chapter 28

2008

The 2008 Democratic race quickly narrowed to two candidates: Barack Obama and Hillary Clinton, two history-making figures Biden worked with in the Senate.

As the contest between Obama and Clinton stretched on, other Democrats faced enormous pressure to pick sides and endorse. Joe decided not to publicly support either candidate but told both he would campaign hard for whichever one secured the nomination.

"If you win, I'll do anything you ask me to do," Joe told Obama.

"Be careful, because I may ask you a lot," Obama said.

Part of Joe's equivocation was strategic. It was likely he would be considered for a senior administration role if either won the White House, and aides calculated that it was best for his future if he remained neutral.

Joe and Obama had run different campaigns. Obama coined one of the most recognizable platform slogans of all time, running on "Hope and Change," while Joe had pitted his experience against the idealism of younger candidates. The contrast in experience was indeed stark. By 2007, Joe had been a member of the Senate for thirty-four years, with experience as chairman of both the Judiciary Committee and Foreign Relations Committee. Obama, on the other hand, had only been a US senator since 2005.

People frequently mentioned the prospect of Joe being Obama's or Clinton's vice president to Jill, but her reaction had always been "Yeah, sure, fine. We'll see what happens." If anything, she thought, he would be secretary of state because he had so much foreign policy experience. "But it wasn't in the forefront of my head."

Joe turned his attention back to the Senate, focusing on war in the Mid-

dle East as the conflicts in Afghanistan, Pakistan, and Iraq were all beginning to blend together. He joined Senators John Kerry and Chuck Hagel on
a tour of the region, for a fresh perspective on the most costly and controversial element of US foreign engagement. Joe made his feelings clear that
without adequate and appropriate attention being paid to each of America's
individual conflicts, none of them would be satisfactorily resolved.

Following Joe's return to Washington, he spoke to Obama about playing a larger role in his potential administration. The two senators began to
find each other with more frequency. "He'd call not so much to ask for
advice as to bounce things off me," Joe said.

By June 2008, it was clear that Obama had the support he needed to
clinch the Democratic nomination. Obama's advisers drafted a list of
roughly twenty potential running mates. Joe was near the top.

———————

Jill had just joined Delaware governor Ruth Ann Minner for a Boots on
the Ground event at her office in Dover. In the car on the way back, Joe
called.

"Barack called me," Joe's voice boomed from the speakerphone, "and
asked if we would be vetted for vice president."

Thrilled for Joe, Jill urged him to hurry home. The vice presidency
could be a new journey for the Bidens, a family adventure.

But Joe had declined Obama's offer.

"I obviously didn't say this lightly," Joe wrote. "I was honored to be
asked, but I had been a United States senator for thirty-five years, a job I
loved, in an institution I revered. I had gained respect as a formidable legislator and had seniority. I was my own man, and I enjoyed what I was doing.
I also believed I could make more significant contributions as chairman of
the Foreign Relations Committee than I could as vice president."

Before hanging up, Obama insisted Joe take some time to discuss it with
his family. Jill called the kids to come over for a talk on the back porch.

To Joe's surprise, everyone was enthusiastic about the prospect, and
explained their own rationales as to why Joe could help Obama chart a
course to the White House.

There were also personal advantages to being based in Washington, a city Joe and Jill had long avoided calling home. Beau and Hunter were now living there with their families, so there would be more chances to see them and the grandchildren. That held more appeal than the constant travel required of the secretary of state, the other position Biden was thought to be in the mix for.

The other person who pressed him to reconsider was his mother. Joe recalled her words in his book *Promise Me, Dad*. "My ninety-year-old mother, who had watched my lifelong fight for civil rights and racial equality, put it this way at a larger family meeting the next day: 'So let me get this straight, honey. The first African American in history who has a chance to be president says he needs your help to win—*and you said no.*'"

Beau, Hunter, and Ashley would call Jill daily to ask where Joe was on the idea. "You've got to push him," they urged her.

"I kept pushing, but it ultimately had to be his decision," Jill said.

For Joe, it was the prospect of working directly for someone else that was most troublesome. As a senator, he had no boss. As long as the people of Delaware were happy, Joe was happy.

"I must have said it to her a good deal more than once," Biden wrote. "'What happens when I have to support administration policy I don't agree with?'...'What's it going to be like to be number two?'...'How am I going to handle this?'"

"'C'mon, Joe,'" Jill finally said. "'Grow up.'"

Being vetted for the vice presidency was an invasive process that involved a deep dive into the Bidens' finances, their personal lives, and their families. It was stressful, exhausting, and emotionally difficult.

Jill was uncomfortable with all the questions that were being asked, but she really wanted Joe to be vice president. She liked Obama, and she thought together they could make a difference.

In terms of assets, there wasn't much. Joe and Jill had a little money, but nothing compared to elite prospects who built their political careers on wealth.

"We had the equity in our home and my pension. Jill had a teacher's pension and some certificates of deposit her mother had given her," Joe wrote. "'This all there is?' Obama asked the team investigating me. The next time I saw him, after the process was concluded, Barack looked at me and joked, 'That was one of the easiest vets in the world. You own nothing.'"

The vetting process, and the state of the race, helped Obama narrow his list of contenders to three: Joe and US senators Tim Kaine of Virginia and Evan Bayh of Indiana.

Two of Obama's top advisers, David Axelrod and David Plouffe, traveled to Delaware to meet with Joe at Val's house. Biden was considered to be more engaging than Bayh, more experienced than Kaine, and more connected to the white working-class voters Obama would need to win over than almost anyone else in the Democratic Party at the time.

But he also had a well-earned reputation for marching to the beat of his own drum and speaking his mind—a trait that Obama liked, but also carried risk, both for a campaign and an eventual administration.

Jill and Beau picked up Axelrod and Plouffe from the airport.

"We got to Valerie Biden's house and a few minutes later, the senator showed up in a pickup truck. And he had a baseball cap on and, of course, his aviator glasses," Axelrod remembers. What struck Axelrod was the natural warmth between Joe and his oldest son.

"Joe and Beau had an interaction, and when they were done, Joe kissed Beau and said, 'I may come by to see the kids later.' And the whole scene was so vivid in my mind that when I went back and spoke to Obama about the day, the first thing I said was, 'There's something really special about this family,' and I talked about just how warm and loving and normal it all seemed to me," Axelrod said.

Axelrod and Plouffe walked away impressed by Joe's command of the issues, and the distinct absence of a hunger for power.

––––––

When word got out that Joe was on the short list, the press camped out with vans and camera trucks at their Wilmington home. The house was set back from the road at the end of a long, curved driveway, but Jill felt held captive.

"My God, we can't even go to the driveway," Jill said one night. They were stuck inside, practically locked in their house. Reporters had trampled the red and white impatiens she'd planted.

Jill turned to Joe one night and said, "Let's sneak out the back." It was dark in their yard and the property next door was wooded; they could slip away.

They hatched a plan for Beau to meet them near their neighbor's house. They walked through the woods, climbed into his car, and ducked down as he pulled out, making their escape.

Jill and Joe walked the city streets, just enjoying being alone in the dark, for some time. Eventually Beau came back and picked them up.

Mary Doody remembered this time as exciting and a little nerve-racking. "You couldn't talk to anybody about it," she recalled. She and Jill went out for a glass of wine after work one day.

"Do you think Joe will be picked?" Mary remembered asking Jill.

"Mary, I cannot tell you," Jill said.

Mary remembered thinking, "Okay, well, maybe that's my answer."

To Mary, the prospect of Joe being chosen as Obama's running mate came with just one major downside.

"I'm so afraid I'll never see you again," she told Jill.

Jill smacked her on the arm. "Of course you'll see me again," she said.

Chapter 29

Instant Connection

Jill walked out of her dentist's office on a Thursday afternoon, mouth numb and immobile after a root canal. She was afraid of needles, and Joe had come along for moral support. After the procedure, he hurried her out of the waiting room and into the car.

As they turned onto Wilmington's Pennsylvania Avenue, he told her the news. "Barack called and asked me to be VP."

He'd accepted. "It felt good to say yes," he wrote.

She immediately teared up, but could still barely speak. "Joe, I'm happy for you," she managed. "You deserve this."

They called Beau, who lived nearby, and met him in the parking lot of a nearby shopping center to share the news. They were ecstatic.

Ashley met her parents at home to celebrate. She recited aloud from one of Joe's favorite poems, Seamus Heaney's "The Cure at Troy"—a message of unity between "hope" and "history."

"Oh great," Joe joked. "He's hope. And I'm history."

The couple spent the next few hours quietly calling other family members to share the good news—but also warning that they needed to keep it a closely held secret for now.

To keep up appearances and give nothing away, Jill went to work the next day at Del Tech, where the fall semester had just started.

———

But life started to change fast, and the scope of what lay ahead for the Bidens quickly became clear. That weekend, Obama campaign officials descended on their house to outline the months ahead. Obama would announce Biden as his running mate at the Old State Capitol in Springfield, Illinois, the same place Obama had launched his campaign months earlier. The team had already hired campaign staff for both Bidens, including the aides they would spend long stretches traveling with.

Jill watched the Secret Service drive up for their initial meeting in the Bidens' library. She knew if they won, they'd need to move to Washington. She was caught up in the swirl of it all. It was exciting and scary all at once. There was so much to take in, and it was all happening so fast.

They couldn't get out to the store, so a friend brought over fruit salad and sandwiches. But Jill found she couldn't even swallow food.

The Bidens had long been surrounded by a close-knit circle of family and friends. Most of Joe's top advisers had been with him for years, and Jill herself had never had a staff. Now, suddenly, their every move was closely managed, often by people they had never met.

At one point, Jill and a staffer were working together to choose what she would wear for the announcement in Springfield, Illinois, trying a number of different outfits.

"My God, I just met you and now you see me in my underwear," Jill said.

On August 23, Obama introduced Joe on an outdoor stage on a sun-splashed day.

It didn't take long for Jill and Michelle to realize how much their aspirations as first and second lady overlapped. The announcement was their first in-person meeting since Joe's selection. Michelle had a "practical yet effortlessly chic look," Jill wrote. "Like me, she had a career of her own—the title of First Lady wasn't one she was seeking, but she believed deeply in Barack's leadership and did everything she could to support him."

"Jill, have you given any thought to what you'd want to work on if we win?" Michelle asked as Obama and Joe spoke.

"Yes," Jill said. "Military families."

"Me too!" Michelle said.

They clasped hands. "We had an instant connection," Jill wrote in her memoir. The idea was born.

Working with military families had become one of the causes dearest to Jill's heart. Both Joe and Jill had learned firsthand what it meant to have a child who could be sent into harm's way at any moment. Beau hadn't deployed yet, although Obama had mentioned in his speech that he was preparing to.

Jill and Michelle had different schedules for much of the campaign but at times they ended up together at events. During one crossover appearance, Jill ran the idea of continuing to teach past Michelle, who encouraged her.

Joe said of course she should continue her career—it's what she had always done.

Still, there would be obligations that would come with being second lady. Jill needed to start thinking about building out a staff.

She reached out to Cathy Russell, her travel companion during the 1987 campaign who had gone on to become Joe's staff director on the Judiciary Committee. Jill and Cathy had gotten to know each other well over the years. Cathy and Tom Donilon had married in 1991, and Donilon was helping with Obama's debate prep. Jill asked Russell to come work for her in the general election.

But Cathy said she wasn't sure she could make it work—Donilon was already off with the campaign, and their kids were in middle school.

It was Jill's confidence in her ability to balance both her family and dual roles teaching and on the campaign—or eventually in the White House—that convinced Russell to sign on.

"The way she talked me into it was she said that she was going to continue teaching" during the campaign, Russell said.

Jill's agreement with the campaign would make for a grueling schedule. She would teach at Del Tech during the week, Monday through Thursday. She headed out on the campaign trail on Thursday nights, then returned late on Sunday. She had to be in the classroom at eight a.m. on Mondays.

Joe would spend far less time than Jill in Delaware during the general election, his schedule packed with campaign events in battleground states across the country. Mindful that a winning campaign would mean four, or even eight, years away from his beloved home state, Joe was wistful when he and Jill appeared at the Wilmington train station for a farewell before heading to Denver for the Democratic National Convention.

"These guys have been my family," he said as he shook hands and greeted train station vendors he knew. Joe took no questions except one about the convention speech, which he confidently told reporters "is all ready."

Jill stopped at a newsstand to hold up a copy of *Newsweek*. Obama and Biden were on the cover.

"Obama looks good, man," Biden said. "Obama looks good."

At the convention, it was Beau who introduced Joe with a rousing speech about character. He talked about his father and the leadership he could provide as vice president. He talked about the ways his mother had both salvaged his family and been the glue that kept it together for so many years.

Of his parents, he said, "They together rebuilt our family."

Beau, who had been serving as Delaware attorney general since 2007, would deploy to Iraq with his National Guard unit that fall. In a nod to his impending service overseas, he said, "My dad has always been there for me, my brother, and my sister, every day. But because of other duties, it won't be possible for me to be here this fall to stand by him the way he stood by me. So I have something to ask of you. Be there for my dad like he was for me."

After Joe took the podium, he expressed his pride in Beau, Hunter, and Ashley, and then voiced a special appreciation for his wife. As the crowd gave a standing ovation, he called her "the only one who leaves me both breathless and speechless at the same time."

Chapter 30

Compartmentalizing

The Bidens arrived in Denver ready to celebrate what at the time was the highlight of Joe's political career. But, as all too often happened with the family, real life intruded.

Joe and Jill were on their way to breakfast with a state delegation when her sister called with grim news of their mother. Bonny Jean Jacobs, at seventy-eight, had been in declining health; lymphoma, chemo treatments, and dementia had taken a toll. Now, Jill learned, her mother had only weeks to live. "I began shaking," she recalled.

The Secret Service agents left the couple alone in the car for a private moment, and Joe held Jill. "All I wanted was to be with my mother at that moment," she recalled. "But I knew it would have to wait. I gave myself a few minutes to be heartbroken, and then I put those feelings away."

It was a skill—compartmentalizing—that Jill had grown accustomed to deploying over the years, including when Joe was sick at Walter Reed, and one she would lean on even more in her years in Washington. There was the space she reserved for her work teaching, the space she kept for her political roles, and the moments when she let the sorrow or worry seep in.

Word of her mother's failing health came on top of the concerns she had about Beau's upcoming deployment to Iraq. Beau's unit, the 261st Signal Brigade, managed the maintenance, installation, and operation of communications systems—a distant echo of his grandfather's days as a Navy signalman—and he served as a lawyer in the Judge Advocate General's Corps.

"Caught between two realities I didn't want to think about," Jill wrote—"losing my mother and my son leaving for war—I turned to the only thing that kept me sane: running." She struggled to eat, to swallow food. She lost ten pounds that fall from the stress.

All through the fall, Jill was suspended in anticipatory grief. In her memoir she recalled going to a campaign event, rushing home to sleep, then going early to Willow Grove to steal a day or two with her mom. When time was tight, she would find a way to fit in a few hours with her. After the always-too-short visits, she would go right back to the campaign trail.

"The worst part of watching my mother slip away wasn't the physical indignities....I wanted to share my life with her, like I'd always done. I wanted her to be *her*. But so much of her was gone." Jill visited often and gave her mother what little comfort she could.

One bright spot during that difficult stretch was Jill's emerging friendship with Michelle Obama. The two traveled together for a week on a bus tour following the convention.

"At the end of that week, she put her arms around me and I put my arms around her and we just hugged one another and she said, 'I love you,' and I said, 'I love you' back," Jill said. "That doesn't happen that often in life, that you have that immediate connection, that friendship, with women."

"I could not be more grateful for her friendship," Michelle later said.

———

During the convention, and in the weeks that followed, it was clear that Joe, as well as his entire family, would turn out to complement the campaign in all the ways the Obama team had hoped. He was relatable, expressed his command of important issues, and as a longtime friend of John McCain, the Republican nominee, he knew the Arizona senator's record well enough to make a strong case against him. In particular, Biden was against McCain's long-standing support of the Bush administration's war efforts in the Middle East.

Jill, meanwhile, dove headfirst into becoming a solo campaigner on behalf of her husband and Obama. "Suddenly, Beau, Hunter, Ashley, and I all started traveling separately around the country, making appearances and giving speeches. The crowds were much bigger than any I'd spoken to before—thousands of people, sometimes in vast arenas—and I had to get used to that very quickly," she wrote in her autobiography. "It still wasn't coming naturally to me, and I still struggled to channel the easygoing demeanor that people can connect with. One reporter noted in a story that I was 'not the most polished political performer, reading carefully from her speeches.' But I didn't give up."

Jill and Cathy Russell found themselves in Iowa again, two decades after their first time there together. Jill was nervous to give speeches but worked hard to prepare. Her staff would write her remarks and then practice them with her.

"It's just like being a teacher, right?" Russell asked. "You're going to get up in front of the classroom" and speak.

"It's not like being a teacher at all," Jill said about speaking in front of campaign crowds. "I'm comfortable in the classroom." Jill began working with a speaking coach and put in many hours of practice. Slowly, her new role became more manageable.

Jill continued to insist that she would teach if Barack and Joe won the election, but the details of how she would make that happen were far from locked in. "There were always different parts and pieces of my life," she said. "So I just saw it as a continuation, which it was."

Then an opportunity appeared. Dr. Jimmie McClellan at Northern Virginia Community College began emailing Jill. I'm a dean at NOVA, he introduced himself. You should come teach here. With six campuses, 160 programs, and more than seventy-five thousand students, NOVA was the largest institution of higher education in Virginia, and the second largest in the United States.

Jill found a lot to like about the school, and McClellan. In addition to his wicked sense of humor, he came from a working-class background and had been a civil rights activist in Texas. As a member of the Army Reserves, he'd protested the Vietnam War. He had been associated with the college since the 1970s. NOVA's Alexandria campus reflected the diversity of the Washington area; while Jill's students at Del Tech were primarily white, here she would teach students from an array of countries and cultures.

Jill found his idea a little crazy at first, but the more she read McClellan's emails, the more she thought she might like NOVA.

"There were different pieces to it that planted the seed in my mind— hey, I want to keep doing this," she recalled.

———

Jill and other Biden family members attended the October 2 vice presidential debate between Joe and Alaska governor Sarah Palin in St. Louis, Missouri. Palin, who said she came from a family of many teachers and valued education highly, praised Joe for his passion for education and Jill for her years of teaching. "God bless her," Palin said. "Her reward is in heaven, right?"

The next day, Beau's National Guard unit began its deployment. The 261st would go to Fort Bliss in Texas for several weeks, followed by Iraq. Back in Delaware, Joe spoke at the deployment ceremony on the Legislative Mall in Dover. He addressed the rows of troops in green camouflage and tan boots.

"My heart is full of love and pride," Joe said, keeping his speech under three minutes after Beau advised his loquacious father to keep it short. Jill later recalled feeling an intense mixture of pride and concern as she watched the ceremony.

As a military lawyer, Beau would be prosecuting violations of military law. "We've made no special considerations for him, nor has he asked for any," a public affairs officer for the Delaware Army National Guard told the press.

Delaware Boots on the Ground co-president Kathy Greenwell told the *Wilmington News Journal* it was an especially emotional time for Jill, given her mother's ill health. "I could see she was ready to break down and cry," Greenwell said.

Joe went back to the campaign trail. The next day, Jill was running in Brandywine State Park when a Secret Service car pulled up beside her.

"Your mother has taken a turn for the worse," the agent said. "I think you need to call home."

Bonny Jean Jacobs died the next morning, surrounded by her five daughters. "In one emotionally racked week," Jill wrote, "my mother was gone, my son was a world away, and my husband was out there somewhere, stretched thin on the campaign trail."

Joe canceled his campaign appearances and came back for the funeral, held at Abington Presbyterian Church in Abington, Pennsylvania.

Despite her grief and the pressure of national attention, Jill remained practical—and kind. She called everyone in her eight thirty a.m. class to tell them not to come to school if they didn't have to. "It would save them the gas," she said.

Bonny Jean had long been a source of strength for her daughter. Now she was gone, at a moment when Jill may have needed her the most. In her mother's absence, Jill found herself saying, "Mom, I need you. Where are you now?"

Chapter 31

Election Day

Joe and Jill started Election Day 2008 in Wilmington, heading to their regular polling place to cast their votes.

"Morning," Jill said chipperly as she walked in. Joe followed behind, holding his mother's hand. She lived with Joe and Jill in a cottage on their property. Each stepped behind the blue curtain and into the voting booth, Jill cheering and hugging her husband after he emerged.

Then they were bound for Chicago, Obama's hometown, where the candidates, their families, and staff would await the results. The atmosphere was jubilant throughout the day. Polls showed the Democratic ticket comfortably ahead of McCain, whose campaign had faltered in the closing weeks of the race, particularly as the nation descended into an economic crisis.

Americans wanted the change Obama represented. Biden, as vice president, offered an insurance policy, the assurance that an experienced Washington veteran would be by the new president's side.

It was an unusually warm November night in Chicago when the race was called. Nearly a quarter of a million people descended on Grant Park, on the shores of Lake Michigan, for a victory celebration. After Obama's remarks, he called Joe to the stage. Then Michelle and Jill walked out to join them, holding hands as they appeared before the crowd.

On election night in Chicago, Mary Doody congratulated Joe and remarked on the transformation she'd seen in Jill's confidence in campaigning.

"How about your girl?" Mary said.

"I know," Joe said. "She just took it on and she just did it."

———————

With Barack Obama's 2008 presidential victory, Joe and Jill finally found themselves living in Washington full-time — a thing they'd avoided throughout Joe's entire Senate career.

The Bidens settled into life at Number One Observatory Circle, on the grounds of the sprawling Naval Observatory in Northwest DC. The Queen Anne–style home that became the official residence of the vice president and his family was built in the late 1800s. Located three miles from the White House and in a more residential section of Washington, the home is surrounded by lush greenery and wildlife that gives the residence a quiet intimacy though it sits steps away from the bustling traffic along Massachusetts Avenue.

Downstairs is reserved for public-facing life; upstairs is private. Jill and Joe furnished their space with leather couches and family pictures on the bookshelves. When they were alone, they ate by candlelight at the small table there.

Jill asked Cathy Russell to stay on and be her chief of staff. She'd never had a staff but knew it was important to surround herself with knowledgeable people who could help.

"I absolutely cannot do that, Jill," Russell said. Her husband, Tom Donilon, was serving in the administration as President Obama's deputy national security adviser. It would be impossible.

"Don't worry," Jill said. "Whatever you have to do for your kids, you can do." Jill lived up to her word. The pace was such that Russell missed the occasional family event, but otherwise the job was unexpectedly flexible. When Russell's mother became ill and passed away in the first year, Jill said, "Just do what you need to do."

After the election, Russell observed, the tremendous platform Jill now had really seemed to sink in. "It wasn't her chosen path, it wasn't where she ever imagined herself going, but she was given an opportunity and she was going to make the best of it."

Jill knew she'd be swept up in Joe's work, and her plans for helping the administration. But she also knew that she would be unhappy if she didn't find a way to keep teaching. "Teaching is my internal compass; I can always count on it to steer me in the right direction," she wrote.

She would do what she'd been telling voters since the '87 campaign—she would teach while Joe held national office.

Cathy told her she was crazy.

"I did think it was crazy," Cathy said in an interview. "I actually really did think it was crazy."

Cathy had seen firsthand during the campaign the intense level of work Jill put into grading papers and developing her students' often-weak writing skills. "She'd sit there for hours reading these things and marking them," Cathy recalled. "I'm like, 'Just give everyone an A, for God's sake.'"

They had no way to gauge yet how busy Jill would be as second lady. "Maybe you should wait and see?" Russell suggested.

"Absolutely not," Jill said.

In retrospect, Cathy said she hadn't fully appreciated how much Jill got out of teaching and how much meaning it gave to her life. She also came to realize it was Jill's way of escaping the weight of Joe's life and career. "This was a way that she's always maintained her own life." Continuing to teach let Jill "hold on to some shred of what it was that she felt made her who she was" before her and Joe's lives changed entirely.

Obama adviser Valerie Jarrett found Jill's determination to continue teaching a welcome surprise. She thought it sent an important message to the country that women didn't have to sacrifice their careers for the sake of their spouses, that they could do more than one thing at a time. And Jill juggled her obligations well: "I can't think of an important White House event that she missed," Jarrett said. "But I also know how much satisfaction she gets from teaching." Jill didn't want to give that up. "I loved her for that. I thought it was great."

Within days of the inauguration, she was standing at the front of a classroom at NOVA. It was different from Del Tech in many ways—including the Secret Service detail that came with being second lady. Agents would be scattered about the classroom in civilian clothes and backpacks, keeping a low profile and trying to blend in. Jill would introduce herself by her real name on the first day, but immediately ask to be called *Dr. B.* Surprisingly, it was enough to help avoid a lot of attention.

"The vast majority of my students are first-generation arrivals from other countries, and for many of them, English is their second language. Most didn't notice the Biden name, and if they did, they didn't put together that I was married to the vice president," she wrote.

Christine Vilsack, whose husband, Tom, was now the secretary of agriculture, wasn't surprised at all when Jill continued teaching; she didn't feel she even needed to ask Jill's reasons. Whenever Jill and Christine spoke, they always talked about education together, and understood each other as fellow teachers. The role gave Jill the opportunity to be a role model, both for children and working teachers, Christine felt. "Teachers have been sometimes maligned and not respected," Christine observed. "She's brought a lot of respect to the profession, which was much needed. She stands up for teachers. She stands up for kids. That really matters to a lot of people, because just about everybody is connected to a teacher."

Chapter 32

Second Lady Puts Education First

Jill and Cathy Russell worked closely together on the policy issues the new second lady hoped to prioritize. Jill wanted the world to understand how important community colleges were as institutions, who the students were who attended them, and the challenges they overcame to do so. But it wasn't the only issue Jill hoped to influence. She wanted to continue her work on preventing cancer, and she wanted to work with Michelle Obama to support military families.

"She was very involved and very thoughtful about it," Russell said of Jill's work on determining her policy priorities. The issues came naturally, but formulating a strategy and following through on it was very important.

"Okay, these are the things I'm interested in, but what does it mean?" Russell recalled Jill saying. "What am I going to do about it? What are we trying to accomplish here?"

Jamie Lawrence, one of the second lady's policy directors, recalled, "She always wants to see tangible results, which I think is really important in government."

Whenever Jill traveled with Joe, they tried to find ways for her to visit military bases and hold roundtables at community colleges. "She wanted to engage, she wanted to be with people," recalled Kirsten White, another of Jill's policy directors. "We would, on the plane home, talk about what she saw and how we could use the experience that really touched her to formulate and pursue policy."

During the year Beau was deployed, Joe often found Jill standing at the sink sipping coffee early in the morning before she left for school. He could see her lips move, and he knew she was praying. "Hoping that car never drove up in front of the house, hoping you never got that phone call," he later said.

Jill regularly kept in touch with the Gold Star mothers and military families she met. As time went by, Jill realized through her travels that it wasn't just her proximity to President Obama or Joe that resonated with people. "She was having an impact on people's lives," Cathy Russell said, "and I think that really meant a lot to her, that she could make people's lives better by the work she was doing."

The *Washington Post* reported that in Jill's first year at NOVA, she taught English as a Second Language. Later she began teaching Freshman Composition and Developmental English—writing courses that taught a highly structured approach to writing research papers, five-paragraph essays, and other necessary college writing skills.

"I would say I ask them to write a lot, but then I give of myself as well," Jill later said, describing her teaching methods. "I give a lot of feedback. And it's why I say that writing is a skill." She compared students learning to write well to basketball players improving their game through constant practice. "The more they write, the better they become. And so you have to write a lot. So I do demand a lot of them." She tried to connect the work she was asking of her students in the classroom to their futures—their ability to get good jobs and provide for themselves and their families.

"People judge you on your writing," she said. "And they're all going for jobs. They're all probably going to have to write some essay for their job application." She recalled having to write an essay when applying to teach at NOVA. "I think a hundred people applied for that job. But there I was, writing that essay as second lady to try to get the job. So it's important that they write well."

The less formal, more creative elements of her class were the weekly journals she asked students to keep. There, with prompts provided by Jill, students shared personal stories, often revealing the hardships in their lives and the difficult road many had taken to get to NOVA. "And I then get to know them," she said. "Sometimes it's more than I want to know."

Education took on a significant role in the early life of the administration as well. In his first address to Congress, President Obama offered a vision for how his administration would steer the nation through the economic recession. Education—and in particular, community college—would be a major part of the blueprint.

"In a global economy where the most valuable skill you can sell is your knowledge, a good education is no longer just a pathway to opportunity—it is a prerequisite," Obama said. In the 1990s, the US had led the world in college graduates, but over the following quarter century, that mark of academic superiority had been lost to other nations. "By 2020, America will once again have the highest proportion of college graduates in the world," Obama said. Instead, by 2021, *Newsweek* reported the US was number eleven in the world, behind countries including Russia and Lithuania.

Although the costs of attending college in the United States had grown prohibitive—in 2008, the average cost of college at a four-year public in-state institution hovered between $10,000 and $20,000 a year—the increased levels of unemployment during the 2008 recession ironically smoothed the way for the administration to urge Americans on unemployment benefits to take advantage of Pell Grants and student loans.

The administration's push "led to the enrollment of at least 500,000 students who otherwise wouldn't have enrolled," author Josh Mitchell wrote in *The Debt Trap*. Hundreds of thousands of Americans began to enroll in community college.

As second family, the Bidens were able to keep their traditional Thanksgiving trip to Nantucket but traded hours in a car on the interstate for the speed and convenience of Air Force Two. They stayed at a friend's house, and things felt nearly normal—the Secret Service gave them as much space as possible and the house was full of grandkids. On Thanksgiving morning, Jill ran in the Turkey Trot run.

Life was undeniably different; military communications officials took over one room to install a secure phone line and secure video hookup that allowed Joe to communicate with the White House Situation Room and make international calls. Joe bent his old rule of not doing any business on the island; it was harder for him to stick to that as vice president than it had been when he was in the Senate.

In those early months, Jill would experiment with which traditional trappings of second lady fit into her life. That Christmas, she had medallions made for her staff with the vice presidential seal on the front and "Love Team Jill" on the back. As gifts, she gave necklaces to the women on the staff and cuff links to the men.

It was tradition for the second lady to serve as president of the Senate Spouses group, but Jill struggled to find time between the administration, teaching, and family obligations to attend the Tuesday meetings. She did find other ways to stay connected, mindful of the support she'd received from the Senate spouses before she became second lady.

"When there was a break, she was diligent in having events and bringing the Senate spouses to the vice president's residence," Marcelle Leahy recalled. Jill hosted them in all the traditional breaks in her teaching schedule—spring break, summertime, and over the holidays in December.

Chapter 33

The American Creed

Barbara Bush once famously noted, "When I was second lady, I could say anything I wanted, and no one really paid much attention. But the minute I became first lady, everything became newsworthy."

Being in the fishbowl of the vice presidency, with staff and Secret Service always around, took some getting used to. But as vice president and second lady, Joe and Jill had a bit more freedom than the Obamas did in the White House. The Naval Observatory was more secluded, and the second family faced much less scrutiny.

The Bidens were also able to spend many weekends at home in Delaware. Jill met her friend Mary Doody at restaurants and would always get a pizza or bagels or dessert for the Secret Service agents. "Oh, my gosh, those guys have been out in the cars waiting for two and a half hours," she'd say. "And this happened over and over again," Doody said.

Once, while Jill was second lady, she insisted on a weeding party to help Mary Doody, an accomplished amateur gardener, get her home ready for an upcoming garden tour.

"We got some friends together and they all came over and we weeded all day," Doody recalled. "And then I made dinner and we listened to Motown music. It was one of the most fun days we had with our friends, and it was her idea."

———

During Joe's tenure as vice president, his longtime staffer Mark Gitenstein served as ambassador to Romania. When Gitenstein and his wife traveled back to the US, the Bidens would host them at the Naval Observatory.

They were staying there when Mom-Mom, Joe's mother, Jean, passed away in January 2010.

Joe had been traveling home by train most weekends to visit her while she'd been ill. Jean had been a tremendous influence on not only his and Jill's personal life but Joe's stances and growth as a political leader. He had long said it was her unrelenting commitment to basic decency that shaped him—"My mother's creed is the American creed: No one is better than you."

Gitenstein remembers Jill's ability to turn a sad and uncomfortable situation into one that was handled with grace and unrelenting hospitality.

"Jill came upstairs and said he was downstairs, and he was obviously distraught. He's very close to his mom. I said, 'Look, we don't need to stay here.' And she said, 'No, no, really, we both really want you to.'"

The house was large enough that each couple had their space, but it allowed the friends to enjoy brief moments of normalcy. Mark and Joe exercised together in the on-site gym, and the couples continued to dine together, as both a way to share company and engage in conversation on American foreign policy, particularly the rise in nationalism Mark was witnessing in Europe, which was in part a response to the increase of migrants fleeing poverty and insecurity in the Middle East and Africa.

Gitenstein's beach house on the Delaware coast was one of Joe and Jill's favorite retreats from the Washington scene. Gitenstein told Joe that they would have to arrange an upcoming trip to the beach house as a thank-you for the Bidens' hospitality—but especially for Jill.

One time while Gitenstein was in Romania, the Bidens stayed at another friend's nearby vacation home. Joe walked over to Gitenstein's house while it was rented out, with the Secret Service in tow, and had a picture taken of himself at the end of the driveway with the house in the background.

Joe sent the photo to Gitenstein in Romania and said, "I'm taking care of it, don't worry." He had a print of the photo made and kept it on the mantel of his vice-presidential office.

It was a reminder: When this is over, I'm getting one of these.

Chapter 34

Blue Star Mom

On a Tuesday morning in May 2010, in the middle of an event focused on community colleges and military families, Jill was notified that Beau, just forty-one years old, had had a stroke. He'd been taken to the Christiana Medical Center in Newark, Delaware, that morning around eight "with a headache, numbness and paralysis."

Jill postponed a tour of the Capital Breast Care Center in Washington to be with Beau. Joe had been in Wilmington for TV interviews about Elena Kagan's nomination to the Supreme Court and had been scheduled to return to Washington for his weekly lunch with Obama and meetings on Afghanistan but stayed in Delaware to join Jill and their son. Reporters staked out the hospital, and state troopers and other security took up posts.

The vice president's office released a short, vague statement just after ten a.m.: "Delaware Attorney General Beau Biden is at Christiana Medical Center undergoing treatment at present. He is alert and awake, and communicating with his parents and his wife, who are with him. We will provide more details as they become available."

Later in the day, Beau was transferred to Thomas Jefferson University Hospital in Philadelphia, the largest stroke and aneurysm care center in the region, for observation and further tests. Doctors seemed to be weighing whether Joe's medical history—the life-threatening brain aneurysm he experienced at forty-five—was in any way connected to Beau's stroke.

Hours after he'd arrived, Beau was able to move his right arm and leg again. Soon, doctors released a statement through the White House that said Beau was fully alert and in stable condition and had full motor and speech skills. He was reported to be in good spirits and talking with his family.

On Wednesday, Joe returned to Washington to host a dinner for Afghan president Hamid Karzai at the Bidens' official residence. Beau was "doing great, thank God," Biden told reporters before heading into the event.

Jill stayed with Beau, missing a summit for the National Military Family Association. First Lady Michelle Obama told the group, "I'm so grateful to be joined in this effort by a truly wonderful partner in this work. She's a Blue Star mom and a champion of our National Guard and Reserve families, my friend, Dr. Jill Biden. As many of you heard, Jill couldn't be here because her son Beau was admitted to the hospital yesterday, but he is expected to make a full recovery, and our thoughts and prayers are with the entire Biden family."

Jill maintained her nearly thirty-year-old running practice during this time. It remained one of the most consistent and calming elements in her life.

"I need to pretend you're not here," she told her Secret Service detail, which both led and trailed her on her five-mile runs.

"I think that running creates a sense of balance in my life, and it really calms me down," Jill told *Runner's World*. "It's a great feeling to just get out and lose myself in a run. I think that's why I continue to run, because… once you get that, you kind of crave that time for yourself."

Even with the agents surrounding her, Jill managed to keep a low profile in leggings and a T-shirt. The agents she ran with were fellow athletes, easily keeping up with her and making her exercise part of their own routines. "I mean, these guys are fit, and they're good runners," Jill said.

It was sometimes difficult to find the time, but she made running a priority. "My office knows that it goes first on the list." For the sake of fitting it in, Jill usually stuck to five-mile runs in the morning. "I've got to build in that time to get back and showered and changed and read my briefing for an event."

Chapter 35

Integrity and Honor

As they settled into Washington, the Bidens forged a connection with Walter Reed National Military Medical Center, traveling there regularly to visit wounded troops.

The enormous facility is famous for its treatment not only of veterans, but presidents, members of Congress, and Supreme Court justices. Service members and their families go through some of the most vulnerable times in their lives there, battling the loss of limbs, eyesight, or any number of complications due to their military service. The families of those being treated at Walter Reed also found support and community with each other.

With his first wife and daughter suddenly taken from him, Joe was no stranger to the pain of losing a loved one, and Jill, who had carried the family through Joe's aneurysm at Walter Reed, knew how hard it can be to keep everyone upbeat while a loved one suffers.

"At just twenty or twenty-two, patients and their partners often had to make the kinds of life-changing care decisions that people three times their age struggle with," Jill wrote in her autobiography. "It's difficult to see people so young, who should be running marathons or biking around town with little kids hitched behind them, now stuck in beds. And their spouses—often caring for a newborn or toddler, just beginning their career, or finishing school—were also confined there, not willing to leave their partner's side. I can't tell you how many times I saw a couple and thought, *That's it, this tragedy is going to define them for the rest of their lives,* only to come in months later and see them not just recovered, not just beating the odds, but actually mentoring the new patients and inspiring them to get better, too."

For Jill, the relationships she made at Walter Reed became true friendships.

"Everyone there was tied together through military service in some way, and it was easy to feel a quick connection with the people I met," she wrote.

She soon began spending more time there, organizing dinners, as well as parties and holiday events for military families that she and Joe would host at the vice-presidential mansion. Such events became a hallmark of the Bidens' tenure as second family.

Being a mom shaped the way Jill wanted to engage with people, recalled Kirsten White. As they worked on ways to make the visits with wounded troops feel natural, Jill recalled how much she loved "when the kids would bring their friends over for dinner and I'd be in the kitchen cooking and having a glass of wine. They would all be gathered around in the kitchen, and we'd be chatting."

At Walter Reed, Jill would set up a room where patients and their families could relax and enjoy a meal prepared by one of the White House chefs. Assisting with the Wounded Warrior dinners became a coveted assignment for the kitchen staff.

Jill asked Sam Kass, who had been the Obamas' personal chef in Chicago and had become an assistant chef at the White House, to prepare one of the first dinners, enough to serve a table of six to eight people.

She didn't tell him what to make, so he kept things easy, serving steak, potatoes, broccolini, green beans, and salad—hearty and fuss-free American cuisine.

Once everything was ready and guests had gathered, Jill was right there beside Sam, helping plate and serve the food.

"Somehow it felt like we were at her house. It felt like her name was Jill, and she invited us over to her house for dinner," he said.

They sat around and talked after everyone had been served, and Jill got them to open up about their families, their injuries, life in the military, and the plans they had for life after the service. Sam remembered one man saying he dreamt of opening a barbershop; another man wanted to run his own restaurant.

He had anticipated a somber evening. Instead, he was surprised by the laughter.

"Humor was clearly a real coping mechanism, and we were laughing. I can't remember laughing as hard as I did that night with her and them," Sam said. "Part of it was just the way she made everybody feel at ease and helped them feel comfortable just being themselves...Once that happened, they just started really showing their true colors and we just had a blast...it was not what I expected."

Around eight thirty p.m., after a few hours had passed and things were winding down, the door swung open.

"Yo! What's going on here?" Joe exclaimed. "I'm on my way home and I hear that Jill decided to come hang with you guys and didn't tell me about it. I just wanted to come see you all, and say thank you for your service and meet you guys."

At the end of the night, Joe pulled Sam in so close that they were nose to nose.

"Thank you so much," Joe said. "You don't know what this means for people. I won't forget it."

Sam was touched.

"I just saw their true character in that moment," he said of the Bidens. "It was a very special night for me."

Food Network star Sunny Anderson recalled a similar feeling when the Bidens hosted a cookout for wounded service members around the swimming pool at their residence in 2010, a short time after Beau's stroke.

She was an Air Force veteran who had followed her grandfather, father, and uncle into the military and who later made a name for herself cooking on cable TV. The Bidens invited her to help and she added colorful beet chips and a patriotic-themed mixed berry dessert to the standard cookout menu of burgers and hot dogs.

The Bidens had also invited her uncle, Major General Rodney Anderson, who had served in Grenada, Saudi Arabia, and Afghanistan and was stationed at the Pentagon.

When Joe and Jill delivered brief remarks recognizing the service and

Senator Joe Biden, D-Del., walks with Jill in Wilmington, Delaware, after announcing his first candidacy for president, June 9, 1987. *(AP Photo / George Widman)*

Senator Joe Biden takes the oath of office with Vice President Dick Cheney (right) and Jill during a mock swearing-in ceremony in the Old Senate Chamber in the US Capitol in Washington, DC, following his fifth reelection to the Senate, January 7, 2003. *(AP Photo / Evan Vucci)*

Jill at a presidential campaign rally with grandchildren Hunter, two, and Natalie, four, in Media, Pennsylvania, September 16, 2008 *(AP Photo / Gerald Herbert)*

Vice President Joe Biden and Second Lady Jill attend the Southern Ball, on Capitol Hill in Washington, DC, January 20, 2009. (*AP Photo / Lauren Victoria Burke*)

First Lady Michelle Obama (left) and Jill escort former Yankee Yogi Berra to the pitcher's mound before Game 1 of the Major League Baseball World Series in New York City, October 28, 2009. (*AP Photo / Eric Gay*)

Jill shakes hands with a Palestinian music student at the Al Kamandjâti music center in the West Bank city of Ramallah, March 10, 2010. *(AP Photo / Abed Omar Qusini)*

Jill poses with children of Beacon of Hope kindergarten and some of their artwork, June 9, 2010. Partially funded by the US government, the facility in Ongata Rongai, Kenya, teaches HIV-positive women skills to help them generate an income and educates the women's children. *(AP Photo / Khalil Senosi)*

Jill greets workers at a UNHCR screening center at Ifo camp outside Dadaab, eastern Kenya (sixty miles from the Somali border), where tens of thousands of Somali famine refugees sought shelter, August 8, 2011. *(AP Photo / Jerome Delay)*

Jill hugs Joe onstage at the Democratic National Convention in Charlotte, North Carolina, September 6, 2012. *(AP Photo / Pablo Martínez Monsiváis)*

First Lady Michelle Obama, President Barack Obama, Vice President Joe Biden, and Jill wave at Obama's reelection night party in Chicago after defeating the Republican challenger, former Massachusetts governor Mitt Romney, November 7, 2012. *(AP Photo / Chris Carlson)*

Vice President Joe Biden dances with Jill during the Commander-in-Chief's Inaugural Ball at the Washington Convention Center during Obama's second inauguration in Washington, DC, January 21, 2013. *(AP Photo / Evan Vucci)*

Santa Claus, Jill, and Kate Wharton, twelve, whose father is Army Major General John Wharton, commanding general of the US Army Research, Development and Engineering Command, pose for a photograph at the Vice President's Residence with two of five Christmas trees dedicated to each of the US military branches during a holiday reception for service members, veterans, and their families, December 3, 2014. *(AP Photo / Cliff Owen)*

First Lady Michelle Obama and Jill visit with children as they make gifts during their annual Mother's Day Tea to honor military-connected mothers at the White House in Washington, DC, May 8, 2015. *(AP Photo / Carolyn Kaster)*

Jill steps up to welcome President Barack Obama at Macomb Community College in Warren, Michigan, September 9, 2015. Obama announced an initiative to expand apprenticeships and make community college free. *(AP Photo / Andrew Harnik)*

Jill greets a graduate onstage at the Girls Can Code graduation ceremony at the Colonel John C. Robinson American Center at the National Archive and Library Agency (NALA), in Addis Ababa, Ethiopia, July 17, 2016. Jill said American-sponsored programs are helping high school girls around the world to learn computer and information technology skills. *(AP Photo / Mulugeta Ayene)*

First Lady Michelle Obama and Jill arrive at the US Capitol in Washington, DC, Friday, January 20, 2017, for the presidential inauguration of Donald Trump. *(Saul Loeb / Pool Photo via AP)*

Jill stands alongside Joe as he speaks at a campaign rally during the Democratic presidential primaries in Columbia, South Carolina, February 29, 2020. (*AP Photo / Gerald Herbert*)

Masked for protection against COVID-19, Jill, Joe, vice presidential nominee Kamala Harris, and her husband, Doug Emhoff, during the fourth (final) day of the Democratic National Convention at the Chase Center in Wilmington, Delaware, August 20, 2020. (*AP Photo / Andrew Harnik*)

President Joe Biden, First Lady Jill, and family walk a portion of the inaugural parade route near the White House in Washington, DC, January 20, 2021. *(Doug Mills / The New York Times via AP Pool)*

President Joe Biden and Jill watch celebratory fireworks from the White House in Washington, DC, on the night of the Inauguration, January 20, 2021. *(AP Photo / Evan Vucci)*

"The Bidens are a National Guard family." Jill greets members of the National Guard with chocolate chip cookies at the US Capitol in Washington, DC, January 22, 2021. *(AP Photo / Jacquelyn Martin)*

President Joe Biden kisses Jill before boarding the Marine One presidential helicopter in Washington to visit wounded service members at Walter Reed National Military Medical Center in Bethesda, Maryland, January 29, 2021. *(AP Photo / Evan Vucci)*

A Valentine's Day decoration, signed by Jill, sits on the North Lawn of the White House in Washington, DC, February 12, 2021. *(AP Photo / Evan Vucci)*

Jill holds a roundtable discussion with six Latina farm workers at Forty Acres, the first headquarters of the United Farm Workers labor union, in Delano, California. They discuss discrimination against farm workers, the need for labor unions, and how they have dealt with work and childcare during the COVID-19 pandemic, March 31, 2021. *(Mandel Ngan / Pool via AP)*

Jill speaks about the benefits for children in President Biden's $1.9 trillion American Rescue Plan at the YWCA Central Alabama in Birmingham, Alabama, April 9, 2021. *(Anna Moneymaker / The New York Times via AP Pool)*

Jill arrives with Second Gentleman Doug Emhoff (far right), husband of Vice President Kamala Harris, before President Joe Biden places a wreath at the Tomb of the Unknown Soldier at Arlington National Cemetery, Arlington, Virginia, on Memorial Day, May 31, 2021. *(AP Photo / Alex Brandon)*

The Bidens wave as they arrive aboard Air Force One at RAF Mildenhall for the G7 Summit in Cornwall, England, June 9, 2021. *(Joe Giddens / Pool via AP)*

Jill and Kate, Duchess of Cambridge, talk with children during a visit to Connor Downs Academy in Hayle, West Cornwall, during the G7 Summit in England, June 11, 2021. *(Aaron Chown / Pool via AP)*

Jill and President Biden with Britain's Queen Elizabeth II, watching a Guard of Honor march past before their meeting at Windsor Castle, near London, June 13, 2021. *(AP Photo / Matt Dunham, Pool)*

Jill holds the hand of a nervous patient receiving a COVID-19 vaccination, at Jackson State University in Jackson, Mississippi, June 22, 2021. *(Tom Brenner / Pool via AP)*

The Bidens pose for a photo with (from left) granddaughters Finnegan Biden and Naomi Biden and daughter Ashley Biden as they watch fireworks during an Independence Day celebration on the South Lawn of the White House, Washington, DC, July 4, 2021. *(AP Photo / Patrick Semansky)*

President Joe Biden and Jill ride bikes on a trail at Gordons Pond in Rehoboth Beach, Delaware, September 19, 2021. *(AP Photo / Manuel Balce Ceneta)*

President Joe Biden and Jill listen as the national anthem is played during a ceremony honoring fallen law enforcement officers at the fortieth annual National Peace Officers' Memorial Service at the US Capitol in Washington, DC, October 16, 2021. *(AP Photo / Manuel Balce Ceneta)*

Jill speaks at the Barbara Bush Foundation for Family Literacy's National Summit on Adult Literacy at the Kennedy Center in Washington, DC, October 20, 2021. *(AP Photo / Andrew Harnik)*

Jill holds the hand of former senator Elizabeth Dole, R-NC, as Dole is acknowledged during a ceremony at the White House honoring children in military and veteran caregiving families, November 10, 2021. *(AP Photo / Manuel Balce Ceneta)*

Jill reads from the Dr. Seuss book *How the Grinch Stole Christmas!* while participating in a Toys for Tots sorting event at Joint Base Myer-Henderson Hall in Arlington, Virginia, December 10, 2021. *(AP Photo / Cliff Owen)*

sacrifice of those who attended, Sunny said she almost lost it when she heard her uncle's name.

"It was like the wind got knocked out of me," she said. She looked over at her uncle and thought how "really, really awesome" it must be for him to be recognized like that.

"There is not a thing in the world that can replace the feeling of being honored by the people who are in charge of actually sending you out there," Sunny said.

As a veteran, she said it's important that regular people understand the courage it takes for an eighteen-year-old to swear an oath to protect and defend the country.

"We're not perfect, but there is perfection in the integrity and the honor of our veterans, and if you love someone who has gone to war and they get honored in that way, you'll never forget it," Sunny said.

Chapter 36

Lighting of a Fire

In 2010, Jill joined Joe for a July 4 visit with troops in Iraq at Joint Victory Base in Baghdad. Joe had gone alone the previous year and visited Beau while he was stationed there. Now Jill explored the base with interest.

There were barbecues and volleyball tournaments taking place to celebrate Independence Day. Wherever she found a gathering, Jill walked in and met with the troops as a surprise. "I couldn't know that Joe was here and not come with him," she told the troops she met in Baghdad. "All I wanted to do the whole time Beau was here was to have a mom give him a hug."

She hugged practically everyone she met that day—countless soldiers.

"I'd love to call your mom when we get home from this trip and tell her I hugged you," she told each of them.

Her staff collected their mothers' contact information, phone numbers written down on slips of torn paper. On the plane back, they made a list. "We then spent two full days after we get back from this trip calling these phone numbers," recalled Kirsten White, Jill's policy director.

They would call each mom, then say, "Will you hold for Jill Biden, the wife of the vice president?"

"I had to call you because I was in Iraq with Joe over the Fourth," Jill would explain. She told each mom she'd met their son while she was there: "I just wanted to tell you he looks great. He looks great, and he can't wait to see you." The conversations were moments of instant connection, "magical sort of moments through a phone line," White said.

There was nothing she wouldn't have done, Jill told the mothers, for a mom to have "called me and said that she hugged Beau while he was deployed."

———————

Leaning on Jill's academic expertise, President Obama asked her to convene a summit on community colleges in the fall of 2010. It would bring together college presidents and professors with business and community leaders as a means of sharing best practices for learning and retention, while publicizing the opportunities that community colleges could offer everyday Americans.

Jill announced the event in an op-ed that ran in the *Chronicle of Higher Education:* "This will be a working summit, a setting where we can shine a spotlight on community colleges, highlight their utility to families and communities across the nation, nurture more collaboration, and generate additional policy ideas and goals for student success," Jill wrote. "As a community-college instructor, I am thrilled to be leading this summit and truly pleased to have the support of the administration."

A number of people in the Obama administration had community college experience, including Transportation Secretary Ray LaHood, but few people in the administration had as much holistic expertise with community college education as Jill.

The second lady's staff was small but dedicated. The community college summit "basically meant we were going to be putting together this enormous summit," Kirsten White recalled. "In the months leading up to an event like that, we never stopped working." They were "the little team that could," she said. But for Jill, it was only one of many ways that she remained steeped in community college life.

The summit was held on October 5, 2010, in front of a backdrop of gold curtains and American flags. Albert Ojeda, a student, gave opening remarks about the migrant farm life his family lived when he was young, and the financial strife they endured. Ojeda hadn't initially considered college, but he decided to give community college a chance—and found a place that "truly cared about my future," he said. It challenged him in new ways and helped him chart a different course. "I stand before you today a product of community colleges—a true testament to the significance these institutions play in our community, in our country, and ultimately in the world," he said.

After finishing his remarks, Jill came to the stage where she and Ojeda shared a hug. They had known each other for roughly a year, and it was clear that Ojeda's journey inspired Jill.

"For more and more people, community colleges are the way to the future," Jill said. "They're opening doors for the middle class at a time when the middle class has seen so many doors close to them." The summit highlighted all types of success stories, ranging from young immigrants like Ojeda, to Ray LaHood, to Billy Crystal—who said his acting career would have never been what it was without community college.

The president made his strong commitment to community college clear, and reiterated Jill's. "I'm so grateful for Jill being willing to lead today's summit," Obama said. "To take this one on, too, on behalf of the administration is extraordinarily significant." He added, "I do not think she's doing it for the administration. She's doing it for the passion she has for community colleges. Jill has devoted her life to education.

"I want it on the record that Jill is not playing hooky today...And this morning, between appearing on the *Today* show, receiving briefings from her staff, and hosting the summit, she was actually grading papers in her White House office."

The spirit of the summit was embodied by a quote that Jill chose from Irish poet W. B. Yeats: "Education is not the filling of a pail, but the lighting of a fire."

Chapter 37

Joining Forces

By 2011, Beau appeared to have recovered from his stroke and was back to his normal schedule as Delaware's attorney general. Jill and Joe pressed forward, too, with their work in Washington, believing that the worst of their son's health issues were behind them.

Jill's latest effort was called Joining Forces, a program she launched with Michelle Obama to help the public better understand and appreciate the sacrifices of military families while also using the government to help improve their well-being and access to education and job opportunities.

Both the president and vice president introduced their spouses, signaling that the commander in chief fully supported the effort. Joe praised the deep devotion exhibited by this generation of soldiers, who had endured two long wars in Iraq and Afghanistan, many of them serving multiple combat tours. "We owe them a lot," he said.

Jill, as she often did when speaking to military communities, emphasized the toll service can take on families and the sacrifices they make when a loved one is deployed. "You are all heroes—from the moms and dads who keep your families together while your loved ones are serving overseas, to the grandparents who step in with much needed support, to the children who are strong and brave while mom and dad are away," she said. "You do it all while carrying a heavier burden than most folks imagine."

She recalled a deployment ceremony she attended the month before where she met three grandparents who had banded together to take care of their three grandchildren, all under ten, when both parents had deployed. "They aren't wearing uniforms. They don't live on a base. But they are serving."

"We can all join forces," Jill said.

Neither Michelle nor Jill had a large staff, so their teams took a divide and conquer approach to setting up Joining Forces, recalled Tina Tchen, chief of staff to Michelle Obama. Jill's office focused on the needs and policy issues that specifically affected the National Guard, as well as military child education.

The collaboration meant double the resources that would normally go to an initiative pushed by a spouse. Michelle and Jill also sought support from a team on the National Security Council, a move aimed at adding some heft—and West Wing buy-in—to the effort.

The two women came to the issue of military families from different perspectives. Jill had lived firsthand the experience of having a family member serve overseas; Michelle could highlight the fact that one didn't need to be a member of a military family to care deeply about the cause.

"The Bidens obviously had a personal connection, given Beau's deployment, and their being a Blue Star family, which Mrs. Obama was very clear when we started Joining Forces that she was not," said Tchen, a major Obama fundraiser who became Michelle's chief of staff in 2011. "She was very representative of the ninety-nine percent of Americans who don't have that connection. And that's something she felt very strongly about forging and learning. In many ways, she learned a lot, I think, from Jill, and from Jill's Blue Star mom experience."

Jill and Michelle wanted to ensure that Joining Forces went beyond symbolic gestures of support. They wanted to tackle the bureaucratic and often overlooked issues that were disruptive or even obstructive to the everyday lives of service members and their families.

The list was long: for-profit colleges that were taking advantage of veterans, helping military spouses whose professions required licensure move their credentials from state to state, military health coverage, and many others. Encouraging employers to hire veterans was another big focus of Joining Forces.

Naturally for Jill, she took the lead on the educational components, specifically focusing on the education avenues available to military children, including partnerships with community colleges.

At the time Joining Forces was launched, the United States had been at war for ten years, and the civilian–military divide was stark. Less than one percent of the US population serve in the military, and frequent moves and service members away on third, fourth, or fifth deployments left military spouses and families isolated from community support systems. Family care was important for morale and readiness.

———

In 2011, Jeremy Bernard took on the role of White House social secretary. The day before he started, he saw Jill Biden shopping at Whole Foods. He thought about approaching her to say something, but he decided not to.

"The next day I saw her at the White House and she was so warm and welcoming," he recalled. He told her he'd seen her at the grocery store.

"Oh, you should have come up," Jill said. "You should have said something." She invited him to join her and her staffers for hot yoga.

"She has that ability to make you feel as if you're family or you've known her for a long time," Bernard said.

As social secretary, one of Bernard's primary responsibilities was organizing state dinners for visiting heads of state—opulent and carefully choreographed affairs that were closely analyzed at home and abroad. The first state dinner Bernard organized was for German chancellor Angela Merkel and her husband, Dr. Joachim Sauer, in June 2011. In a break from tradition, the Obamas held the black-tie event outdoors, with a reception on the Truman Balcony and dinner in the White House Rose Garden. Four long rows of tables for the 220 guests filled the garden with eye-pleasing symmetry, set with china and elegant centerpieces of yellow calla lilies. The National Symphony Orchestra played for guests, and singer-songwriter James Taylor performed.

Jill sent Bernard a handwritten note on Office of the Vice President stationery shortly afterward: "What a magical evening. Seeing the beautiful setting in the Rose Garden just took my breath away. It was wonderful, Jeremy. Love, Jill."

Jill often sent similar notes that made the staff feel very appreciated, Bernard recalled. Jill, who had never had a staff before becoming second lady, was also forming a bond with the team she had hired in the East Wing.

Out on the road, Jill and her aides didn't scatter to different hotel rooms after events. "We went out for martinis and french fries together," Kirsten White recalled. "We curled up with hot tea and talked. We would sit by the pool and catch up." Sometimes staffers would accompany Jill on runs, especially when they were in a different city and looking to get out for some fresh air and to explore.

When White left Jill's staff and moved to Boston, she had to take the Massachusetts state bar exam to practice law there. "She called me the morning of the test," White recalled. She and other former staffers "still get calls on our birthday" from Jill.

Chapter 38

Global Issues

In August 2011, Jill saw news coverage of a terrible drought in East Africa. Thousands of Somalis were fleeing to refugee camps in Kenya to escape famine.

She called Cathy Russell. "What can we do?" Jill asked. "Can we do anything?"

That issue was outside the bailiwick of the second lady's office. So Russell called Denis McDonough, the deputy national security adviser.

"Dr. Biden really wants to do something. She'd like to try and bring attention to this," Russell explained.

The White House organized a trip for Jill, former senator Bill Frist, and other officials to travel to Kenya to visit the Dadaab refugee camps. She met with Kenyan officials, pledged US support, and highlighted the need for both aid and long-term solutions. The visit generated considerable media interest, with CNN's Anderson Cooper and Dr. Sanjay Gupta reporting from the region.

"I just couldn't imagine, being a mother myself, that someone wouldn't help my children," Jill said in an interview with Cooper. "It's a desperate situation." She asked Americans to donate "to help the children live."

"Then we got on the plane, went back," Russell recalled. "I think she really felt, I have some power here to make a difference. I can do something."

Jill continued to use her travels abroad to highlight issues there that rarely received attention in the US. She focused on countries that were less likely to be visited by her husband, or the president, whose foreign trips were often anchored around international summits and visits with key allies and heads of state.

On a 2014 trip to Zambia, the Democratic Republic of the Congo, and Sierra Leone, Jill visited Panzi Hospital, run by Congolese gynecologist Denis Mukwege. Dr. Mukwege, who received the Nobel Peace Prize in 2018, had set up the Panzi Hospital in eastern Congo's Bukavu in 1998 to work with women who had been subjected to sexual violence in war. Cathy Russell, who by then had left Jill's staff for the State Department and had become the US ambassador-at-large for global women's issues, went on the trip, too. Jill also brought her granddaughter, Finnegan, one of Hunter's kids.

Jill and Cathy spotted Finnegan playing with a little girl at the hospital and initially thought she was the child of one of the women at the hospital. "No," Dr. Mukwege said, "she was a victim, too."

"I think for Jill it was a devastating moment for her to really see that and to understand," Russell said.

Chapter 39

National Tragedies

The atmosphere surrounding Obama and Biden's reelection campaign in 2012 was far different from their first joint appearance on the Democratic ticket four years earlier. The US economy had been battered by a recession, and while a recovery was underway, it was grindingly slow. Millions of Americans remained out of work or underemployed. The president had staked his political capital on passing the "Obamacare" healthcare law, a sweeping measure that Republicans would brand as a government takeover and a detour toward socialism. Democratic lawmakers suffered stinging defeats in the 2010 midterm elections and it was a distinct possibility that Obama could suffer the same fate in his reelection campaign.

Jill kept a low profile at first, staying focused on teaching, but she helped out during the campaign's final months by showing up at fundraisers and grassroots events in key states on weekends. "We want as much of her time as we can get," David Axelrod, one of Obama's senior advisers, said at the time.

Jill was a far more experienced campaigner at this point, but also a more efficient one than her husband, who drew energy from his one-on-one interactions with voters. During an event in New Hampshire, Joe spent fifteen minutes working the crowd along the rope line, while *Politico* clocked Jill's time at two minutes and twenty seconds.

In June 2012, Ashley Biden married otolaryngologist and plastic surgeon Howard Krein. Beau had introduced them two years before. They married in Delaware and Jill and Joe hosted their reception lakeside at their home in

Wilmington. In the family tradition, Joe's office released a statement after the private event, largely surprising the press.

Ashley had studied cultural anthropology at Tulane University, where she was arrested for possession of marijuana. It is unclear if she was charged, but she was not convicted. She later earned a master of social work degree from the University of Pennsylvania and went on to develop foster care, mental health, and juvenile justice programs for Delaware's Department of Services for Children, Youth, and Their Families. She held leadership roles at the Delaware Center for Justice until 2019 and launched a line of unisex sweatshirts called Livelihood that donated proceeds to "education, work-place development, and job placement initiatives" in Wilmington and Washington, DC.

The centerpiece of Jill's role in the campaign was her address at the Democratic convention in Charlotte, North Carolina, in early September. Angie Flores, a student at Miami Dade College, introduced Jill, who gave Angie an enthusiastic teacher's hug and kiss on the cheek as the audience cheered.

"Hello!" Jill called out to the crowd gathered in the cavernous arena. She introduced herself as the wife of the vice president, a full-time teacher, and a military mom. "Tonight, thanks to the leadership of President Obama and my husband, Joe, the war in Iraq is over," she proclaimed.

It was a key talking point of the Obama campaign—the president had officially ended the US combat role in Iraq and most American troops had left. But the situation in Iraq would grow complicated and continue to vex the Obama administration in the ensuing years, with the rise of the Islamic State and the instability of the Iraqi government.

Most of Jill's address that night focused on domestic matters. She also leaned heavily into Joe's character and personal story—the early loss of his first wife and daughter, and their family history together.

"People started questioning whether I could keep teaching" after becoming second lady, Jill said. "Not Joe. He was there, standing by my side, saying, 'Of course you should. It's who you are, Jill.'"

She also talked about his policy work. "Two decades ago, when Joe started working on the Violence Against Women Act, domestic violence was often treated as a private family matter rather than the crime it is. But Joe knew that he had to bring this issue out into the open." Jill, who had initially been skeptical of the law, told the crowd, "In the years since that bill passed, I've had women tell me that their sisters or their friends wouldn't be alive today if it weren't for Joe."

Jill concluded her speech with Joe's signature closing line—"God bless our troops"—and added one of her own: "And God bless our military families."

The fall campaign was filled with highs and lows. Obama struggled in his first debate against Republican nominee Mitt Romney, the former Massachusetts governor. His subpar performance upped the stakes for Joe in the vice-presidential debate against Wisconsin representative Paul Ryan, at the time a rising star in the Republican Party.

Joe made a vigorous case for Obama's agenda—more compelling than the one Obama had made, many Democrats noted—and seemed to revel in poking holes in Ryan's counterattacks. Joe was credited with helping ease anxieties within the Democratic Party over Obama's performance and getting the campaign back on track.

Jill sat with other family members in the audience. When the face-off was over, she joined Joe onstage and warmly greeted Ryan and his young family.

After a fall spent sprinting from one battleground state to the next, Joe and Jill found themselves back in Chicago on election night. Democrats' margin of victory was narrower than in 2008, some of the sheen of Obama's hope and change message having come off during a difficult first term. But Obama and Joe—and Michelle and Jill—now had four more years ahead of them in Washington to complete the work they had started.

The two couples spent a few private minutes celebrating their victory in the hotel suite where the Obamas watched the results come in, then stepped before a cheering crowd that had gathered to help them celebrate.

Obama had been fond of saying during the 2012 election that he was running his last campaign. He was term-limited and there was no higher office for him to seek.

Attention would soon turn to whether that was the same for Biden.

———

Like most Americans, and as a longtime educator, Jill was appalled by school shootings. But the events of December 14, 2012, at Sandy Hook Elementary School, where a gunman killed twenty-six people—including twenty young children—were especially shocking.

President Obama was moved to tears as he addressed the nation. Joe was put in charge of a renewed, but ultimately failed, effort to get Congress to pass gun control legislation. Michelle Obama offered condolences and support in an open letter.

Jill became inspired by the story of first-grade teacher Kaitlin Roig, credited with saving fifteen children by huddling with them inside a bathroom during the shooting. Jill invited Roig to be her guest of honor at Obama's State of the Union address in February 2013. For those speeches, Jill got to invite a guest or two to join her in the first lady's box in the House chamber in the Capitol building.

Jill felt a deep connection with Roig and other Sandy Hook teachers, none of whom ever expected the circumstances that confronted them just before Christmas in 2012.

"She was without question an inspiration" to Jill, said Kirsten White, the policy director.

Only a few months later, tragedy struck again. On April 15, 2013, a bombing near the finish line of the Boston Marathon killed three people and injured hundreds. The culprits managed to escape, putting the nation on high alert for four days. While on the run, the Tsarnaev brothers shot and killed a twenty-seven-year-old police officer from MIT.

Jill and Joe visited Boston in the days that followed, a few days after the

Obamas. After Joe's remarks of sympathy at the officer's memorial service, Jill paid a solo visit to a memorial at the scene of the attack that was filled with flowers, running gear, and messages of strength. Dressed in black, she spent a few moments in silence taking in the scene. Before leaving, she left flowers and a pair of her running shoes that she had signed, "Boston Strong! Love, Jill Biden."

Chapter 40

Battle Together

With the 2012 reelection behind them, Joe began to think about his and his son Beau's political futures. "He had all the best of me, but with the bugs and flaws engineered out," Joe wrote.

Beau was serving as Delaware's attorney general, but Joe believed that a winning bid for the Delaware governorship in 2016 could give Beau a path to the White House a few years down the road. And while Hunter had been chairman of the board of directors for World Food Program USA since 2011, Joe thought Beau would have a strong chance at winning the presidency if his brother became his speechwriter and adviser. Joe was thinking of "shifting the family's focus to Beau's political future" after the Obama administration.

But three years after his stroke, Beau's health was again in crisis. After what White House officials said was "an episode of disorientation and weakness" as he drove to Indiana for a family vacation, Beau was referred to the University of Texas MD Anderson Cancer Center in Houston, one of the nation's leading cancer institutions, for testing and a more thorough medical evaluation.

Joe postponed a bus tour with President Obama to be with his son and Jill in Houston. With Beau's health deteriorating, the doctors grew worried that Beau could be dealing with glioblastoma multiforme, a highly aggressive form of brain cancer.

In Joe's book *Promise Me, Dad*, he described how the family had been drawn to MD Anderson by Beau's neurosurgeon and his reputation as one of the world's best at awake craniotomy. The high-stakes procedure "allowed the surgeon to remove the greatest part of a brain tumor without doing damage to speech, cognition, or motor skills." Seven hours after it began, the procedure concluded without Beau incurring any lasting complications other than a scar.

His diagnosis, however, was grim. Some cancer cells couldn't be reached without affecting key arteries; success depended on the removal of ninety-eight percent or more of the tumor. Biopsy results revealed that not only did Beau have stage IV glioblastoma, he lacked a mutation that could slow the growth of the cancer, and had two additional mutations that accelerated it. Following the surgery, all attention shifted to the critical next stages of Beau's treatment. Beau was in his early forties, fit and strong, and the doctors' plan was aggressive.

Beau's treatment was a full-family effort. Joe spoke with any doctor that would see him. Jill, Ashley, and Beau's wife, Hallie, focused on easing the burdens of everyday life, not only for Beau but for his children. Hunter, who had been Beau's protector from day one, stayed by his side during the darkest moments.

Even with a difficult road ahead, doctors sent Beau home to Delaware with a hopeful outlook. Beau's doctors told him he should resume as much of a normal life as possible, with goals and ambitions for the future. If he wanted to coach a soccer team or run for governor of Delaware, he should do it.

"I knew, deep down in my gut, that he would beat the odds," Jill wrote in her autobiography. "Yes, they were one in a hundred. But Beau was invincible. I felt like if I believed hard enough, if I prayed hard enough, we would all look back on his battle together. It would be another challenge we overcame as a family. I never gave up—as a mother, you can't."

Chapter 41

Worsening Conditions

Back in Washington, Joe asked his chief of staff, Steve Ricchetti, to help keep him busy. "Unfortunately, I've lived through this before," Joe said. "The only way I survived, the only way I got through it, was by staying busy and keeping my mind, when it can be, focused on my job."

Jill soon saw the strain that approach put on her husband. Over the next months, Jill would pull Ricchetti aside. "Joe's working too hard," she said. "He's exhausted. He's not sleeping. It's going to kill him."

"I would be happy to do anything he'd let me do," Ricchetti said.

Sometimes at home, Jill would talk to Joe directly about it. "You've got to stop, Joe. You're going to get run down and you're going to get sick. I'm really worried about you."

———

During Jill's spring 2014 semester, her sister Jan was also diagnosed with cancer and hospitalized. Doctors gave her a low chance of survival and told her stem cell replacement therapy was her only real hope. The treatment meant Jan would be kept isolated in quarantine for six weeks. Jill and her sisters had worked out a schedule to keep Jan from being alone. Jill told her students she would miss their next class for personal reasons.

"Where are you going to be, Dr. B?" they asked.

She told them about her sister's situation. "I need to be with her," Jill said. The words caught in her throat and, needing a moment, she turned to face the chalkboard. With Beau and Jan sick at the same time, Jill knew she had to be strong for Joe and the rest of the family—but it was so hard.

"I brought out my reassuring smile for my family as much as I could, but standing in front of my class, I suddenly lost my composure," she wrote in her memoir.

Her students stood and lined up to give her hugs, one by one.

The stem cell treatments were successful, and Jan's lymphoma later went into remission.

———————

That summer, Jill began to accept how sick Beau really was. The doctors warned the Bidens that with all the therapies they were trying, Beau's condition could appear to worsen as he dealt with side effects of the treatments. But if they worked, his condition would suddenly improve.

"So as bad as it would get," Jill recalled, "I would say to myself, I can live with this because I know it's going to get better."

Close friends tried to connect with Jill, concerned both about Beau and her own well-being. But she just wouldn't talk about it. It was too emotionally fraught, and she was protecting Beau.

It was a stark contrast to the Jill her friends were accustomed to—she was normally warm and open. For her to close herself off this way, friends concluded, Beau must be really sick.

———————

Over Thanksgiving 2014, with the family gathered in Nantucket, Beau and Hunter cornered their father in the kitchen. Joe had to run for president in 2016, they said.

"You've got to run," Beau said. "I want you to run."

"*We* want you to run," Hunter said.

"It was the conviction and intensity in Beau's voice that caught me off guard," Joe wrote. "At one point he said it was my obligation to run, my duty."

Joe began to test the waters. Steve Ricchetti and Mike Donilon, Cathy Russell's brother-in-law, laid the initial groundwork, meeting Joe and the boys at the Naval Observatory to discuss a twenty-two-page memo they had written. Joe remembered the February 2015 evening in DC as frigid, but the room "determinedly upbeat."

If he ran, Biden would effectively be asking the country to stay the course he and Obama had charted over eight years. The economy had improved and the administration's signature healthcare law was becoming increasingly popular—but Americans often looked to switch parties after two-term presidencies.

Biden's advisers, however, believed Joe had key advantages compared to others in the likely Democratic field—particularly Hillary Clinton, who was expected to run. The country was looking for authenticity, something long seen as one of Biden's strengths. He could run on his experience as vice president, his foreign policy expertise, on his calls for campaign finance reform. Simply put, Ricchetti told Biden he had a platform he could sell.

Ricchetti's memo ended with a blueprint that Biden would need to follow from that point forward, if he considered running a viable option. It touched on everything from speech topics and locations to key staff picks and campaign infrastructure and lead up to the announcement of Joe's candidacy in April, only six weeks away.

Beau was gaunt and gray, and clearly tiring although it was still early in the evening.

"For more than twenty years, at any meeting about any political campaign," Joe wrote, "I had looked to Beau for counsel. He was the only other person in the room that night who had ever stood for and won elective office. Beau's advice was the advice I would have most valued at that moment. But that night he mainly just sat and observed."

Joe had a sense that the meeting was an important charade. "We all understood how much Beau wanted me to run for president. We all knew that, more than anything, Beau did not want to be the reason I did *not* run," Joe wrote.

———

April arrived. There was still no public announcement of a Biden presidential campaign, or even a set plan for one.

On April 12, the Bidens had a family day planned. Beau and his wife, Hallie, were bringing their children, Natalie and Hunter, over for a taping of *Reading Rainbow*. The segment would feature Jill, Joe, and their youngest grandchildren, Beau's children, reading from *Don't Forget, God Bless Our Troops*. Jill had written the children's book for military families based on her grandchildren's experience when Beau had been deployed to Iraq.

While everyone was gathered in front of the television crew, Beau quietly lounged with his aunt Val in the sunroom of Joe and Jill's home in Wilmington, enjoying the fresh breeze with the doors open. The house was one of his favorite sanctuaries. He was in pain, no doubt, having received a few days earlier the most recent step in his cancer treatment, an experimental live-virus injection that caused inflammation across his body as it attacked the cancer cells. No one knew for sure what to expect except a painstaking wait. The idea of any more Biden children losing a parent was too painful to bear.

A TV was turned to the news, and the networks were covering Hillary Clinton's announcement that she would run for the Democratic presidential nomination, as had been widely expected. There was also an expectation that she would clear the Democratic field—early polls showed her with a fifty-point lead over the next most popular option, Joe Biden.

Earlier in the week, at Obama's request, Joe had met with a group of pollsters who all but told him that the Clinton campaign machine was too well funded and organized to defeat, so it would likely be best to refrain from entering the race. That news didn't matter to Joe, nor did it weaken Beau's resolve.

"He was reading all he could about the Clinton campaign—its message, its candidate's travel schedule, its early field operation. He wanted to be up on everything, so he would be ready to pitch in the minute I announced my own candidacy," Joe wrote. "In my own head, the race was more than anything a matter of daring. And if I had my two sons behind me, anything was possible."

Clinton's head start didn't worry Joe, he still believed he had a viable path to the nomination and could close the gap with Clinton once he jumped into the race. But he wanted to push off an announcement until Beau had emerged from his current treatment. Family first, then politics, was a natural order for the Bidens, to the extent that the two could be distinguished.

Shortly after, Joe's brother Jimmy took Beau to his next appointment, for more tests and to receive his second dose of the live virus. The treatment was yielding promising signs—Beau wasn't reacting negatively to the injections, and his tumor growth was rapidly slowing. "We really may have something," Jimmy said. "We may have cracked the atom."

Joe and Jill, eager for any good news about their son, welcomed the positive developments. But they also knew there was still a long road ahead. They had been through enough as a family to know not to get their hopes up too high.

Chapter 42

Hope

Soon the early success of Beau's treatment began to slow. Until that point the Biden family had kept the full extent of Beau's illness to themselves. None of Jill's NOVA colleagues knew. Nor did most of their colleagues at the White House. They looked for ways to cope with the devastating situation largely on their own.

"I used to exercise a lot to get me through that time period," Jill recalled. She tried to be there for her other children, her grandchildren, and Joe. "You just go through it," she said. "You feel like you're walking underwater. You feel like that's what it feels like every day."

It was a secret even from their closest friends. "People would see Beau in public and say 'Wow, he's lost a lot of weight,'" Jill's close friend Mary Doody said. "And I knew he was sick. I probably knew he had cancer, but I did not know the gravity of his illness."

Over time, the Bidens began telling more people, confiding in the Obamas early on. Beau's illness became an open secret in Washington — but no one wanted to discuss it, well aware of how much pain Biden had already endured during his life.

Obama, whose working relationship with Biden had grown into a friendship, was shaken by news of Beau's illness. During a meeting in the Oval Office, staffers had trouble getting Obama's attention. Disengaged, he looked out over the South Lawn. He'd just been told that Joe had left to be with Beau. "I don't know how Joe's going to live — survive — if something happens to Beau," Obama said.

About a week later, Joe returned to the White House. When Obama heard he was there he went quickly to the foyer of the vice president's office, almost sprinting, and met him in an embrace.

Treatment was hard on Beau, and watching him go through it was devastating. Beau's athletic body began to grow weak, and Jill and Joe began considering a second mortgage on their home to help finance his treatment.

Despite his political prominence, Joe had never accumulated significant wealth. He was consistently ranked as one of the least wealthy members of the Senate, a distinction he normally wore with pride. But it left his family, like so many others in America, financially vulnerable when an unexpected illness struck.

In a sign of how close their families had become, it was Obama who offered to help.

"I'll give you the money," Barack told Joe. "I have it. You can pay me back whenever."

Joe and Jill didn't accept the offer. But it was among the most meaningful gestures either had ever received.

One of the few people Jill opened up to about Beau's condition was Mary Doody. Over a private lunch, Jill revealed just how gravely ill Beau was. "Mary, I just have to keep finding joy in every day," Jill told her friend. "And today you're my joy."

When Beau's condition worsened, he was moved to Walter Reed National Military Medical Center, in Bethesda, Maryland, where the facility offered security measures, allowing Jill and Joe easy access to visit their son.

A Catholic priest stopped by the room. Jill said thank you, but asked him to leave—and not to return. "She didn't want Beau to get the idea he was there to perform last rites," Joe wrote. "In fact, there would be no discussion about last rites."

It was one of many parallels Jill saw between Beau's illness and Joe's near-death experience in 1988. "There's just so many ironic moments throughout life," she said, recalling the appalling ICU rule that kept Joe's parents from seeing him after his surgery. "And then what happened to me," with Beau. She couldn't imagine being kept from her son when he needed her.

Returning to the classroom while Joe was still in the hospital had also been a good lesson in her ability to cope by compartmentalizing her pain. "It was the same thing when Beau was sick," she said. "I was still teaching. Nobody knew what was going on. But I knew I had to walk into that classroom and I had to be there. And that helped me, because I could compartmentalize." Before school and after school were another matter, "but at that moment, I had to be there."

Carrying on with teaching, friends said, also helped Jill keep alive the prospect that Beau might recover and life might return to normal.

"She just never, never, never, never gave up hope," Cathy Russell recalled. "She believed till the bitter end that he could make it."

Joe, too, continued to project optimism.

Valerie Jarrett, Obama's senior adviser, recalled riding back from an event alone in the car with Joe.

"I really believe he's going to pull through," Joe said. "I really do." He squeezed Jarrett's hand.

She felt he was talking as much to himself as to her, trying to keep hope alive for Beau and the rest of the family.

But the medical reality was that Beau's condition had reached a point where his team had no real expectation that he would pull through. The Bidens relished in the small moments, like the mild May days when they could take their son outside to savor the sunshine.

Chapter 43

The Last Light

When Beau became unresponsive, the doctors at Walter Reed gathered the family but didn't fully communicate the simple reality that they had reached the end. Jill and Joe and the rest of the family were headed back to Beau's room when Dr. Howard Krein, Ashley's husband, called them back into the meeting with the medical staff. He had translated the medical-speak throughout Beau's treatment.

"You have to tell them the truth," Howard told the doctors.

"He will not recover," they told the Bidens.

On May 29, 2015, the family gathered as doctors prepared to remove Beau's life support. Hunter recalled in his memoir, *Beautiful Things*, there were "twenty-four Bidens slipping in and out of the room, wandering the hospital's halls, lost in thought, waiting."

After Beau's tracheostomy tube was removed, "the morning seeped into the afternoon, then into the evening, then late into the night. The sun came back up, its light scarcely leaking through the room's drawn shades," Hunter wrote.

In the final hours, Jill whispered to her son. "Go to a happy place, Beau," she said. He'd loved the lake at their home in Delaware. "Go to the dock, with Hunter."

Beau slipped away just before eight that night.

Jill and Joe arrived home in Delaware on Air Force Two the next night. They took their dog Champ and walked down to sit beside the lake.

Jill saw a white egret on the water. Together she and Joe watched it for twenty minutes until it flew off, circling several times overhead.

"It's a sign from God," Jill said. "Beau being at the lake one last time, and heading for heaven."

Chapter 44

Peanuts

The first of two viewings to pay respects to Beau was scheduled at St. Anthony of Padua Roman Catholic Church in Wilmington at one p.m. on June 5. But the line of mourners began to queue hours earlier, with thousands gathering to pay their respects and offer condolences to the Biden family. It was as if all of Delaware had arrived to honor the state's most prominent family.

Joe and Jill stood in front of Beau's flag-draped casket, hugging longtime friends and strangers. They were drained, the sadness and exhaustion of the moment evident on their faces. But they also laughed and took comfort in the personal remembrances of Beau that so many shared.

"All of Delaware went through that, because Beau was a native son," Sherry Dorsey Walker, a Delaware state representative and member of the Biden Breast Health Initiative, said. "And in this state, when one of us was hurting, we all hurt. And so we as a state went through that with them. We prayed with them. We loved them through it, and they saw the culmination of all of that at Beau's homegoing, when people stood in line for seven and eight hours just to give them a hug...

"And just to be in the midst of that, and to feel the love that the state of Delaware showed to our very own Jill, Joe, and to the rest of the family, to Ashley, Hunter, and the children, and Hallie. It was just, it's something that, unless you were there to see it and feel it for yourself, some may find it to be indescribable."

The next day, a thousand people filled the pews of the same church for the funeral service. Hunter and Ashley spoke movingly about their big brother. Beau was posthumously presented with the Legion of Merit and a gospel choir sang "Amazing Grace" before Coldplay's Chris Martin, one of Beau's favorite musicians, performed "Till Kingdom Come." But it was President Obama's eulogy that affected the Bidens most profoundly. He called Beau "an original" who "made you want to be a better person" and embodied the "Biden family rule: If you have to ask for help, it's too late."

"I will tell you what, Michelle and I, and Sasha and Malia, we've become part of the Biden clan. We're honorary members now. And the Biden family rule applies. We're always here for you, we always will be—my word as a Biden." Jill remembered the strength that she and Joe gathered from his words, and the way that it wreathed all the support that Barack and Michelle had given them throughout Beau's struggle.

Jill stayed close throughout the viewing and funeral services to Beau's children, wrapping her arms around them protectively. When her husband was overcome with emotion, she placed a hand on his shoulder.

———

Joe and Jill managed their immense grief over Beau's death differently. Joe leaned into his role as vice president and sought comfort in close friends and confidants. His emotions flowed without hesitancy. Axelrod remembers seeing Joe for the first time after Beau had passed: tears quickly swelled in the vice president's eyes as they spoke.

Jill was less vocal about her pain. Old friends saw that she was crushed after Beau died; she had adored him. And she definitely wasn't ready to return to the White House.

———

Following Beau's funeral, the Bidens went down to a friend's home in South Carolina to retreat from Washington for a while.

"We were raw from those final weeks of Beau's illness and needed a place to recover. Wilmington had poured out love for us, and yet, the reminders of Beau were everywhere; we felt like we could never catch our breath," Jill wrote. "And so we gathered up the kids and grandkids and headed to the beach, hoping for some healing from the clean salt air."

While the Bidens were secluded on Kiawah Island, a white gunman opened fire at Mother Emanuel AME Church in Charleston, one of the oldest Black churches in the country, with a deep history in the civil rights movement. Eight Black worshippers were killed during a Bible study led by Reverend Clementa Carlos Pinckney, the church's pastor, who was also killed.

The Bidens joined President Obama at the funeral for Reverend Pinckney, where Obama delivered yet another eulogy. Joe said he had seen Pinckney—who was also a South Carolina state senator—at a prayer breakfast the year before his death. In his speech, the president recognized all nine victims and gave a soulful rendition of the first verse of "Amazing Grace."

With Beau gone, Jill had struggled to hold on to her belief in God.

Being at Mother Emanuel that day to remember those who were killed reminded her of just how empty she felt without both her faith and her son.

Jill wrote in her memoir that she felt her heart in her throat as she walked with Joe into the cavernous convention center for Pinckney's memorial. At their seats, music from the gospel choir flooded over her as it had at Beau's funeral in Delaware about a month earlier.

She marveled at the sense of joy emanating from a community that had suffered so deeply yet had come together in grief to celebrate Pinckney's life.

"Their collective faith seemed undaunted, and I wished that I could share it with them. Where was my faith?" Jill wrote.

Despite the outpouring of support for the Bidens, the political world did not stand still.

On their last day in South Carolina before returning to Washington, the *Wall Street Journal* published a story speculating about a Biden campaign for president. The article highlighted Beau's dream of his dad being president in a way that got under Joe's skin—as if he would be letting Beau down by not having enough emotional fuel left in the tank.

"Everything we talked about is over," Joe told Ricchetti, his chief of staff. "If Beau had never gotten sick, we would already be running…the thought of doing it without him was painful," Joe wrote.

To many, including Jill, the timing of running in 2016 was too soon—there was too much to do, too much to consider—during a time when their emotional coffers were so totally drained. Yet for Joe, who had been sworn into the Senate in 1973 from Beau's hospital bedside, politics could be his refuge.

Hunter and a friend talked amid the Washington speculation that his father might actually be considering a run for the White House.

"Hunter, this doesn't make any sense to me," the friend said. "He seems fragile, you know, emotionally."

"He is fragile," Hunter said, "but one of the things he does to just deal with life is, he runs. He's a politician. This is what our family does.'"

The discussion of running was hard on Jill, who took far less comfort in politics, or even the basic idea of moving ahead with their lives. But Hunter encouraged Joe to press forward with the process.

By mid-July 2015, Mike Donilon and Ricchetti reported to Joe that they thought there might still be time if he wanted to enter the field. With his closest council—Jill, Hunter, Ashley, Val, Donilon, Ricchetti, and Ted Kaufman—there were long discussions about the realities of a run. The effort it took to campaign was only the first challenge, followed by either the immense pressure of governing or the draining task of losing.

"Understand, if you lose, it will be a big loss," Biden recalled them saying. But after Beau's death, the idea of losing an election was peanuts.

Chapter 45

Potential Candidate

By midsummer, Jill began inching back into the spotlight. She'd needed the time away from Washington, and the summer break at NOVA had allowed her to step away without missing any time teaching. But now it was time to get back to work.

"I stayed home that summer for a while, just trying to get through it," she said.

One of her first major endeavors was a trip to South Korea, Vietnam, and Laos to promote girls' education and support military families.

Her team kept the traveling delegation purposefully small. Val and Cathy Russell, now the US ambassador-at-large for global women's issues, were on the trip, as was Jill's longtime friend Christine Vilsack. She'd joined the administration in 2013 as the head of international education at USAID.

Jill was quiet, and Val and Cathy were protective of her. Christine, there in an official capacity and sensitive to Jill's grief, tried to keep her distance from the close-knit group. "I felt honored they invited me to come along," Christine said. "It was a tough trip for her. She was doing it, but it was difficult."

On the way back, Jill stopped in Japan for a USO block party at the base in Okinawa. "My son Beau also served in the Iraq War," Jill said. "As a military family member, I understand how proud you are of your service and the sacrifices you make for our country."

Even in grief, Jill's focus was on military families. Jamie Lawrence, one of Jill's policy directors, recalled a woman who asked about military coverage of in vitro fertilization at a Joining Forces event. "I had no idea. And two weeks later, Dr. B turns around to me, she's like, 'Hey, did you ever get back to so-and-so on that?' I was like, wow."

In late August 2015, Joe and Jill Biden gathered by the pool of their home at the Naval Observatory with some of the vice president's closest political advisers. It was a meeting the advisers had been putting off, sensitive to the couple's heartbreak.

The vice president's political advisers had spent the weeks following Beau's death treading carefully around the topic of Joe entering the 2016 field, but there was work to be done and decisions to be made.

The Democratic campaign was well underway, with Hillary Clinton, Obama's former secretary of state who had long been considered the 2016 front-runner, and Vermont senator Bernie Sanders battling it out for the party's nomination. Biden could still run but the window was closing fast.

Jill and Joe sat side by side as the team ticked through fast-approaching deadlines to get on state ballots. Biden would need thousands of signatures on petitions around the country and a campaign headquarters that could establish a command over the moving pieces.

Labor Day, the team told the Bidens, was the latest recommended time to launch the campaign.

Jill grabbed Joe's arm. "We can't be ready by then," she said, according to a person with knowledge of the meeting. Despite her own reservations, Jill tried to create space for her husband to make his decision with a clear mind, unperturbed by graphs, deadlines, and fundraising needs.

"Joe, this is your decision," she told him. He had to make up his mind for himself.

But from the beginning, Jill was acutely aware that neither Joe nor anyone else in the family had the strength or capacity for a presidential campaign.

"You can't just lose a child and then think you can get out on the campaign trail and go talk to people," she said later. "You just can't."

While Joe watched the Democratic field take shape without him, President Obama found himself caught between two former rivals who had become friends and close advisers.

Hillary Clinton started out strong but was saddled by ethics questions surrounding her use of a private email account and internet server at the State Department and the fundraising practices of her family foundation. Her approval ratings steadily declined as Vermont senator Bernie Sanders gained momentum, particularly among younger voters.

Joe was seen by some Democrats as a potential candidate who could split the difference. He had deeper experience than even Clinton, and was viewed as more authentic and more critical of the big money political apparatus she was associated with and that Sanders was railing against. Yet Joe was also seen as a more moderate and less risky choice as a general election candidate than Sanders.

In public, Obama stayed stridently neutral, even with his legacy on the line. Clinton had been instrumental in helping Obama accomplish many of his foreign policy goals, but it was Joe whom he had formed a truly lasting friendship with. "Certainly, he's got something at stake here," said White House spokesman Josh Earnest, about Obama's decision to refrain from promising an endorsement.

Chapter 46

Give It One Hundred Percent

Earlier in 2015, Obama had called for $60 billion in funding to finance a program for free community college, but the proposal was going nowhere in Congress. Eager to build national support, Obama turned to Jill Biden.

On September 9, 2015, Jill and President Obama traveled to Michigan, to visit Macomb Community College. They flew together on Air Force One, and then shared the president's limousine as they drove to the campus for a tour of a technical educational center. To a group of about a thousand spectators, Jill and Obama applauded MCC's success in creating new innovative programs that worked with the local business community to support student opportunities. The headline announcement was the creation of the College Promise Advisory Board, an independent group that Jill, Obama's "favorite community college instructor," was set to co-lead.

Jill hadn't been briefed on the correct pronunciation of "Macomb" and she placed undue emphasis on the first syllable as she spoke. The crowd yelled out how to properly say the name of their town, and they shared a laugh. "You're correcting the teacher," she joked.

To Obama and Jill, the case for free community college was clear. They argued that greater access to community college would bolster the US workforce, and ensure that young graduates wouldn't be so debilitated by debt.

The College Promise Advisory Board was to be an independent group that worked with other organizations to build momentum behind the push for free community college by highlighting similar, smaller programs that had already proved successful.

"It's important that you give your friends, your families, your classmates, a heads-up to join the movement to make two years of community college free because education is the key to America's future," Jill said.

Every public appearance by both Joe and Jill at that moment was being scrutinized for clues about their next steps. Was Jill speaking as a second lady making a final push for her policy priorities before her moment on the national stage passed? Was she test-running campaign messages and her role in an upcoming White House run?

In either case, her connection with the audience was evident, particularly when she drew in her personal experiences. She confessed that she had been grading essays from her students at Northern Virginia Community College aboard Air Force One.

"If you didn't know she was the wife of a vice president, you'd think she was just one of the teachers," said Ross Neba, a student who watched Biden's speech.

———

Labor Day slipped by without a campaign announcement from Biden, or even a decision on whether he planned to run.

On September 11, while in New York for a 9/11 memorial, Joe appeared on *The Late Show with Stephen Colbert*. The conversation between the men was honest and emotional, with Joe publicly revealing his private doubts and internal deliberations about his ability to launch a presidential campaign while mourning his son.

"Look, I don't think any man or woman should run for president," Joe said, "unless, number one, they know exactly why they would want to be president; two, they can look at the folks out there and say, 'I promise you, you have my whole heart, my whole soul, my energy, and my passion, to do this.' And I'd be lying if I said that I knew I was there. I'm being completely honest. Nobody has a right, in my view, to seek that office unless they're willing to give it one hundred percent of who they are."

It was a moment that both accelerated calls for Joe to run for president and revealed just how difficult that would be.

While Joe's primary considerations in those days was the impact a campaign would have on his family, he was also weighing practical political considerations. Some Democratic leaders worried that if Joe jumped into the race at this stage, he and Clinton would split the votes from the party's more moderate, establishment-minded voters, clearing a path for Bernie Sanders to grab the nomination. It was a prospect that also concerned Joe, who worried about Sanders's prospects in a general election campaign.

Chapter 47

Knowing the Time

Biden huddled again with his small inner circle of advisers on October 5. It was six months after his team's original target for a campaign launch and just over four months since Beau's death on May 30.

Once again, the team told Joe there was still a small window of time to meet the necessary filing deadlines and build out the infrastructure for a legitimate campaign. Funding prospects were solid, as were a list of people who offered to give Joe their endorsement.

"By the end of the meeting it was clear to everybody in the room that we had the ability to staff a first-rate field operation and the capacity to raise the money to get us through the first four contests. I hadn't been sure of any of that at the beginning of July, but I was certain of it on October 5. Only one thing could stop me now—and that was me," Joe later wrote.

———

The next day, *Politico* ran a story that upended things. "Exclusive: Biden himself leaked word of his son's dying wish," read the headline, with a subhead reading "The vice president is mourning. He's also calculating."

Joe felt sickened by the idea that he would use his son's death for his political advantage.

"I didn't think anybody would believe the charge," he later wrote, "but I could feel my anger rise. And I understood the danger of that, especially in my present emotional state. If this thing about Beau came up somewhere in my hearing, I was afraid I would not be able to control my rage."

———

On October 20, the vice president's advisers were once again summoned to the Naval Observatory to brief Joe and Jill on their options one final time. The vice president seemed to want his advisers to tell him it was over—that there was no way to launch a successful campaign this late in the race. But the team informed him that the window remained open if he wanted it. In the absence of a decision, some members of his team remained waist-deep in planning for the race, in case he suddenly decided to run. They had no idea whether their work would ultimately be in vain.

The atmosphere in the green-walled library was tense as the meeting stretched on for several hours; Jill sat listening, choosing to say very little.

The meeting ended without a clear resolution. But the next day, in a surprise to even some of his closest aides, Joe was ready to make an announcement.

"Come to the Rose Garden," read the cryptic email that Biden's team received just before noon.

Joe emerged from the Oval Office flanked by Jill and President Obama. He would not, he announced, be running for the presidency of the United States.

"Unfortunately, I believe we're out of time, the time necessary to mount a winning campaign for the nomination," Joe said in a thirteen-minute speech. "But while I will not be a candidate, I will not be silent."

The news came as a disappointment to some members of the team. To others, uncertain that Joe had a favorable chance of winning, the vice president's decision was a relief. Biden spoke that day like a politician who knew his moment in the spotlight was coming to an end.

"We intend—the whole family, not just me—we intend to spend the next fifteen months fighting for what we've always cared about, what my family's always cared about, with every ounce of our being," he continued.

Chapter 48

The Couple's Farewell

Joe's decision also provided clarity for him and Jill. No matter what happened in the 2016 election, they would be leaving Washington as private citizens.

They started to plan life after the White House, including looking for a beach house in Rehoboth Beach, Delaware. Jill had always loved the beach, and Joe wanted to have a house by the ocean. It would be difficult financially, but Joe promised his wife they would make it work.

Jill also threw herself back into work, both as a teacher and as second lady. Joe and Jill led the US delegation to the 2016 World Economic Forum in Davos, Switzerland. While there, Jill surprised her old friend Sam Kass, who had been the chef at her first Walter Reed dinner, by attending a lunch and talk he was hosting on the intersection of human dietary habits and the climate crisis.

Kass, by then a senior food analyst for NBC, spoke before a group of more than a hundred people, "telling them food is killing us and the world's going to end if we don't do something about it" as they ate a lunch of responsibly sourced ingredients.

"And in the middle of it," Kass recalled, "in walks Jill. And she sits down in the back, gives me a smile and a wink and just sits there and listens to me talk and stays for a half hour, forty-five minutes, just about to the end of the event."

Kass later heard through a Biden aide that she had noticed he was hosting a lunch, and simply wanted to come by and show support.

"Everything there is intense, there's a million people," Kass said of the scene at Davos. "There's just not many people of her stature who would have come to a chef policy guy's little food and climate talk," Kass said.

Back home Jill spent time campaigning for Hillary Clinton, sometimes on her own, other times alongside her husband. They were frequently dispatched to the kinds of places where Clinton was viewed with more skepticism—a union hall in a working-class neighborhood outside Pittsburgh or alongside singer Jimmy Buffett in more conservative-leaning areas of Florida.

In his final State of the Union address, President Obama borrowed a phrase of Joe's about curing cancer being a new moonshot and announced "a new national effort to get it done."

He surprised Joe by adding, "I'm putting Joe in charge of mission control. For all the loved ones we've all lost, for the family we can still save, let's make America the country that cures cancer once and for all. What do you say, Joe?"

On TV, Joe could be seen mouthing "I didn't know" to House Speaker—and his former rival for VP—Paul Ryan. "I didn't know that."

Most polls and prognosticators believed Clinton was positioned to handily defeat Donald Trump. In July 2016, Jill took center stage at the Democratic National Convention in her hometown of Philadelphia to introduce her husband—not for the speech they once envisioned he might deliver, but one seen at the time as a farewell to politics for the couple.

"He remains today, even after all he's been through, the most optimistic person I know," Jill said.

Chapter 49

Inauguration 2017

On election night 2016, the Bidens gathered a small group of family, friends, and advisers at the Naval Observatory for what many expected to be a historic victory party for Hillary Clinton.

Even with staff on hand, Jill was a hands-on hostess, making sure guests were comfortable and that their drinks were full.

The polls still favored Clinton. But the Bidens' travels across battleground states on her behalf had left them nervous. During a trip back from Wisconsin days before the election, the vice president remarked to aides that something about the situation on the ground didn't feel right.

Trump had run an aggressive and highly personal campaign against Clinton. He also seized on a growing strain of nationalism in the US and emboldened racist elements in the country that had already been on the rise during the tenure of the nation's first Black president.

Even so, Jill's confidence in the Democratic candidate was unwavering. "I truly believed Hillary was going to win," she said. "I'm telling you, just like half of America."

By about nine p.m., as results from the first wave of battleground states began trickling in, a Clinton victory looked like less of a certainty. Jill left the room and returned carrying a tray with bottles of beer and wine. She grabbed a bottle of wine for herself and retreated upstairs.

"I went to bed thinking Hillary was going to win," she said. "It just didn't cross my mind that Trump was going to win."

At 10:39, Ohio, the canary state that had gone for the winner of every presidential election since 1964, was called for Trump. By 10:53, Florida went red. Next to be confirmed for Trump were the hotly contested battle-ground states of North Carolina and Pennsylvania.

By 2:35 a.m., Clinton had called Trump to concede.

In the morning, Jill turned on the little TV in her bathroom to watch the five thirty news while she got ready to teach. She was shocked to hear that Trump had won.

She went into the bedroom and shook Joe awake.

"What happened? Why didn't you wake me up and tell me?"

———

Trump's victory threatened everything that the Obamas and Bidens had spent eight years accomplishing. Still, Joe and Jill were determined to help ensure a smooth transition, particularly for the incoming vice president and second lady, Mike and Karen Pence.

On November 16, they invited the Pences to the vice-presidential mansion. The two couples greeted each other warmly and smiled in front of the press before the Bidens showed the Pences inside for lunch. Jill walked Karen through the house.

Afterward, the second family and the second-family-to-be emerged to the press. "I hope they enjoy this home as much as Jill and I have," the vice president said.

Jill stayed mostly silent, a somewhat bemused smile affixed to her face as her husband bantered with Pence. Joe was getting on a roll, fielding question after question, when his wife stepped in.

"Thank you, thank you, everyone," she said, easing her husband away from the throng of journalists.

The next night, at a swanky Washington party honoring foreign diplomats, Jill told a story of trying to tidy up the house before the Pences' visit, stashing papers and books from her community college classes in a closet and instructing her husband to keep it closed.

"I said, 'Joe, for gosh sakes, do not open that closet,'" she said, according to the *Washington Post*. "And what do you think he did? But that's Joe for you."

———————

On January 6, Jill joined Joe for a ceremony in his office where, like other departing vice presidents before him, he would sign the interior of his desk drawer.

"Fast company here," he joked of his predecessors, a list of names that included Gore, Bush, Truman, and Rockefeller, among others. Jill and the press looked on as Joe, grinning, with a marker in hand, said the signing was only "to prove I was vice president."

———————

During the weeks between Trump's victory and Inauguration Day, Obama and Biden wanted to celebrate what they saw as their signature achievements, even as they worried their efforts would be wiped away by the incoming administration. They worried about Trump's "America First" policy, which seemed to leave even close allies out in the cold. They worried whether Trump was up for the job.

Still, they were proud of the work they had done, particularly considering the state of the economy when they took office. They were handing off an economy that was on an upward trajectory and appeared poised for more growth. Millions more Americans had health insurance, Osama bin Laden, the mastermind behind the 9/11 terror attacks, was dead, and the US had led efforts to forge a global climate change agreement.

The first and second ladies had put the wheels in motion for addressing childhood obesity in an era when children were being born with Type 2 diabetes for the first time, advocated for increased funding for community colleges, and new employment pipelines, and their work with military families was a substantial bridge between the White House and America's troops.

There was significant work left undone. The US withdrawal from Iraq left a vacuum that extremist groups exploited, and the Middle East seemed as unstable as ever. Partisan rancor in Washington had reached new heights, with Republicans fighting Obama on all fronts, keeping the country lurching from one potential fiscal crisis to the next. Nuclear threats from North Korea and cyber threats from Russia loomed large.

In the closing days of the administration, the internet was awash with memes celebrating Obama and Joe's "bromance." The "JoBama" movement was born. When asked about it in an interview with *People* magazine, Jill and Michelle started to crack up. "Oh, is that just *hysterical*?" Jill said.

In one meme, Joe is pictured sitting next to Michelle, eyes locked in intense discussion.

> *Joe: I think it's clear I should get custody of Barack.*
> *Michelle: He's my husband, Joe.*
> *Joe: Ugh fine. I'll take him weekends. Final offer.*

In another, Joe sits calmly in the Oval Office, legs crossed, while Obama is seated next to him holding his head in his hands.

> *Joe: I'm not giving them the WiFi password*
> *Barack: Joe...*
> *Biden: I said what I said.*

When Jill and Michelle were asked what the two men would do after they left office, they parried jokes.

"Oh, they'll find each other," Michelle said.

"Probably off eating ice cream somewhere, I'm sure," said Jill.

"They'll go for long walks together, looking into each other's eyes...I miss you, I miss you, too," Michelle said.

"But that has become a truly beautiful friendship. And I don't think we've really seen a lot of that, especially in politics. But I think they really love one another," said Jill.

"They do. They do," Michelle concurred.

Chapter 50

Highest Honor

As the administration drew to a close, Jill got a phone call from President Obama.

"Jill, I want to give Joe the Medal of Freedom," he said. "But no one at all can know about it." Obama wanted it to be a complete surprise. The Presidential Medal of Freedom, awarded with distinction, is the highest form of the highest civilian honor.

This is going to be one of the best days of Joe's life, Jill thought. She told no one, not even the children. Obama needed her help to bring their children, grandchildren, and scores of other relatives and friends to the White House — and to get Joe to the ceremony without giving away the surprise.

On January 12, just days before they would leave the White House, Joe went to what he thought was a gathering with Obama and Michelle, Jill, and their kids for a goodbye toast to the eight years they'd served together.

Instead, they walked into a room that was packed with family, people he'd grown up with, even a distant cousin from Ireland. *What in the hell is going on?* Joe thought.

When he saw the military personnel standing ready, he realized the president was going to give someone an award. *I don't know why the hell they didn't brief me on this*, he thought. Then it dawned on him. Jill could read the look of shock on his face.

"I just wanted to get some folks together to pay tribute to somebody who's not only been by my side for the duration of this amazing journey, but somebody who has devoted his entire professional life to service to this country," Obama said. "The best vice president America's ever had, Mr. Joe Biden."

Obama spoke from the podium while Joe stood to his side, struggling to keep his emotions in check.

"This also gives the internet one last chance to talk about our bromance," he joked.

Obama said Joe's counsel had made him a better president and commander in chief. "This has been quite a ride. It was eight and a half years ago that I chose Joe to be my vice president. There has not been a single moment since that time that I have doubted the wisdom of that decision."

The president also acknowledged Jill, and the role he had watched her play over the last eight years. He commended her teaching and her work on community colleges and Joining Forces. "When our administration worked to strengthen community colleges, we looked to Jill to lead the way," he said. "As a Blue Star mom, her work with Michelle to honor our military families will go down in history as one of the most lasting and powerful efforts of this administration."

He also highlighted her lighter side, revealing to the room one of her best pranks—the time she hid in the overhead compartment of Air Force Two to scare whatever poor soul tried to stow their suitcase. "Because why not?"

He singled out her ability to sense when someone needs a friend. Her thoughtful, always handwritten notes of appreciation and support. And her undying admiration for her family.

"She is one of the best, most genuine people I've met, not just in politics but my entire life. She is grounded, caring, generous, and funny, and that is why Joe is proud to introduce himself as Jill Biden's husband. And to see them together is to see what real love looks like, through thick and thin, good times and bad. It's an all-American love story."

Obama called the military aide up to the stage. He hung the gilded star around Joe's neck while the vice president fought tears. They warmly embraced.

"I was so excited for him," Jill said later. "He deserves it. It's a great honor."

Chapter 51

Post-Vice-Presidential Life

After the 2016 election, Jill was eager to move past politics. After eight years dealing with the stresses of the White House, and the loss of their oldest child, Jill and Joe both appreciated the time and space that post-vice-presidential life provided, for them and for their family.

The absence of daily political requirements also meant they were able to direct their attention to causes and projects that they connected with personally. In 2017, Joe began work with the Biden Domestic Policy Institute at the University of Delaware and the Biden Center for Diplomacy and Global Engagement at the University of Pennsylvania. He continued with his initiative working toward cancer cures. Jill and Joe also quickly signed with the Creative Artists Agency, a Hollywood talent firm, for representation for upcoming writing projects.

Jill briefly kept in touch with Karen Pence, who sent her notes and some pictures that Karen, a watercolor artist, had painted. Going forward, they occasionally saw each other at events—"mostly funerals, unfortunately," Jill noted—and were cordial and friendly.

———

Jill also kept teaching at Northern Virginia Community College, an institution to which she had developed a deep attachment.

Nazila Jamshidi enrolled at NOVA shortly after she moved to the United States from Afghanistan in 2017. At twenty-eight, she was eager to take advantage of educational opportunities that weren't afforded to women in her home country.

She soon applied for a part-time job at the college's women's center, seeing it as a way to both integrate herself more fully into the campus and explore her passion for women's rights. After she was hired, she found herself occasionally working with an English professor at the school who participated in regular meetings at the center, a petite blond woman named Dr. Biden.

"There was no difference between her treatment of the students and other faculty or staff," Jamshidi said. "She was nice, she was listening, she was open to new ideas, just like any other faculty member."

Jill was particularly focused on efforts to help retain female students and keep them enrolled, something Jamshidi had noticed was a particular problem for immigrant women, including many she had gotten to know who had emigrated from Afghanistan. Some Afghan women who were enrolled at NOVA attended for a while to work on their English, Jamshidi said, but didn't continue on with their education. Jamshidi drafted a proposal for a program that would specifically focus on retention of Afghan women at the college and submitted it to the retention committee. She was soon invited to present her proposal to the committee members, including Dr. Biden.

"She was so open to the idea.... She encouraged her colleagues to support my idea, to help me," Jamshidi said. "When I was explaining, she was carefully listening to the proposal."

The result was a summit for Afghan students at NOVA that Jamshidi helped coordinate. It was attended by more than one hundred people and was followed by the creation of an Afghan American student council.

Jamshidi also recalled Jill sharing stories about her students during regular meetings at the women's center. At one meeting, Jill said she had received a text message that morning from a pregnant student who was on her way to the hospital to give birth, but still wanted her professor to know she had submitted an assignment that was due.

"She was telling the story so excitedly," Jamshidi said. "She was repeatedly saying to her colleagues, we need to make ourselves familiar with our students and their circumstances and do whatever we can do to help them." Jamshidi said she later learned that the student Jill was referring to was also from Afghanistan.

It was only after months of working closely with Jill that Jamshidi realized that the professor, who showed up to campus without any visible security or staff, had once been second lady of the United States. She was sitting in class when a fellow student asked another professor if Joe Biden's wife was still teaching at the college. The professor confirmed she was.

"I said, 'Oh, my god, that's Dr. Biden!'" Jamshidi exclaimed.

She continued: "I was so impressed by her behavior. Especially at NOVA, you find a lot of immigrant students like me. When I started at NOVA, I had very broken English, there was no sentence I could speak without broken grammar or mistakes. Many other students were just like me. And she would listen carefully, without any expression like, 'Hey, I can't understand you very well' or 'Hey, your broken English is hard to understand.'"

———

By April, Jill and Joe had an $8 million multibook deal to provide accounts of their White House years, and a memoir of Jill's past. The couple was broadly popular, and Beau's passing in 2015 brought both sympathy and greater interest in the couple and their family from people across the nation. Although Joe had published an earlier memoir, and Jill had published a children's book, their prospects as re-minted authors were promising.

The book deals also brought financial freedom to the Bidens for the first time, easing their recent purchase of their dream house in Rehoboth Beach, Delaware. They'd turned to their longtime friend and Rehoboth resident Mark Gitenstein for help finding a house. He kept an eye out in the area, flagging listings he thought the Bidens might like.

One house in particular caught their eye.

The home was on a cul-de-sac and sat in an unusual way, opposite the ocean across a coastal savannah. Though not on the beach proper, the house was blocks from the Atlantic Ocean and a short drive from downtown Rehoboth Beach. Its setting had a similar feel to Cape Cod—another place that was near to the Bidens' hearts—and featured a swimming pool that overlooked Cape Henlopen State Park.

"We want to come down right now," Jill said. "I have to see that house."

They fell in love with it after their first viewing.

Joe called Gitenstein and told him the news: they were going to put in an offer. The price was steep, but Joe had no choice.

"Jill said to me that she would love to have this house for her birthday" in June, Joe said.

"Joe, you're a dead man," Gitenstein said.

With advances from their book deals in hand, Jill finally got her big wish. They bought the $2.7 million vacation home in Rehoboth Beach. Jill was ecstatic. "I wanted it to be the kind of place where you can come in in your wet bathing suit and bare feet and I can just take the broom and brush out the sand," she said. "And that's what this is. Everything's easy."

The Bidens put up two signs on the house. One read "Beau's gift"; another, "Forever Jill."

Chapter 52

The Loud Roar

As the Bidens embraced their life outside of politics, the chaotic early days of the Trump administration stirred quick conversation about who might run against the president in 2020.

Jill constantly found everyday people encouraging Joe to run against Trump. It started as a trickle and built to a stream. At the grocery store, at the drugstore, at school, at the train station—wherever she went, people told her, "Joe's gotta run. You have to make him run." She told them they'd moved on.

"I think I could have won," Joe told students at Colgate University that spring. "I don't regret not running. Do I regret not being president? Yes."

Jill watched the news and knew what was happening in the country. By late summer, mere months into the Trump administration, Jill was fed up with it.

"The louder the roar," for Joe to run, she said, "we couldn't ignore it."

On August 11, 2017, the Unite the Right rally began in Charlottesville, Virginia. The two-day event brought hate-spewing groups together from across the country, displaying torches, Nazi paraphernalia, and Confederate flags as they recited anti-Islamic and anti-Semitic chants. By the time the event was over, violent clashes between the alt-right groups and dissenting demonstrators left dozens injured. One white supremacist deliberately drove his car into a crowd of counterprotestors, killing thirty-two-year-old Heather Heyer. Virginia governor Terry McAuliffe had called a state of emergency due to the chaos.

Much of the nation, including the Bidens, looked on in horror. To Jill, it was Trump's response that would make the disturbing event even worse.

"After Donald Trump praised those people as they came out of the fields in Charlottesville and said that there were these white supremacists and that there were good people on both sides, that was the turning point," Jill later said to a Phoenix news station.

Joe and Mark Gitenstein had a long talk the day after Charlottesville. Through Gitenstein's work in Romania, where he'd served as US ambassador, he'd been engaged on issues of democracy and rule of law. When he found a good book on the topic, he'd send it to Joe. They discussed several books on saving democracy, especially Jon Meacham's 2018 book *The Soul of America*.

Through their conversations, Gitenstein thought it was increasingly obvious that Joe should run against Trump, that he was the only one who could win. Gitenstein believed Jill thought so, too.

Joe began to speak out against Trump more forcefully.

At an Axios event in Philadelphia, Jill and Joe sat together onstage. "Did any one of you ever think that you would see, in one of the historic cities in America, folks coming out from under rocks and out of fields with torches carrying swastikas literally reciting the same, the same exact anti-Semitic bile that you heard and we heard in the '30s?" Joe spoke. "And then have those that were protesting compared as the moral equivalent to those people?

"Folks, this is eating at the fabric of this country....It is undermining the social fabric of the nation...this phony nationalism," Biden said. "The reason why the world is [compared] to America is not just because of the exercise of our power, but it's the power of our example," he added. "It's because of who the hell we are."

Side by side onstage that day, Jill and Joe's final race for the White House, for their legacy, for "the soul of this nation" began to take form.

"I haven't decided to run," Joe said. "But I've decided I'm not going to decide not to run. We'll see what happens."

Chapter 53

Going for It

Jill knew a presidential campaign was something you had to be one hundred percent in on—you couldn't run at sixty or seventy-five percent. Campaigning was just too hard.

And it was hard to think about giving up the life she and Joe were creating outside of politics: their beach house, uninterrupted time with their family and friends.

She reached out to Michelle Obama to ask the former first lady for advice. Their relationship, warm and loving, picked up right where they'd left off. "If you and Joe want this, go for it," Michelle said. "Just run as hard as you can. Just go for it."

Many of the people involved in Joe's decision to run in 2020 were the same as in his previous runs: his longtime political advisers Mike Donilon, Steve Ricchetti, and Ted Kaufman, his children Hunter and Ashley, and, of course, Jill. Unlike previous campaign cycles, like 2004, when she was adamantly opposed to a run, or 2016, when she worried about the emotional toll on her family, Jill was now viewed as a strong supporter from the start.

A final decision would stretch on, as was often the case with Joe, though the outcome this time around was never really in doubt.

Despite their decades of experience in politics, the Bidens faced a new nation, and media environment, in the 2020 campaign. Television media was more partisan. Social media was an echo chamber, one where powerful progressive voices often had outsized influence, and the #MeToo movement had brought about a new era of accountability for powerful men.

Joe quickly found himself in the crosshairs.

In March 2019, before Joe had officially announced he was running or launched his campaign, former Democratic legislator Lucy Flores of Nevada published a *New York Magazine* op-ed accusing Joe of touching her shoulders, sniffing her hair, and kissing the back of her head as they waited to be introduced at a Las Vegas rally.

"I had never experienced anything so blatantly inappropriate and unnerving before," Flores wrote. "Even if his behavior wasn't violent or sexual, it was demeaning and disrespectful."

Women on both sides of the aisle spoke up in support of Joe. But Flores's comments had resonance: Joe was indisputably a hugger and a toucher of men and women. It had long been one of his greatest strengths as a campaigner—the quick, personal connections he built, the ways he tactically engaged with people he met. But with the #MeToo movement, his style was being viewed in a new light.

A spokesperson said Joe did not remember kissing Flores. Joe said in a statement that he never intended to make women feel discomfort and if he did so, "I will listen respectfully." Joe said he had listened, learned, and would respect people's personal space going forward. "We have arrived at an important time when women feel they can and should relate their experiences, and men should pay attention. And I will."

Jill defended her husband, addressing the matter as a "space issue" when questioned and saying he had "learned that he needs to give people their space."

She was careful to note the courage it took for the women to come forward with their allegations and described—though not in any detail—what she said was a "similar situation" she faced years earlier. She said she didn't talk about her experience at the time because "women never used to say anything."

"Now they speak up. Now they have the courage to come forward and I think that's a good thing," Jill said in a May 2019 interview with *CBS This Morning*.

"I think that's a good change, and Joe has heard that message," she said.

Joe formally announced his candidacy in April. "If we give Donald Trump eight years in the White House, he will forever and fundamentally alter the character of this nation," Joe said. "I cannot stand by and watch that happen."

The Biden team knew that his decades in politics would provide his competitors plenty of fodder. Many of the positions and statements he'd made in the early phases of his career were out of step with where the Democratic Party was in 2020. And Joe had gone through his own personal evolution on some issues, too.

He was particularly aware that there would be a focus on his handling of Clarence Thomas's Supreme Court confirmation hearings. So he reached out to Anita Hill, the law professor who had accused Thomas of sexual harassment, to apologize.

"I cannot be satisfied by simply saying, 'I'm sorry for what happened to you,'" Hill, who by then taught social policy, law, and women's studies at Brandeis, told the *New York Times*. "I will be satisfied when I know that there is real change and real accountability and real purpose."

Again, Jill stepped in to defend Joe.

"We believed Anita Hill," she reiterated in an NPR interview. "He voted against Clarence Thomas." Asked why Joe had waited until he was running for president to contact her, Jill acknowledged, "He didn't know whether she would take his call, and he was so happy that she did."

Jill said Joe had told Hill that he felt badly. "He apologized for the way the hearings were run. And so now it's kind of—it's time to move on."

Jill was also getting more comfortable telling her own story. Two years after Joe released *Promise Me, Dad*, his emotional book about Beau's death, Jill's memoir, *Where the Light Enters*, was published in May 2019.

"This book was a little dreamlike to write," Jill said on her book tour. "Growing up, I never imagined that I would write something like this. Being vulnerable in front of such a large audience is not really my nature."

As the former second lady who was now hoping to become first lady, Jill drew laughs on the book tour when she reminded audiences that Joe had promised her decades ago, when she was a young teacher, that her life wouldn't change. "My life changed, and changed, and changed, and is still changing as we speak!" Jill said.

The book received favorable reviews and was praised for its candor. Jill was candid about her family's struggles, including Beau's death. The timing was notable, putting Jill in the spotlight in a warm, personal way days before her husband would officially announce his candidacy.

—————

Jill revealed during that time the ways she struggled with her faith after Beau's death, a striking revelation given how crucial religion had been to Joe during that time. Jill, however, found she couldn't pray or go to church for about four years after losing Beau.

That began to change after the campaign trail took the Bidens to Brookland Baptist Church, a Black church in West Columbia, South Carolina. Both Bidens found the choir music moving.

Joe leaned over to the pastor's wife, Robin Jackson, and said, "This sounds so beautiful. It reminds me of my son's funeral."

Jackson could see Jill's pain and "felt called" to help her.

"Jill, it's okay," she said. "Would you mind me just praying with you? I would like to be your prayer partner."

"And I thought, 'Prayer partner? What's a prayer partner?'" Jill later recalled. "But I thought it was so kind."

They each wrote their numbers down on the church bulletin and stayed in touch. Jackson prayed for Jill daily and texted her each Wednesday to let her know she was praying for her and Joe.

"Thank you, my friend," Jill would text back. "I needed that."

Later Jill would say, "I thought maybe God was saying to me, 'Hey, Jill. It's been four years. Come back. Come back.'"

In 2021, Jill returned to Brookland Baptist, telling the congregation that their church had "changed my life." Jill said that Jackson's "kindness, mercy, and grace pushed past the calluses on my heart and, like the mustard seed, my faith was able to grow again."

Chapter 54

New Campaign

The lineup of candidates vying for the 2020 Democratic presidential nomination was deep. With just under a year until the general election in November, Biden was facing off against several prominent senators—Elizabeth Warren, Bernie Sanders, Kamala Harris, and Amy Klobuchar—and rising stars within the party, including Texan Beto O'Rourke and Pete Buttigieg, the mayor of South Bend, Indiana. Biden led in early polls, but much of his strength was assumed to be based on name recognition, given his eight years as vice president. The campaign was considered to be wide open, and after Trump's unexpected success four years earlier, few political pundits felt confident predicting who would emerge to lead the pack.

Jill was a near-constant presence on the campaign trail in the fall of 2019, delivering formal speeches to large crowds and having one-on-one conversations with voters in coffee shops and diners.

Cathy Russell joined Jill again in Iowa—their third time doing this together. The difference between watching Jill campaign in 1987 or 2007 and 2019 was striking—almost like watching a different person, Russell thought. Back then, Jill had been nervous; she'd been trying to get through what she needed to as quickly as possible.

Now, Jill engaged with people easily and directly, more confident in herself and the role she played in Joe's campaign.

"Sometimes in between events, she was agonizing over her students," Christine Vilsack recalled of the campaign's time in Iowa. Jill and Christine wound up talking about their students on the campaign bus. "I remember having a conversation with her because she teaches the same kind of kids that I taught," Christine recalled. They both worked with college freshman English students who struggled academically. Jill was grading papers and struggling with how best to assess work from her most challenged students. Christine commiserated. "There's a certain standard that you have to live up to," she said, "and at the same time, she was very much aware of their personal circumstances, and trying to really think through some of her students and figuring out what's best for them."

On September 6, 2019, in Mason City, Iowa, Christine watched Jill give an unusual speech at the opening of a Biden campaign office. "Joe really is the perfect person to run this time," Jill said. Joe was "known for bringing people together" and "known for his integrity," she said. "People are looking for a president that they can look up to and be proud of."

Wow, Christine recalled thinking. *She has found some kind of fire.* She'd always known Jill to be eloquent, poised, and graceful with people, but that day she was on fire. "She wants to win and she wants her husband to have this job, and she wants this job, too," Christine remembered. Jill put aside her notes and started speaking from the heart. "She was going at it," Christine recalled. "She came to play on that mission and she wasn't just a political spouse. She sounded more like a candidate."

———

For Jill, her evolution as a political spouse wasn't an accident. She had spent years honing her skills, understanding how she could best advocate for her husband and be herself.

"It is a lot of work," Jill said. "You have to read your briefings. You have to know who people are. You have to know relationships."

One thing that hadn't changed over the years was Jill's commitment to using her platform on the campaign trail to advocate for education policy. Joe, she said, would "lift up the profession of teaching," provide additional funds for teachers and mental health services in schools, and expand free community college "on a national scale."

"One thing I've tried to say to Joe throughout the years—I've seen what teachers want, because I talk to teachers every single day," she said. "I've made it a mission to talk to all the teachers here in Iowa and across the country when I was second lady. And I've seen what we need in an education policy. I've seen it firsthand in my classroom."

In July 2019, the Vilsacks held an early campaign event for Biden at their home. Like the Bidens, the Vilsacks had suffered personal tragedy when their six-year-old granddaughter Ella died in 2017 from flu complications.

Ella's parents — the Vilsacks' son and daughter-in-law — were at the fundraiser. Joe and Jill took them into a separate room before the event and spoke to them as fellow parents who knew the pain of losing a child — or in Joe's case, two children.

"It's that empathy that made them president and first lady and has made them that for a reason at this particular time when empathy was going to be really, really important," Christine said in 2021.

The road to the White House, however, didn't look so certain for the Bidens in Iowa. As the leadoff state in the primary process, Iowa voters took their responsibilities seriously. But the state's Democratic voters had something of a progressive bent, making Sanders a popular option. The state also liked to play a role in anointing a new generation of political talent, as it had in 2008 when Obama won the caucuses. All those factors made Iowa a challenge for Biden, a more moderate Democrat who had been in politics for decades.

Biden's campaign also frequently noted that Iowa hardly represented the whole of the Democratic Party. The state was overwhelmingly white and rural. Biden was counting on voters of color, particularly African Americans, to carry him to victory in later contests, most notably South Carolina.

The challenge for his team would be making sure they could maintain enough momentum — and money — to get that far if Biden stumbled badly in Iowa.

In a sign of how critical Jill was to the campaign, she made a decision she'd only ever made before for personal reasons, never politics: She stopped teaching for the upcoming spring semester.

"Iowa was a hard one," Christine Vilsack conceded. The Bidens used the time to hone and clarify their message, a process Christine likened to writing an essay: "You write your rough draft, and then you go back and edit and refine and you finally get it right. And I think that was kind of what was happening in Iowa."

She continued: "The worst things in the world have happened to them," she said. "So what more can happen? Keep going on, and put one foot in front of the other, and you work through it. I just felt like that was going to be what was going to sustain them through a tough campaign, and I think it did."

No one on Biden's campaign was surprised when he didn't win the caucuses, but Jill was surprised by just how bad the results were. She'd expected Joe to come in second or third. Instead, he dropped to fourth place, trailing both Buttigieg and Sanders by more than ten percentage points and losing out on third place to Warren.

"I've been disappointed by Iowa before," she said. "Once you've been stung, you don't forget that, and you learn from that."

Joe tried to project optimism coming out of Iowa; his team hoped for a stronger showing in New Hampshire, the next state to vote, and kept pointing ahead to South Carolina. But the campaign's war chest was running dangerously low. While some campaigns spent millions of dollars a day on voter outreach across the country, the Biden team was down to less than $1.5 million in total.

Difficult discussions within the Biden camp ensued about how to pay for the remainder of the campaign. "There was a discussion about asking them [the campaign staff] to put in their own money," one campaign insider said, adding that Jill and Joe "refinancing their home" was "on the table," as Jonathan Allen and Amie Parnes reported in their book *Lucky*.

Chapter 55

State by State

New Hampshire, the next state to vote in the primaries, didn't give Biden the bounce he was looking for. The campaign hadn't expected to win, but believed the former vice president would have a stronger showing than in Iowa, something they could build on heading into South Carolina.

Instead, Biden did worse, finishing fifth. Jill was stunned.

Biden was committed to staying in through the first southern primary, the first contest where Black voters—a crucial Democratic constituency—had their say.

"We weren't going to drop out," she said. They had put in too much time, energy, and money. "No way we were going to drop out."

But the couple was also having honest conversations about next steps. They didn't want to keep afloat a campaign that failed to make good on salary commitments to staff or accrued debt. With money so tight, everyone knew that the Biden train could only travel so far unless there was a significant shift in momentum.

"Hold on 'til South Carolina," Joe kept saying.

Biden had built deep relationships over the years with Black voters and political leaders, particularly in South Carolina. That was due in part to his connection to the nation's first Black president and his ties to southern religious leaders.

The Bidens arrived in South Carolina before the final votes in New Hampshire had been counted. A crowd gathered to greet them and Jill could feel an uptick in enthusiasm.

Okay, we're on track, she thought.

There was one key South Carolina endorsement Joe sought: the backing of Representative Jim Clyburn, the highest-ranking Black member of Congress and the kingmaker of South Carolina's Democratic political orbit, as well as a personal friend. Clyburn was on the fence about endorsing at all, a decision that itself would have been seen as a repudiation of Biden.

Establishment Democrats were getting worried. The results so far had put Sanders in command and in position to represent Democrats in the general election against Trump—a face-off many in the party thought would lead to defeat given Sanders's far-left policies and embrace of democratic socialism. Michael Bloomberg, the billionaire former New York City mayor and another moderate, made a late entrance into the race in a bid to block Sanders because he didn't think Biden was capable of overtaking the Vermont senator.

The late maneuvering and the worries about Biden threatened to thrust the primary—and the Democratic Party—into chaos. With just days until the South Carolina primary, Clyburn urged voters in his state to rally behind Biden.

In a deeply personal endorsement of his longtime friend and colleague, Clyburn declared: "I know Joe. We know Joe. But most importantly, Joe knows us."

The endorsement moved Joe to tears.

It also shifted the dynamics of the primary, both in South Carolina and in states to come. By the time primary day rolled around in South Carolina on February 29, Biden felt confident enough to spend much of the day campaigning in neighboring North Carolina—one of the fourteen states that would vote in the upcoming Super Tuesday contests, when nearly one-third of the convention delegates needed to win the Democratic nomination would be up for grabs.

After hours of talking with voters in North Carolina, Joe headed back across the state line for evening Mass in Columbia, South Carolina. As he left church to meet up with his campaign team, one of his top advisers called with good news. Early indications showed Biden was cruising to a landslide win.

By the end of the night, Biden had clinched nearly fifty percent of the vote, while Sanders, the second-place contender, finished with only twenty percent. The remainder of the field had been crushed. It was a strong indication that Biden carried much of the faith of the Black community—a voting bloc that no Democratic primary candidate could afford to lose.

While Joe refrained from mentioning Sanders by name in his victory speech, his message was clear: "Most Americans don't want the promise of revolution.... Talk is cheap. False promises are deceptive, and talk about revolution ain't changing anyone's life.... This isn't an election to spend all our time in a battle for the soul of the Democratic Party. This is a battle for the soul of the United States of America."

"It was incredible, it was so reaffirming," Jill said of the victory.

In a sign of the campaign, and Jill's new confidence in the state of the race, the Biden team deployed Jill for a round of live television interviews, the first time she had talked with reporters on a primary night.

"I'm a marathon runner," she told CNN. "This is just the beginning of our marathon... I think we're going to take it the whole way."

After her TV appearances, Jill joined Joe backstage where he was greeting supporters and taking photos. Ashley had joined her parents for the celebration and the family marveled at the size of Joe's margin of victory.

Joe and Jill departed together, holding hands as they walked toward the separate motorcades that would take each to their next destination. They were planning to spend the next seventy-two hours apart, part of a divide and conquer strategy to blanket the Super Tuesday states.

"You guys need to stop working her too hard," Joe told Jill's aides.

The couple kissed before parting ways.

Chapter 56

A Good Philly Girl

Jill's first Super Tuesday stop was Arkansas, where she spoke at a Sunday church service in Little Rock. The scene was chaotic; members of the congregation rushed toward her after she spoke. Local reporters peppered her with questions about a paternity lawsuit in the state involving Hunter. Jill's normally mild-mannered staff was on edge, with one aide shouting down a reporter who had asked about her son.

From Arkansas, Jill was scheduled to make stops in Memphis and Nashville, Tennessee, as well as Birmingham and Montgomery, Alabama.

She woke up in Nashville on March 2, the day before Super Tuesday, to learn that the campaign was in discussions with two of Joe's rivals, Pete Buttigieg and Senator Amy Klobuchar. Both had dismal showings in South Carolina and it was clear they had little support among Black voters. Both were also worried about Sanders's chances of success in a general election showdown with Trump.

Events would unfold quickly. Jill toured a school in Nashville and dropped off donuts for the teachers, then flew to Birmingham. By the time she arrived, word was leaking out that both Buttigieg and Klobuchar were dropping out of the race and planning to endorse Biden. They were also planning to travel to Dallas that night to join Biden—as well as Beto O'Rourke, another former primary challenger—for a high-profile show of party unity.

"It felt like a whirlwind," Jill said. "It was happening so fast."

Jill still had one more event in Montgomery. But all the energy was in Dallas, and Jill and her staff thought she should be there, too. They cut short her remarks in Montgomery, then diverted to Dallas. But she wanted her appearance there to be a surprise, even from her husband.

"He didn't know I was going to fly in," she recalled. "So we did, we surprised him."

On Super Tuesday, the Biden ticket was a steamroller. Joe carried ten of the fourteen states, with a double-digit lead over the second-place candidate in nearly every contest he won. It was one of the most remarkable turnabouts in modern politics. In a month's time, the Biden campaign had gone from broke and on the ropes to front-runner status.

Joe and Jill greeted supporters that night in California, both newly energized by their rapid change in political fortune. Joe vowed that a Biden presidency would help the country move past the divisive politics of the moment.

Roughly five minutes into the speech, a handful of protesters condemning the dairy industry rushed the stage from behind, waving signs and chanting "Let dairy die!"

Jill placed herself between the first protester and Joe, giving a Secret Service agent a moment to subdue and drag the woman away.

Moments later, another protester rushed from the other direction. Jill met her with outstretched arms, holding the screaming woman back from Joe. Symone Sanders, a senior adviser on the campaign, also ran onto the stage and tackled the protester.

Just as quickly as Jill had stepped into protective action, she was ready to help revive the celebratory moment.

As Joe returned to the podium to continue his speech, Jill stood alongside, clapping her hands to lead the crowd in a "Let's go, Joe!" chant.

"People called me up and said, 'Oh my God, did you see what Jill did?'" her aunt Barbara recalled. "That's Jill. That's who she is. That's what she's about."

It was the second time during the campaign that Jill had stepped in to physically protect Joe. A few months before, at a February event in New Hampshire, a large man approached the podium from Joe's right. Moving without hesitation from the other side of the stage, Jill intercepted the aggressor until security was able to remove him.

Interviewed about it by the *Philadelphia Inquirer*, Jill shrugged and said, "I'm a good Philly girl."

Chapter 57

The Start of a Pandemic

Just as Biden was surging, the campaign, the country, and much of the world ground to a halt. A global pandemic was bearing down and no one knew quite what to do, or how long normal life would be put on hold.

The campaign went from planning travel itineraries to building a basement television studio for Joe. Aides washed groceries and packages on the back porch of the Bidens' Delaware home, taking every precaution to keep the candidate and his family from getting sick with the new coronavirus.

Jill marveled as she recalled the dizzying early days of the pandemic.

"We were doing Zoom after Zoom after Zoom with so many groups of people," she recalled.

Joe's forte was being out among the people, shaking hands and hearing stories. Campaigning by Zoom was a struggle.

David Axelrod and David Plouffe wrote an op-ed in the *New York Times* urging the Biden campaign to make better use of digital tools. "Mr. Biden is mired in his basement, speaking to us remotely, like an astronaut beaming back to earth from the International Space Station," they wrote. "'Biden in the Basement' is not a strong enough show to hold the audience."

Joe's virtual campaign was a stark contrast to Donald Trump's, who resumed traditional campaign travel despite warnings from public health experts about the coronavirus's spread. Trump sought to use the contrast to his advantage, casting Biden as old and not up for the rigors of a campaign, let alone the presidency. The Trump campaign released an ad using doctored photos of Joe to suggest that he "sits in his basement. Alone. Hiding. Diminished."

Joe, too, embraced the contrast, eager to use his willingness to follow public health guidelines to send a message about how he would approach the presidency.

"The idea that somehow we are being hurt by my keeping to the rules and following the instructions that [have] been put forward by doctors is absolutely bizarre," Joe said on *Good Morning America* in response to Democratic hand-wringing and Republican mockery.

"This is not politics," Joe said. "This is life."

In May, Joe began easing back into campaign travel, making stops about once a week in Delaware and eastern Pennsylvania that were a short drive from his home in Wilmington. It wasn't the campaign he expected to be running, but the events still gave him opportunities to deliver his message and engage with small groups of business owners and others.

Joe's other priority that summer was picking a running mate. It was a process he was intimately familiar with, having gone through the intense vetting in 2008 before he was ultimately selected as Obama's running mate. And from personal experience, he knew the importance of having a number two who could both offset his vulnerabilities as a candidate and serve as a trusted adviser in the White House.

From the start, Kamala Harris was seen as the favorite. She was among the most prominent Black women in politics and had shown flashes of brilliance during her own short-lived presidential campaign. She would be a historic pick, a running mate who would add youth and diversity to the ticket.

But there were also skeptics. Harris had launched one of the most searing attacks on Biden during the Democratic primary, attacking his record on civil rights and busing.

"There was a little girl in California who was part of the second class to integrate her public schools and she was bused to school every day," Harris had said. "That little girl was me."

The verbal assault on Joe in the nationally televised encounter was especially jolting to Jill because Harris and Beau had become close friends when both served as attorney general in their respective states, working together on a multistate settlement with banks over mortgage financing.

It took a couple of days for the scrappy Philly girl within Jill to say what she really thought about that viral debate moment.

"With what he cares about, what he fights for, what he's committed to, you get up there and call him a racist without basis? Go f—k yourself!" the future first lady exclaimed to some of her husband's closest supporters during a telephone call a week after the debate, according to people on the call, as reported in Edward-Isaac Dovere's *Battle for the Soul*, a book about the 2020 Democratic presidential race.

Her anger toward Harris is said to have festered for months. But Joe didn't want to carry a grudge. He genuinely liked Harris and saw the advantages she would bring to the ticket and to the White House.

In her memoir, Jill wrote that "*I* end up being the holder of the grudges" in the family because of Joe's capacity for forgiveness. "I remember every slight committed against the people I love."

Reflecting the oddities of pandemic campaigning, Biden made Harris the formal offer to serve as his running mate over Zoom.

Jill knew firsthand the whirlwind that was about to consume Harris's family. She and Joe made it a priority to develop a relationship with Harris's husband, Doug Emhoff, inviting the couple to spend time with them in Delaware. They also made calls to Emhoff's parents and his children, Cole and Ella.

"The gist was like, 'You're Bidens now.' And you really felt the warmth," Emhoff said.

Chapter 58

Going Virtual

It took Joe Biden more than three decades and three presidential campaigns to become his party's nominee. But there would be no cheering crowds, no convention center packed full of delegates on hand to watch him formally accept the nomination.

From beginning to end, the 2020 Democratic National Convention was unique. As COVID-19 continued to ravage the world, the convention was converted to a virtual event, creating myriad challenges for Biden's team. How would they generate enthusiasm? How would they give voters a sense of connection to the candidate? Would anybody watch? Organizers arranged a robust lineup of speakers and musicians.

The convention was the Democrats' highest-profile opportunity to draw a contrast with Trump, at a pivotal moment for the nation. Everyone at the convention, including Republicans who came to speak against a party that had become unrecognizable to them, did their best to remind voters of just how high the stakes were.

One speaker, Kristin Urquiza, brought the point home with a chilling story about her father, who had died from COVID-19. "My dad was a healthy sixty-five-year-old. His only preexisting condition was trusting Donald Trump—and for that, he paid with his life."

———

On the second evening of the convention, Jill addressed the nation from Brandywine High School in Wilmington, where she had taught for two years. It was her third straight appearance at a Democratic convention, but the first time her husband's name was at the top of the ticket.

She juggled several jobs at once: she had to tell her story, let Americans take the measure of her, humanize her husband, and validate him as a would-be president.

Over the next nine minutes, she spoke to the camera and gestured broadly as she slowly walked down the hallway toward her former classroom. In an emerald-green dress, Jill spoke about the silent classrooms across the nation and the difficulties parents faced while navigating working during a pandemic—many from home, others risking their health by working outside the home—trying to support their children's remote learning.

"I am heartbroken by the magnitude of this loss—by the failure to protect our communities—by every precious and irreplaceable life gone. Like so many of you, I'm left asking: How do I keep my family safe?"

She told the story about finding Joe, Hunter, and Beau at a time when they were still deeply affected by the loss of their "wife, mother, daughter, and sister."

"We found that love holds a family together. Love makes us flexible and resilient. It allows us to become more than ourselves—together. And though it can't protect us from the sorrows of life, it gives us refuge—a home. How do you make a broken family whole? The same way you make a nation whole. With love and understanding—and with small acts of kindness. With bravery. With unwavering faith."

Jill was weaving Joe's leadership credentials into their joint biography. COVID-19, she said, should remind us of the strength that still bonded Americans together.

"We're coming together and holding on to each other. We're finding mercy and grace in the moments we might have once taken for granted. We're seeing that our differences are precious and our similarities infinite. We have shown that the heart of this nation still beats with kindness and courage. That's the soul of America Joe Biden is fighting for now."

Joe, she said, was one of the rare individuals who could dig deep enough in the most challenging of times, to keep the ball moving forward for those who relied on him.

"Four days after Beau's funeral, I watched Joe shave and put on his suit.

I saw him steel himself in the mirror—take a breath—put his shoulders back—and walk out into a world empty of our son. He went back to work. That's just who he is."

Jill ended with a promise. Joe would be there for the people if they were there for him; he would "do for your family what he did for ours: bring us together and make us whole."

Following Jill's speech, Joe joined her in the classroom. Before addressing the cameras, he had a hug and kiss for her.

Chapter 59

Accusations and Investigations

The 2020 presidential debate on September 29, between Joe and Donald Trump, was chaotic, bitter, and made all the more unusual by precautions necessitated by the pandemic. There was no friendly handshake to kick things off, and the debate played out before a socially distanced audience of about a hundred people in a debate hall built in an atrium at Case Western Reserve University that had previously been used as an emergency hospital for patients with COVID-19.

The Biden family featured prominently in the debate.

Joe held Beau's military service up as an example of the sacrifices of so many service members and their families. He rebuked Trump for reportedly calling those who served "losers" and "suckers," comments Trump denied uttering.

"My son was in Iraq. He spent a year there. He got the Bronze Star. He got the Conspicuous Service Medal. He was not a loser. He was a patriot and the people left behind there were heroes."

Trump wanted to focus on Biden's other son, Hunter, a frequent target of the president for his controversial work overseas while his father was vice president, as well as for his struggles with substance abuse.

"Are you talking about Hunter?" Trump asked.

"I'm talking about my son Beau Biden," Joe said.

"I don't know Beau," Trump said. "I know Hunter."

Joe was prepared for the moment. Trump and the Republicans had turned Hunter into a boogeyman of sorts in the 2020 campaign.

Although Joe was a famous teetotaler, having watched members of his family suffer from alcoholism in his childhood, Hunter had developed drug and alcohol problems in his youth. He'd been arrested at eighteen for cocaine use shortly after Joe's health issues erupted in the 1980s.

Being arrested "scared me straight—for a while," Hunter wrote in his memoir. "Beau was surprised I did cocaine, but he helped me get through it. "I knew I'd let down Dad. He was still recuperating, still in rough shape, and while he surely was upset, I also knew even then that there was nothing I could do that would stop his love. He was the strictest of any of our friends' parents—we had a curfew; if we stayed over at a friend's house we had to call him at midnight. Yet if you screwed up and it wasn't something done out of meanness or intended to be hurtful, he would love you through it."

In 2013, when Hunter was forty-two, he joined the Navy Reserve as a public affairs officer. He got a waiver for his age, which was three years over the maximum limit, and was allowed to enlist despite his past drug use and arrest. After serving in the role for just over a year, Hunter was released in 2014 without an official statement from the Navy, which cited privacy laws. Eventually, a leak revealed that Hunter had failed a drug test after cocaine had been found in his system. Hunter made a statement of apology, but there was no comment from the vice president's office.

Hunter also joined the board of Burisma in 2014, a private Ukrainian gas company, just as the Obama administration was working to wean Ukraine off Russian energy and spur the nation to make ethical reforms and clean up corruption. Joe was particularly involved in the administration's work with Ukraine, raising questions about Hunter's ties.

At the time, the vice president's office responded to questions about the arrangement by saying Hunter was a "private citizen."

Hunter's entire life seemed to disintegrate after Beau's death. "In the last five years alone," he wrote in 2021, "my two-decades-long marriage has dissolved, guns have been put in my face, and at one point, I dropped clean off the grid, living in $59-a-night Super 8 motels off I-95 while scaring my family even more than myself."

In an attempt to help her son regain control of his life, Jill gave him a call.

"One day out of the blue, three or four weeks into this madness, my mother called. She said that she was having a family dinner at the house, that I should come, even stay in Delaware for a few days...I was in lousy shape but it sounded appealing. I pulled out of a motel parking lot, said goodbye to all that, and headed to Wilmington."

As Hunter walked into the warmly lit home, he found himself at an intervention. His three daughters, Naomi, Finnegan, and Maisy, had all traveled to be there, sitting beside Jill and Joe, his sister-in-law, Hallie, and two counselors he had met during a previous stint in rehab.

After cursing out his father, Hunter turned to leave the house; Joe raced after him. Jill was joined by the rest of the group as she followed to watch her husband pull Hunter in a hug. Joe broke down in tears. "I lashed out at my mother for deceiving me," Hunter wrote. "It was a raw, appalling experience for all of them."

Hunter left that night for a facility in Maryland, driven by Beau's widow, Hallie. As soon as they parted ways, Hunter ordered an Uber, informed the staff he'd be back the next morning, and proceeded to hole up in a hotel room for the next two days with the crack he had brought to Wilmington in his travel bag.

"I don't think I knew the extent of his addiction, but as a mother, it's just hard to see," Jill said. "That's Hunter's to talk about."

Following his brother's death and after his marriage disintegrated, Hunter began a relationship with Hallie. "If ever there was a star-crossed coupling, it was ours," Hunter wrote. "It made perfect sense except for how it made no sense at all....It was an affair built on need, hope, frailty, and doom."

When the *New York Post* reported on the relationship, Hunter asked Joe to release a statement of support. Though the relationship had created some strains within the family, the Bidens publicly gave the relationship their blessing. "We are all lucky that Hunter and Hallie found each other as they were putting their lives together again after such sadness," Joe said. "They have mine and Jill's full and complete support and we are happy for them."

After the article ran, Hunter wrote, "Our lives of quiet desperation were suddenly on full display. I was madly trying to hold on to a slice of my brother, and I think Hallie was doing the same."

In his memoir, Hunter recounted hitting rock bottom and credited a whirlwind romance and marriage with helping him achieve sobriety and restart his life. On his first dinner date with Melissa Cohen, Hunter told her he was addicted to crack. "Not anymore. You're finished with that," Cohen responded. Joe thanked Melissa for "giving my son the courage to love again."

The comments echoed the words Joe's mother had said to Jill decades earlier about the impact she'd made on her son's life.

The Biden family knew going into the 2020 campaign that Hunter's struggles would be picked apart. Still, the ferocity of the attacks—and the lengths Trump was willing to go to dig up dirt on the Bidens—were jarring.

Trump was particularly focused on the discredited claim that while vice president, Joe pushed for the removal of Ukraine's corrupt top prosecutor as a means of protecting his son. In fact, this removal was the official stance of the Obama administration and supported by many other democratic Western nations.

Trump's fixation led to his impeachment in December 2019 after a whistleblower reported a conversation in which Trump seemed to offer $400 million in stalled military aid as a quid pro quo to Ukrainian president Volodymyr Zelensky in exchange for publicly announcing an investigation into Hunter and Joe. "I would like you to do us a favor," Trump had said on the call, asking Zelensky to work with Trump's personal lawyer Rudy Giuliani and Attorney General William Barr to investigate Joe and Hunter.

"It was unbelievable to me that he focused so much on Hunter, and he was relentless," Jill said. "And as a mother, of course it was hurtful. This was my son they were attacking, and he just would not give up."

Hunter wanted his dad to fight back, particularly when Trump focused on his addiction.

"I told Dad not to duck when Trump brought me up, as I was sure he would," Hunter wrote. "I told him that I wasn't embarrassed about what I'd faced to overcome my addiction. I told him that there were tens of millions of families who would relate to it, whether because of their own struggles or the struggles being faced by someone they loved. Not only was I comfortable with him talking about it, I believed it needed to be said," Hunter wrote.

In the debate, Trump launched into his litany of accusations: "Hunter got thrown out of the military. He was thrown out, dishonorably discharged, for cocaine use. And he didn't have a job until you became vice president. Once you became vice president he made a fortune in Ukraine, in China, in Moscow, and various other places. He made a fortune and he didn't have a job."

Joe had punctuated each of Trump's allegations with a quick, firm denial.

Then he acted on Hunter's advice, saying, "My son, like a lot of people at home, had a drug problem. He's overtaking it. He's fixed it. He's worked on it. And I'm proud of him, I'm proud of my son."

When Trump tried again, moderator Chris Wallace of Fox News cut him off, saying, "We've already been through this. I think the American people would rather hear about more substantial subjects." As Trump kept needling, Wallace said, "I'd like to talk about climate change."

"So would I," Joe said, and the subject of Hunter was, for the moment, closed.

Chapter 60

Election Day

Jill Biden spent much of the campaign's final hours focused on Florida, the behemoth of a battleground state that had been increasingly tilting toward Republicans. Trump had narrowly won the state in 2016 and spent considerable time as president at his Mar-a-Lago estate in Palm Beach.

Still, after months of anticipation and hectic schedules, Election Day itself can often have an odd feel for candidates and their families. The work is done, but the wait to know whether it paid off is long.

Jill, not inclined to wring her hands, packed her Election Day schedule with a final fly-around, holding campaign events in Tampa and St. Petersburg, Florida, and Cary, North Carolina.

"Our next first lady," a supporter shouted as she arrived at a polling place at Mills Park Elementary in Cary.

"We've been on this campaign trail for, gosh, a year and a half," Jill said, "so now it's down to the final hours."

The Bidens reunited on election night in Delaware, where a small group of family and friends had filled the house after quarantining. Every bedroom was in use.

It was "heartbreaking," Jill said, not to be able to gather with everyone who had supported Joe through the highs and lows of the campaign.

The earliest electoral announcements came from states with the most predictable outcomes. Biden was winning in the Democratic strongholds: New England and the West Coast, while Trump was dominating the breadbasket, middle-west, and much of the South.

However, following Joe's win in Minnesota at 12:13 a.m., they simply had to wait. As the Bidens watched the electoral map together, the next twenty-two minutes proved painful.

At 12:19, Ohio, the state that so commonly sides with the successful president-elect, supported Trump for the second time. At 12:21, Iowa fell red. And by 12:35, Florida also went for Trump.

The AP's decision to call Florida for Trump was both a blow to the Biden campaign and not entirely surprising. The biggest of the battlegrounds, Democrats had been wrestling with how much effort to put into the sprawling state to begin with. Still, a win in Florida—Jill's last stop before the polls closed—would have blocked Trump's path to the presidency, so the investment of time and money was decidedly worth the effort for the Biden campaign.

Both campaigns began to settle in for a long night.

At 1:05, Texas went for Trump. Despite Texas's Republican loyalty since voting for Jimmy Carter in 1976, Democrats were intrigued by the changing demographics of the state, as well as excitement created by Democrat Beto O'Rourke's narrow loss the previous year in a Senate race against Republican Ted Cruz. While Biden won the most support a Democratic presidential candidate had earned in Texas since Carter, it wasn't enough to flip the state.

Finally, in the middle of the night, Biden's campaign got a shot of good news. At 2:51, the AP called Arizona for the Democrat, the first time the party had carried the state in a presidential election since 1996. Trump's campaign would dispute the outcome, arguing that the AP would be forced to reverse its call and the race would tilt back toward the president.

That never happened. Biden won the state by about ten thousand votes.

What followed next was a slow-motion swing state sweep that cleared Joe Biden's path to the White House. At 2:16, the battleground state of Wisconsin went for Biden. Next, at 5:58, Michigan also went to Biden.

Biden had spent months arguing that he was the Democrat best positioned to pull those midwestern battlegrounds back toward the party after

Trump's stunning victories there four years earlier. Biden's theory of the case—that he could make credible appeals to working-class white voters and achieve the necessary turnout levels in urban areas—had proven to be true.

Biden's path to the White House was also clear—he just needed to win Pennsylvania. But the votes there were being counted slowly as the state grappled with a surge in mail-in voting, which had become popular during the pandemic.

The Bidens were glued to the TV for much of that stretch. Finally, Jill couldn't take it anymore.

"I swear, I felt like I was going to kill Steve Kornacki," she joked. The khaki-clad MSNBC election analyst whom colleagues dubbed "part political junkie, part human calculator, part Energizer bunny" rarely left their screen, doing electoral math and moving wildly around his map of blue and red states.

Saturday after the election was a beautiful, sunny day. Jill and Joe sat outside by the lake in their Adirondack chairs.

Suddenly, they heard screaming from the house. The AP had called Pennsylvania and the presidency for Joe at 11:25 a.m. on November 7, followed shortly after by Nevada at 12:13 p.m.

"We all ran to the porch and screamed at the top of our lungs, 'We won! We just won!'" Hunter wrote.

"It was just incredible," Jill recalled.

That night, the Bidens got to have the victory celebration they had long sought. Like everything else that year, it didn't look anything like they had imagined. "We just did the best we could," Jill later said, reflecting on the uniquely difficult campaign. "And obviously it worked, because we got elected."

To allow for social distancing, the Bidens invited people to drive their cars to a parking lot in Wilmington for a so-called car rally. The family's home state supporters arrived in droves, setting up lawn chairs next to their cars and honking their horns as the Bidens walked onstage to greet them.

Jill stepped onstage in a pale pink coat and a black mask bearing words of encouragement for a beleaguered nation: "Breathe Positivity," it read.

Chapter 61

"Her Name Is Dr. Jill Biden"

On December 11, 2020, the *Wall Street Journal* published an op-ed by Joseph Epstein, the longtime former editor of *The American Scholar* magazine, addressed to Jill. The opening line read: "Madame First Lady—Mrs. Biden—Jill—kiddo." It went on to disparage her doctorate in education. "'Dr. Jill Biden' sounds and feels fraudulent, not to say a touch comic," Epstein wrote.

"A wise man once said that no one should call himself 'Dr.' unless he has delivered a child," Epstein continued. "As for your Ed.D., Madame First Lady, hard-earned though it may have been, please consider stowing it, at least in public, at least for now. Forget the small thrill of being Dr. Jill, and settle for the larger thrill of living for the next four years in the best public housing in the world as First Lady Jill Biden."

The blowback was fierce, and the support for Jill came from all corners.

Doug Emhoff, Kamala Harris's husband, tweeted, "Dr. Biden earned her degrees through hard work and pure grit. She is an inspiration to me, to her students, and to Americans across this country. This story would never have been written about a man."

Indeed, Emhoff has also taught while serving as second gentleman. He transitioned out of his legal practice and took a position at Georgetown's Institute for Technology Law & Policy in December 2020.

Reflecting on the attack on Jill, Emhoff said it upset him "on a very visceral level."

"Here's a woman who went out there and raised a family, got a great education and continued her education while she was doing all the things she was doing, helping Joe in his career and then, you know, to be 'degree shamed' like that…the whole thing was infuriating."

Jill's predecessors as first lady, some of whom had their own prominent careers before their lives in the White House, also weighed in with support.

"Her name is Dr. Jill Biden," Hillary Clinton tweeted. "Get used to it."

And on Instagram, Michelle Obama wrote, "For eight years, I saw Dr. Jill Biden do what a lot of professional women do—successfully manage more than one responsibility at a time, from her teaching duties to her official obligations in the White House to her roles as a mother, wife, and friend. And right now, we're all seeing what also happens to so many professional women, whether their titles are Dr., Ms., Mrs., or even First Lady: All too often, our accomplishments are met with skepticism, even derision.…Dr. Biden gives us a better example. And this is why I feel so strongly that we could not ask for a better First Lady. She will be a terrific role model not just for young girls but for all of us, wearing her accomplishments with grace, good humor, and yes, pride."

Retired senator Barbara Boxer later compared the dustup to the pushback she'd received in the Senate decades earlier for saying people should call female senators by the title of senator, rather than ma'am. "All of us in these positions are really staking it out for those who come after," Boxer said.

A few days later, Jill responded via tweet. "Together, we will build a world where the accomplishments of our daughters will be celebrated, rather than diminished," she wrote.

Jill felt fortified by her bruising years of campaign politics. "I hope it's helped make me stronger and more resilient," she said. "My expectations for people aren't so high."

After the dust settled, Epstein's attacks would become a regular rallying cry. Jill's fellow faculty at NOVA surprised her with a group photo of thirteen of them wearing T-shirts that read, "Doctor, First Lady, Jill Biden" and calling her the "Teacher-in-Chief."

The focus on Jill and her career did highlight anew the nation's complicated expectations for first ladies, and the ways those expectations had changed over time.

No one is elected to serve as first lady, and the role is not enshrined or defined in any statute. Its occupant receives no salary and has no authority to develop or establish policy. Yet first ladies have long been expected to walk an imaginary line, being both a high-profile representative of the president while staying out of the work of the presidency.

"The American public does still get a little uncomfortable when you cross the line," said Anita McBride, First Lady Laura Bush's chief of staff.

That was never more true in the modern political era than during the Clinton administration. Bill and Hillary Clinton's arrival in Washington after the 1992 election signaled a generational shift in politics. When Bill Clinton put Hillary in charge of overhauling the healthcare system, it was the first time that a president's spouse had been deployed as both a political surrogate and policy adviser.

"Things are qualitatively different with Hillary Clinton," said Rider University professor Myra Gutin, who studies first ladies.

As Hillary became both a lightning rod and role model, she drew significantly more media attention to the office of the first lady. Her words were parsed, her actions scrutinized.

Laura Bush and Michelle Obama each put their own stamp on the role, but within more familiar confines. Neither held a job outside the White House but both embraced initiatives they were passionate about. Laura Bush was an advocate for women, focusing on women oppressed by the Taliban in Afghanistan. Michelle Obama prioritized nutrition and exercise, along with her work with Jill supporting military families.

During the Obama administration, Michelle had marveled at the normalcy of Jill's work. "Jill is always grading papers," she said. "Which is funny because I'd forget, 'Oh yeah, you have a day job!' And then she pulls out her papers and she's so diligent and I'm like, 'Look at you! You have a job! Tell me! Tell me what it's like!'"

Melania Trump spent the opening months of the Trump administration living in New York while her then-ten-year-old son, Barron, finished the school year. When she rolled out her signature initiative—an anti-cyberbullying effort named "Be Best" that also focused on child well-being and opioid abuse—she was roundly criticized, given her husband's prolific use of Twitter to attack and demean people.

Melania's public appearances would also ebb and flow in curious ways. Weeks often passed without her being seen publicly.

Chapter 62

Historic Day

On Inauguration Day, January 20, 2021, and clad in a custom blue Markarian dress and coat studded with Swarovski crystals that glittered in the winter sun, Jill held the five-inch-thick Biden family Bible as Joe placed his hand on it. He was sworn in as the forty-sixth—and, at seventy-eight, oldest—president of the United States. They gazed out on a cold Washington morning dotted with snow flurries to see more than two hundred thousand American flags planted on the National Mall, symbolizing those who could not attend in person given pandemic restrictions.

Also making history that day was Kamala Harris, sworn in as the first woman, the first Black person, and the first person of South Asian descent to serve as vice president.

The weeks between Election Day and Inauguration Day had been tense, with no less than American democracy coming under attack from Trump and his supporters. The outgoing president vigorously fought the election results, arguing without any evidence that the contest had been marred by widespread voter fraud. Even his attorney general, William Barr, made clear that wasn't true, but Trump vowed to fight on, whipping his supporters into a frenzy.

On January 6, the day Congress was slated to formally certify the election results, Trump addressed his supporters at a rally in the shadow of the White House, urging them to "fight like hell" and march up Pennsylvania Avenue to the Capitol. They did, violently storming the building, endangering the lives of lawmakers, staff, journalists, and others inside.

It was a stunning moment, one that made abundantly clear just how deeply divided the nation Joe would soon lead was.

Jill and her friend Mary Doody traded texts expressing disbelief. Responding to the events from Wilmington, Joe denounced the rioters as "insurrectionists, domestic terrorists. It's that basic."

The riots added to the surreal nature of Joe's inauguration. Security was heightened, with twenty-five thousand National Guard troops securing the streets of Washington. The blocks around the Capitol were cordoned off with tall chain-link fences. Military vehicles regularly rolled through neighborhood streets in the nation's capital.

Joe was plainspoken about the enormous difficulties that lay ahead and the understanding that his legacy would be judged by his ability to overcome them.

"We have much to do in this winter of peril, and significant possibilities. Much to repair, much to restore, much to heal, much to build, and much to gain," Joe said in his inaugural address. "Few people in our nation's history have been more challenged, or found a time more challenging or difficult than the time we're in now."

He also nodded to some of the reasons for optimism on the horizon, including the rollout of COVID-19 vaccines and an economy he believed was poised to rebound when the pandemic ultimately passed.

Biden was surrounded as he spoke by the traditional array of former presidents and high-ranking American political leaders. Mike Pence was there, too, four years after he'd taken over the vice presidency from Biden.

But there was one notable absence: Trump. Defying tradition, he had left Washington earlier that morning for his house in Florida.

Joe never mentioned his predecessor by name, but his speech was an implicit rebuke of Trump, including his denunciation of "lies told for power and for profit."

Joe, Jill, Kamala, and Kamala's husband, Doug, walked the last short part of the route to the White House after an abridged inaugural parade. Washington, all but deserted downtown and in its federal areas, was quiet.

Trump did adhere to one tradition and left a personal note for Biden in the Oval Office. Biden would only tell reporters that it was "a very generous letter."

In lieu of the traditional inaugural balls, Tom Hanks hosted a ninety-minute concert broadcast live from the Lincoln Memorial, with Joe and Kamala watching along and giving brief remarks. The proceedings ended with a lavish fireworks show in the Washington night sky. Joe and Jill watched from a White House balcony, with Jill wearing a wrist corsage of gardenias that Joe gave her.

———————

Two days after the inauguration, Jill visited the Whitman-Walker Health clinic, a Washington, DC, institution with a history of serving HIV/AIDS patients and the LGBTQ community, to highlight services for cancer patients.

Afterward, she took an unannounced detour to the US Capitol to deliver baskets of chocolate chip cookies to National Guard members, thanking them "for keeping me and my family safe" during the inauguration. The cookies, wrapped with red and blue ribbon, were a bright and colorful distraction on the bleak winter day.

"I just want to say thank you from President Biden and the whole, the entire Biden family," she told a group of Guard members. "The White House baked you some chocolate chip cookies," she said, before joking that she couldn't say she had baked them herself.

"I'm a National Guard mom," she said, adding that the baskets were a "small thank you" for leaving their home states and coming to the nation's capital.

"I truly appreciate all that you do," the first lady said. "The National Guard will always hold a special place in the heart of all the Bidens."

Chapter 63

Unity, Hope, and Love on the North Lawn

On February 12, Jill gave the American people a Valentine's Day present: She had giant pink, white, and red hearts bearing calls for *unity*, *hope*, and *love* installed on the North Lawn of the White House.

"I just wanted some joy," Jill told reporters, standing on the lawn with Joe and their two German shepherds, Champ and Major. They appeared casual, Joe in jeans and a bomber jacket, Jill in a raspberry-colored coat, and both holding coffee mugs. "With the pandemic, everybody's feeling a little down, so it's just a little joy, a little hope, that's all."

The oversized hearts, also emblazoned with the words *kindness*, *healing*, and *compassion*, were intended to be seen by millions of Americans. Jill had them erected in front of the row of cameras where White House correspondents deliver their live reports so the hearts would be prominently featured on the news all day. One of the hearts was signed, "Love, Jill."

Jill signaled early on that she would be a more active first lady than her immediate predecessor, Melania Trump. That included surprisingly normal activities around town, where she made no effort to hide her identity.

She visited a Dupont Circle newsstand in late January, owned by Stephen Bota, a Kenyan immigrant. "I was kind of 'Oh my God, it's the first lady,'" Bota said. "I told her that we are so grateful that she came to see us."

For Valentine's Day weekend, Jill dropped in at the Sweet Lobby, a Black-owned bakery on Capitol Hill, to pick up desserts before the trip to Camp David, where her family was spending the weekend.

The first lady's official Twitter account shared a photo of Jill at the counter beside a rainbow selection of macaroons and a note that said she had "Dropped by @TheSweetLobby earlier to pick up some Valentine's treats for the weekend. Shhh—don't tell Joe!" She wore a candy-pink coat and had her blond hair gathered into a powder-blue scrunchie.

The photo ricocheted across the internet, unbeknownst to Jill, who said she found out when Ashley called to tell her the scrunchie had gone viral.

Jill later drew scorn from conservatives when she returned from California in April 2021 wearing a short dark skirt, patterned hosiery, and high-heeled ankle boots.

"It's kind of surprising, I think, how much commentary is made about what I wear or if I put my hair in a scrunchie. I put my hair up! Or the stocking thing," she told *Vogue* in 2021, marveling at the amount of attention people spend on her fashion.

She defended the patterned stockings.

"They weren't fishnets. They weren't lace," she said. "They were very pretty stockings."

———

But fashion critiques were something first ladies had to become accustomed to. Their outfits, and who designed them, were closely watched for hidden messages.

And sometimes not so hidden messages.

In June 2018, Melania Trump flew to Texas to visit migrant children held in US custody wearing a jacket with "I Really Don't Care, Do U?" scrawled on the back.

Nancy Reagan drew scrutiny for secretly borrowing and wearing expensive designer gowns. Hillary Clinton's fondness for pastel-colored pantsuits was initially mocked, then became a symbol of female empowerment. Michelle Obama used her power and platform to boost the careers of up-and-coming designers.

Jill, who initially went to college to study fashion merchandising, did not bring a stylist with her to the White House. Rather, she chose her wardrobe herself, alternating between a closet of patterned and solid color dresses. She almost always wore high heels.

Although there were no inaugural balls in 2021—and therefore no inaugural ball gown to donate to the Smithsonian, as first ladies traditionally do—she wore a white dress with sheer sleeves designed by Gabriela Hearst on inauguration night. The matching cashmere coat included a Ben Franklin quote embroidered on the inside: "Tell me and I forget. Teach me and I remember. Involve me and I learn."

Jill wore the same dress in black for the president's first speech to Congress. Both dresses were embroidered with flowers from every US state and territory, with the flower of Delaware placed over her heart.

She has worn dresses by Narciso Rodriguez, Tom Ford, Brandon Maxwell, and Michael Kors, often paired with matching or custom-embroidered face masks. She's shown a fondness for Veronica Beard jackets.

Samantha Barry, the editor in chief of *Glamour*, said, "Dr. Biden is the queen of brilliant monochrome outfits; there are countless examples of her looking elegant in all the colors you can imagine."

She frequently rewears dresses and other items, a decision that is both notable and relatable to other women.

"By rewearing her clothes, she is underscoring their value," *New York Times* fashion critic Vanessa Friedman wrote. "The idea that when you find a garment you love, that makes you feel effective and like the best version of you, you keep it. If it made you feel that way once, it will do so again. That such a garment is worthy of investment for the long term."

In October 2021, Jill spoke reflectively about being first lady at an event for Barbara Bush's literary foundation. "Everything you do or say carries more weight. And while that can be intimidating at times, it's also what makes the role so special."

Chapter 64

Life Is Calling

When Jill decided to keep teaching as first lady, she became the first presidential spouse in history to keep their day job. It marked another significant shift in the role of first lady, making her as much of a barrier breaker as Eleanor Roosevelt, Lady Bird Johnson, or Hillary Clinton.

"Until Dr. Biden, everybody else gave up their careers for public life," Anita McBride said.

Jill set a new standard, making clear that a spouse need not give up their career for their marriage, even if they're married to the president of the United States.

Valerie Jarrett observed that Jill was "the same person she was when she was a community college professor before she became the second lady, and now the first lady, and she gives her students her full, undivided attention. She's really comfortable in her own skin and being first lady won't change that."

At the beginning of the 2021 spring semester, responding to a proposed mention of her as first lady in a flyer for NOVA, Jill emailed her colleagues. "I am an English teacher at NOVA—not First Lady....I appreciate your enthusiasm, but I want students to see me as their English teacher. I am not mentioning it in my classes AT ALL. Thanks for honoring my teacher identity."

That semester, Jill faced the same COVID-related struggles as other teachers across the country. She had initially asked to be allowed to return to campus instead and "zoom for classes...to keep work separate from WH," but her request was denied by administrators who were determined to keep faculty off campus.

So Jill taught remotely from her office in the White House East Wing or hotel rooms when she traveled. She fit her travel schedule and other political obligations around her classes, always prioritizing her students.

Mary Doody was impressed that she taught via Zoom during the pandemic. "One thing she never loved was computers," Doody recalled.

Joe joked in a speech that Jill had always planned to teach as first lady, "but I don't think she bargained for having to teach online initially." He said she'd spent "four hours a day for about a month learning how to teach online."

Online learning created other obstacles as well. Jill wondered how she would create a sense of community among her students, who came from varied backgrounds.

What she found was that the pandemic and the unusual learning environment itself ended up bonding the students, even as they built their relationships with each other virtually. "They really depended on and supported one another," she said. "It gave me such joy." Jill said the personal stories that students shared with one another through writing assignments brought them together as "a writing family."

On March 31, after Jill spoke at a Cesar Chavez Day event in California, honoring the American labor leader and civil rights activist, the flight back to DC was delayed until the next afternoon to accommodate Jill's virtual class session.

As a treat for their patience, a flight attendant with short black hair distributed Dove ice cream bars to the press, Secret Service, and first lady's staff, passing through the cabin in a black face mask and black pantsuit.

Minutes later, "Jasmine" the flight attendant returned, laughing and without a wig, to reveal that she was the first lady.

"April Fools!" she said.

The reporters were completely fooled. None of Jill's staff had recognized her in disguise, either. The mischievous first lady returned to her cabin looking pleased with the prank.

"It brings her joy," Valerie Jarrett said of Jill's propensity for practical jokes. "If she can ease the stress through humor and she's good at it, then that's what she wants to do."

––––––––

On May 1, Jill posted grades for her college class. The grueling online spring term was over.

Shortly after, Jill gave the 2021 virtual commencement speech for George Mason University in Fairfax County, Virginia, a four-year school where many of her students transferred after their coursework at NOVA.

"Historians will study this time," she told the graduates. "Generations will wonder what it was like. Our world has been changed in ways we don't even know yet....Each of you walked through the fire of a global pandemic and you made it to the other side....No one can promise you that life will always be beautiful. But there will always be beauty....Life is calling. It will be heartbreaking and hopeful. It will be bruised and beautiful. Give in to it. You're ready for whatever comes your way."

Jill didn't teach over the summer but kept up with some of her students through a book club and mentorship program organized by NOVA's women's retention program.

Jill saw herself in the women she mentored, recalling how she'd had three children and taught full-time while going to graduate school. The average age of her students was twenty-eight, and they had varying needs that affected retention—childcare, computer skills deficits, anxiety over math skills.

The mentorship program showcased the diversity Jill loved about NOVA, with students from many countries and walks of life. One of the students she mentored was a female revolutionary from Ukraine.

"It was fascinating to me that this whole world opened up, that I learned about their lives," Jill said. "And of course as a writing teacher, they write about their lives."

Nazila Jamshidi, Jill's former student, said she was proud to see a community college professor serving as first lady. After two years at NOVA, Jamshidi had been accepted as a transfer student to Georgetown University and planned to start a master's degree in human rights at Columbia University following her 2021 graduation.

Jill had "seen firsthand the difficulties and obstacles that students of color, financially disadvantaged students, immigrant students are facing as they are pursuing their education," Jamshidi said. She believed Jill's experiences at NOVA were guiding her approach to the role and the understanding she has of the struggles facing many people in the US. "They have their own dreams, let's call them American dreams," Jamshidi said. "NOVA wasn't like an Ivy League institution where people come there with a lot of money, not at all. She was seeing firsthand all of those struggles, all of those challenges."

Indeed, Jill found it deeply satisfying to see her students start to recognize their skills and build on them. She was struck by their confidence. "And then they just sort of soar," she said. "I love that."

After months of teaching English and writing to community college students in boxes on a computer screen, Jill resumed teaching in person in September from a classroom at NOVA. She taught on Tuesdays and Thursdays, with other days of the week reserved for official duties and travel.

She was anxious to see her students in person after more than a year of virtual teaching.

The *Washington Post* noted that "As the 'Teacher in Chief,' as her peers have called her, she's also the one person in the White House who is heading back out to the front line of the pandemic." The *New York Times* reported that students had to put their backpacks through a metal detector for security, but that Jill "does not know if her students, who are required to wear masks, are vaccinated."

"It's going great," Jill said of her in-person classes in late September. "It's going really well."

Reflecting on Jill's devotion to education, Mary Doody said, "She can do a lot of good, frankly, as first lady—but having a tangible relationship with a student in a classroom over the course of a semester is something that you just can't get anywhere else."

Chapter 65

Vaccines, Vaccines, Vaccines

By mid-October 2021, Jill had taken nearly thirty solo official plane or car trips outside Washington, including a handful of overnighters on the West Coast and in the Southwest and to Japan for the delayed 2020 Olympic Games. Not included are local stops in Washington or joint trips with the president. Her pace of travel was on par with Joe's, who had taken thirty-seven trips aboard Air Force One for official business by the same time.

Most of Jill's journeys were focused on a combination of children's education, community colleges, and encouraging reluctant Americans to get vaccinated against COVID-19.

"She's really trying to do her part to get out there and encourage people to get vaccinated," Cathy Russell observed. "I think until we break the back of this COVID problem, it's going to be hard to get the rest of the work done that we need to get done."

At a middle school in Pennsylvania, students told her of their difficulties during the pandemic. Some struggled with distractions from their phones; others, with their schedules and the self-control needed to consistently mask up.

"What I try to tell my students is to reflect on this time and journal it somehow," Jill said. In fact, Jill often encouraged her students to write in detail about the pandemic as a unique time in history and their role in it. "We have to remember what this time was like."

She told her students that writing about the pandemic was a way to preserve their unique version of history, and let their grandchildren know "what it was like for you to go through this really horrible, tough time, hard time."

———

Valerie Jarrett thought the Bidens had likely learned during the Obama years "how important it is to stay out in the country and visible and touching people and letting them, you know, feel you, and that it is replenishing." Connecting with Americans individually and collecting their stories enriched the governing process, she said.

In April, Jill's motorcade rolled out of Albuquerque for the long drive to the Navajo Nation. The vast, remote reservation—the country's largest—encompasses parts of Arizona, New Mexico, and Utah. Residents waved from their front porches and roadside hay stands as Jill went past. The trip was Jill's third to the twenty-seven-thousand-square-mile reservation, and her first as first lady.

Part of her focus there was encouraging residents to get vaccinated against COVID-19. Jill noted that about half the reservation's population was fully vaccinated, roughly twice the US rate at that time.

Early in the pandemic, the Navajo Nation had one of the country's highest per-capita infection rates; but by the time of Jill's visit, the tribe recorded just one coronavirus-related death in the previous twelve days, and was reporting far fewer daily cases. Some of that recent success was attributed to the fact that the tribe had approached reopening in a much more cautious manner than surrounding states. Face masks were required and travel was restricted to essential activity only. Tribal roads had also been closed to visitors.

"It's on all of us together to find the path back to hózhó—harmony and beauty, the world as it should be," Jill said beneath a red sandstone arch that had given the tribal capital of Window Rock its name. "Despite the challenges that you faced, the Navajo Nation lives that truth again and again." She said she was proud to address the Navajo Nation on a day that highlighted the protection of Mother Earth, a reference to Biden's climate change agenda.

On an earlier visit to the reservation, in 2019, Jill had been surprised to learn that a cancer treatment center in Tuba City, on the reservation's west side, was the first center of its kind on tribal land. Now, Navajo Nation first lady Phefelia Nez thanked Jill for supporting the center but noted it had received more patients than expected and needed to be expanded.

"That sort of breaks my heart, having so many of my own family members who have been victims of cancer," Jill said.

Dottie Lizer and Phefelia Nez were among a group of women who met with Jill at the library of the Navajo Nation Museum in Window Rock. The women wore traditional crushed velvet or ribbon skirts, moccasins, and jewelry made of silver and turquoise—stones sacred to the tribe. Some wore their hair in customary buns tied with yarn.

Navajo Nation Council delegate Amber Kanazbah Crotty said Jill's choice to meet with women leaders first set the tone for the trip.

Later, Jill spoke to a crowd of Navajo officials and dignitaries, including Miss Navajo Shaandiin Parrish. The Navajo Nation Council gifted Jill a Pendleton blanket that was wrapped around her as the temperature dropped and a chill set in.

Parrish earned the title through a competition that celebrates Navajo women's role in society as caretakers, leaders, and protectors. It also includes butchering a sheep and preparing traditional foods. She said she was excited for the partnerships that Jill would create in Indian Country.

"Everybody on the Navajo Nation has a deep respect for women, and her position as first lady is tremendous," Parrish said. "We all look up to our mothers, and she's the first lady, the mother of the US."

Jill also visited with students at Hunters Point Boarding School, a small, aging grade school. The students spoke to Jill for an hour about challenges they've faced during the coronavirus pandemic, including poor internet service and feelings of isolation. The school had a tainted nineteenth-century legacy from when Native American children were taken from their homes and sent to boarding schools where they often did more labor than learning, as a means of forcefully assimilating them into the culture of white settlers. Such schools continually struggled with sub-par facilities.

Across the Navajo Nation, students had been learning remotely, some given flash drives with schoolwork or paper packets if they had no access to computers. School buses were turned into Wi-Fi hotspots. Yet school board members said on windy days, the internet was "questionable," caus-ing delays to standardized testing, and that some of the school's equipment dated back more than a half century.

Jill met with the students in the common room of the school's dormi-tory, which had a mural of crops planted in rows and the geographic feature Hunters Point. She sympathized with their struggles during the pandemic, losing loved ones and attending classes via Zoom. As with all students, she encouraged them to keep journals.

"If you could write a journal and just look at this time," Biden said. "Don't forget it and think about what did you learn about yourselves. Were you stronger than you thought?"

Throughout the summer, Jill continued her wide-ranging travels around the United States to encourage Americans, often in traditional Republican strongholds in the South, to get vaccinated against COVID-19.

"I'm here today to ask all of the people who can hear my voice, who can see my face, to get their shot," Biden said after visiting a clinic at Jackson State University in Mississippi, one of the largest historically Black univer-sities in the country.

"The vaccines might feel like a miracle, but there's no faith required," Jill said. "They are a result of decades of rigorous scientific research and discoveries, and they have been held to the very same safety standard as every single vaccine that we've had here in America."

It was often a hard sell. Gulf Coast resident Sherie Bardwell was uncon-vinced. She told a reporter that Biden's comment about a miracle with "no faith required" sounded like "a dig at people with Christian beliefs."

———————

In late June, a crowd gathered for Jill and country music star Brad Paisley at the Ole Smoky Distillery and Yee-Haw Brewing Co. in Nashville, Tennessee, where bartenders served beers and shots over loud country music as people got vaccinated outside in a pop-up clinic.

Paisley noted that the COVID-19 virus had hit the country music artist community very hard and that icons like John Prine and Charley Pride had died before a vaccine was available.

"Vaccine, vaccine, vaccine, vacciiiiiine," Paisley sang, laughing and playing the tune of Dolly Parton's famous song "Jolene." With a sly grin he tweaked the next verse, too: "Don't say no just because you can."

Only three in ten Tennesseans had been vaccinated, Jill had told the crowd before the music started.

People booed.

"Well, you're booing yourselves," she said. "The vaccines are the only way to get back to the open mics and the music festivals and the concerts that make this town so very special."

Jill made another folksy vaccine-related stop soon after, clinking cups of beer with Second Gentleman Doug Emhoff at an Astros baseball game in Houston designed to help showcase a vaccination push by Major League Baseball.

The partnership that Jill and Doug began during the campaign, when they appeared together several times, was now solidifying. Emhoff was making his own mark on the role of political spouse with his frequent social media posts and casual style. He credited Jill with being his White House mentor, and said the guidance had helped them forge a bond.

"I couldn't be doing what I'm doing, and doing it pretty well, but for her," Emhoff said in October 2021, noting how much more polished he thought he'd become in the year-plus since his wife joined the ticket. "I'm more focused, I'm more effective, and really into it. And it's really a testament to my relationship with her."

Later in Savannah, Georgia, promoting vaccinations with Senator

Raphael Warnock, Jill stopped by the Green Truck Neighborhood Pub, a farm-to-table burger joint that Warnock, a Savannah native, recommended. The Green Truck had weathered the pandemic by relying on take-out orders before reopening its dining room with a fully vaccinated staff a month before.

To support the restaurant, Jill ordered two pecan pies to go and had some of it served to reporters on their next flight.

Chapter 66

Sense of Unity

Until the modern era, the first lady's diplomatic duties were to host gatherings of and entertainment for foreign dignitaries. Eleanor Roosevelt was a trailblazer, adapting the role of first lady to the fraught international affairs of her day. Rather than play the role of "silent partner and grand hostess," she spoke globally about human rights and served as US representative to the United Nations and chair of the UN Human Rights Commission.

Later first ladies began to get more daring with their international travel.

Pat Nixon became the first first lady to visit a combat zone when she joined President Nixon on a trip to Vietnam in 1969. Her trip to Peru to aid earthquake victims was praised by a Peruvian official as more meaningful than anything else Nixon could have done.

Rosalynn Carter undertook a controversial diplomatic trip to South America in 1977. She toured seven countries in thirteen days, discussed American foreign policy with heads of state, and reported back to President Carter on ways to improve relations with Latin America, focusing on human rights and the nuclear arsenal. The trip garnered mixed reactions from the public, more than a quarter of whom believed a first lady should not represent the United States in talks with foreign countries.

Shortly after a brief retreat to their home in Rehoboth Beach to celebrate her seventieth birthday in June 2021, Jill joined Joe on his first overseas trip to the United Kingdom for the Group of Seven summit—a gathering of leaders from the world's largest economies.

Jill later said Joe had been "studying for weeks" to get ready for the trip. "Joe loves foreign policy. This is his forte," she said. She joked that he was "overprepared." Jill had prepared diligently for her role, too. Her staff tweeted a photo of her sitting at a desk on Air Force One, studying briefing books and newspapers. "Prepping for the G7," the caption said.

The Bidens began the trip at a place Jill loved: the beach. But this was no low-key day by the sea; it was a highly choreographed walk with British prime minister Boris Johnson and his wife, Carrie, at Carbis Bay. The two couples looked out at the ocean and traded pleasantries, while a crowd of journalists looked on.

There was an uncomfortable history there—Joe had once called Johnson a "physical and emotional clone" of Donald Trump—and the upcoming summit talks were shadowed by thorny issues like Joe's opposition to Brexit, Britain's withdrawal from the European Union, and concern for the future of Northern Ireland.

The Bidens and the Johnsons both held hands as they walked. Jill wore a black jacket with the word *love* outlined on the back in silver beading. She'd worn it two years earlier, to kick off Joe's presidential campaign.

"We're bringing love from America," she told reporters, who had asked about the message on her back. "This is a global conference and we are trying to bring unity across the globe and I think it's needed right now, that people feel a sense of unity from all the countries and feel a sense of hope after this year of the pandemic."

The mood was light by the time Joe and Boris Johnson began their one-on-one sit-down.

"I told the prime minister we have something in common. We both married way above our station," Joe joked.

Johnson laughed and said he was "not going to dissent from that one." But then he seemed to hint at a desire to improve relations with his American counterpart. "I'm not going to disagree with you on that," said Johnson, "or indeed on anything else."

As Joe delved into summit meetings, Jill set out on her own. She visited a preschool for children who had experienced trauma with the Duchess of

Cambridge, formerly known as Kate Middleton. Kate has made early childhood education a major cause of hers.

As part of the school's program, the children planted vegetables and flowers and tended to rabbits and hens. Jill and Kate joined the four- and five-year-olds to feed the rabbits, making quiet small talk and giggling together. Jill had met Prince Harry, Kate's royal brother-in-law, several times through their work and support of military veterans, but this was her first time meeting the duchess.

Jill and Kate returned to a silent classroom filled with young students in navy and white uniforms.

"They're scared to death," Jill joked.

"It's the quietest class I've ever been to," Kate said.

The women sat beside each other to address two different groups of children, looking at their drawings and helping them sound out words. They read *Greta and the Giants*, a book about the young Swedish climate change activist Greta Thunberg.

Jill and Kate also took part in a talk about the role of early childhood education in life outcomes with experts from the UK and some from the US who joined via Zoom. Jill thanked the news media for covering the appearance "because early childhood education is so important to lay the foundation for all of our students."

Both Jill and Kate took notes during the discussion, which centered on children's mental health and the importance of early education in childhood development. They also discussed how to get parents involved early on.

"I just don't know where to begin," Jill told the group, "but as an educator myself so much of what you're saying has certainly touched my life in that I taught in a psychiatric hospital for five years." She'd seen firsthand the effects of a negative environment on children.

Jill praised the others for the work they were doing, especially their efforts to educate fathers. "For the longest time, it was always the mother, right, who was doing the caregiving," Jill said. "But I think one of the positive parts of this pandemic is that now we've seen both of the parents, because they've both been home, and the fathers are saying, 'Hey, this is hard work.'"

"I'm committed to this for a long time," Kate said. "I hope our two countries can continue on this and share data."

Later in the week, Jill and Kate published a joint op-ed on the CNN website, writing, "The two of us believe that early childhood care and education should be seen as among the defining, strategic issues of our time."

As she departed the school with the duchess, reporters asked Jill if she had sought her advice for an upcoming meeting with Queen Elizabeth II.

"No, I didn't," Jill replied. "We've been busy. Were you not in that room? We were talking education."

During the trip, Jill managed to weave in visits with veterans before and between Joe's official events. Together they met with American troops and their families stationed at a Royal Air Force base and held a roundtable with military families.

Jill also met with members of Bude Surf Veterans, a volunteer organization based in Cornwall, England, that offers social support and surfing outings to military veterans, emergency workers, and their families to help them cope with trauma. They bonded over a shared love of the water, and Jill shared a laugh over her surfing attempts and the butterfly surfboard she'd owned in her youth.

The Olympics are typically a global celebration, with athletes, their families, and fans descending on the host city. But as with so much else during the pandemic, the summer games in Tokyo would be far different.

The games had already been delayed a year because of the coronavirus. Fans were also banned from all venues in the Tokyo area, meaning athletes would compete without the in-person support of their family and friends.

There was a chance for countries to send dignitaries to represent them and cheer on their athletes. The Biden administration chose Jill.

She arrived in Tokyo in late July with a robust agenda for her forty-eight hours on the ground. It was her first solo international trip as first lady.

Her presence gave an instant boost to the American athletes. She cheered them on from the stands at the opening ceremony and from the empty stands at several events. She hosted a US vs. Mexico softball watch party at the US Embassy for staff and their families. She met Emperor Naruhito at the Imperial Palace and had dinner with Prime Minister Yoshihide Suga and his wife, Mariko Suga, at the Akasaka Palace state guesthouse.

"She sees it as an act of patriotism to support our team," Valerie Jarrett said of Jill's attendance at the games. "They're putting themselves at risk to a certain degree, and so she wouldn't ask them to do anything she's not willing to do herself. And she appreciates the symbolic importance of supporting Team USA from the very top of the administration."

Chapter 67

Public Mourning

If the American president is supposed to be the nation's consoler-in-chief, the first lady is expected to be there, too, by his side.

That expectation has been part of the role for decades.

During World War II, it was Eleanor Roosevelt who addressed the nation by radio before her husband gave his famous "day of infamy" speech after the Japanese attack on Pearl Harbor. "We know what we have to face and we know that we are ready to face it," she said. "You cannot escape anxiety. You cannot escape a clutch of fear at your heart and yet I hope that the certainty of what we have to meet will make you rise above these fears."

In the late 1980s, Nancy Reagan "was deeply involved in the recovery of the families affected by the Space Shuttle Challenger accident," according to NASA. "Her compassion helped them and our nation through a difficult time, and we never forgot her care and heartfelt sympathy in a time of national and international mourning." During the memorial service for the crew killed in the shuttle disaster, Nancy held the hand of June Scobee, the mission commander's wife, as she sobbed.

After 9/11, Laura Bush drew from her background in childhood development to write comforting letters to children. "She appeared on multiple networks to tell parents to turn off their television sets, to share meals with their children, to read and comfort them," wrote Erika Cornelius Smith. She went on *The Oprah Winfrey Show* and *60 Minutes* to share advice on how children could cope with images of the terrorist attacks.

And when a gunman murdered twenty-six children and staff at Sandy Hook Elementary School in Newtown, Connecticut, in 2012, President Obama asked Michelle to return to the White House from a speech right away. "My husband needed me. This would be the only time in eight years that he'd request my presence in the middle of the workday, the two of us rearranging our schedules to be alone together for a moment of dim comfort," Michelle later wrote. "When I walked into the Oval Office, Barack and I embraced silently. There was nothing to say. No words."

There was no shortage of tragedy around the country when the Bidens arrived at the White House. More than 340,000 people had been killed by the coronavirus by the time Joe took office, a number that would more than double by the fall. The night before the inauguration, Jill, Joe, Kamala, and Doug presided over a memorial ceremony for COVID-19 victims at the Lincoln Memorial reflecting pool.

In the melancholy moments just before it started, Jill caught Doug's eye.

"So, you're ready?" she asked.

"Yeah, I'm ready."

"Let's do this together," Jill said.

The four walked out into a sea of cameras, security, and lights. The pair of spouses stood together, looking out over the reflecting pool. Emhoff watched Jill carefully and followed her lead. When she took Joe's hand, he realized it would be okay to hold Kamala's.

In the moving service—the first national recognition of the toll that COVID-19 had taken on the country—prayers were said, lights were lit around the reflecting pool, and church bells rang across Washington.

"There was no way she could have explained that moment to me," Emhoff said. "I'd have to experience it. But I was glad I got to experience it with her."

Jill has joined Joe on other public occasions of mourning, meeting with families in Florida whose loved ones were lost after the Surfside condo collapse. Jill laid a large bouquet of white irises on the curb of a memorial near the site of the collapsed building. On the twentieth anniversary of September 11, Joe and Jill traveled to all three 9/11 memorial sites to commemorate the day and pay their respects to the nearly three thousand people killed.

During the chaotic drawdown of the US military from Afghanistan in the summer of 2021, eleven Marines, one Navy sailor, and one Army soldier were killed by a suicide bomber while securing Kabul Airport for the evacuation of American citizens and Afghan allies.

Jill and Joe returned home to Delaware to attend the dignified transfer service at Dover Air Force Base for the slain troops and met privately with their grieving families. They watched in hushed reverence with hands over their hearts under a gray sky as, one by one, the flag-draped transfer cases were removed with solemnity from a military aircraft.

The only sounds that could be heard during the mournful ritual were the quiet commands of the honor guards in battle dress who carried the transfer cases, the hum of the hulking C-17 aircraft that had transported them, and the sobs of those attending. Five of the dead were just twenty years old, born not long after the September 11 attacks that triggered the beginning of America's longest conflict.

There had been significant public support for ending US involvement in Afghanistan, but the rapid and chaotic drawdown during the final two weeks of August drew sharp criticism from across the political spectrum. The Trump administration had reached a prior agreement with the Taliban, which called for an end to Taliban attacks on American soldiers and military installments in exchange for a US commitment to remove all American troops and contractors by May 2021.

Joe announced in April that although May was unrealistic, he would have all US forces out by September 11, later moving up the deadline to August 31. Having appeared to miscalculate the capability and will of Afghan security forces, Joe was suddenly facing a serious foreign policy crisis in the first year of his presidency.

Jill said she didn't think anyone should be surprised that Joe had ended the war in Afghanistan. "That was a campaign promise he made, and he was firm in his conviction," she said. She believed no one could have anticipated the obstacles or the outcome.

Shortly after the trip to Dover, Jill traveled to Marine Corps Base Camp Lejeune for private meetings and a listening session with military families. One of the slain Marines was twenty-three-year-old Sergeant Nicole L. Gee, who had been stationed at Camp Lejeune as a maintenance technician with the 24th Marine Expeditionary Unit. At a memorial in Midway Park, thirteen pairs of boots lined the grass, replete with photos, flowers, and mementos left by friends and families.

"We are a military family," Jill said. "I just wanted them to feel loved and supported."

She also visited Joint Base Charleston in South Carolina to commend the pilots and crews based there for participating in the airlift from Afghanistan.

Jill and Joe also went to Walter Reed to visit some fifteen Marines who were wounded in the Afghanistan bombing, and their families.

It was difficult for Jill to visit the hospital after Beau died there. The sights and smells brought the memories flooding back. She asked the staff to take her through the hospital a different way so she wouldn't have to pass by Beau's old room.

Chapter 68

Under Scrutiny

Hunter came under scrutiny once again after Joe was elected president.

He had moved to Los Angeles and began painting art that garnered attention. He lacked formal training, but his pieces were praised.

Alex Acevedo, owner of an art gallery in New York, said he'd been in the art business since 1956 and was not at all impressed with modern art, "but I was floored by that guy," meaning Hunter. Acevedo was quoted in a *New York Post* article headlined "Hunter Biden's Art Is Actually Good."

In his memoir, Hunter wrote, "Whether anybody likes it or not isn't what drives me to get up to paint. I paint no matter what. I paint because I want to. I paint because I have to." Jill was very proud. She'd always believed that Hunter would be an artist, and it brought relief to her as a mother to see her son find his footing after years of addiction and struggle.

But his art sales created complications for the administration. To address potential conflicts of interest, the White House established an arrangement whereby Hunter would sell his work through a private gallery that set prices and handled bids and sales, and was supposed to keep anonymous the identities of any buyers.

The arrangement required the art dealer selling Hunter's work to reject any buyer or offer that seemed out of the ordinary, including any that came in above the asking price. The prices started out considerably steeper than typical for a new artist—anywhere from $75,000 for a piece on paper to half a million dollars for large-scale paintings.

The arrangement marked one of the first high-profile tests of Joe's commitment to more stringent ethics rules for his family and administration officials.

Richard Painter, a White House ethics lawyer during the George W. Bush administration, said any complications presented by Hunter's art sales were "minimal compared with Trump." Trump's daughter and son-in-law worked in the White House, though they did not collect a government salary, and Trump often spent taxpayer dollars at his properties. "We definitely have far fewer problems with Biden," Painter said.

But Hunter's arrangement continued to raise questions.

The Biden administration's efforts to draw a sharp ethical contrast with the Trump White House also brought some scrutiny to the handling of Jill's $80,000 salary from NOVA.

There were meetings with lawyers and long weeks of negotiations to figure out how to avoid the emoluments clause. The constitutional provision prevents presidents from taking compensation beyond the salary they earn as president. The Trump White House had repeatedly triggered foreign and domestic emoluments clause investigations and a lawsuit.

"The clause is specific to the President and not the First Lady...But since NOVA is a state school and Jill and Joe file [taxes] jointly," a dean at the school wrote in an email, there was some concern.

The issue was resolved by a decision to fund Jill's salary from a foundation run by NOVA and "not attributable to any specific donor."

Chapter 69

Just Round One

Between her previous White House experience and watching First Lady Michelle Obama up close for eight years, Jill understood the power of her platform and the range of issues she could influence as first lady.

"She was never afraid to show up in her most authentic form," Michelle said of Jill. "She's taking on causes that reflect her passions and her brilliance."

Even before the election, Jill said, "I knew exactly what I wanted to work on. I knew exactly who I wanted to work on the issues with."

It came as little surprise that one focus would be on teachers, children, and community colleges.

In late April, Jill visited Sauk Valley Community College in Illinois, a school whose funding depended in part on corporate grants, which attempted to make college free by offering tuition breaks to students who completed community service.

"Community colleges meet students where they are and help them become the people they want to be," Jill said in her remarks. She stressed the important place in the economy community colleges occupy, offering flexible classes to working students, providing job skills, and welcoming students from nontraditional and working backgrounds. "We can't continue to exclude some people from continuing their education just because they're from the wrong income bracket."

Following her address to Sauk Valley, Jill gave a virtual talk for NOVA. The apparatus of staff, reporters, and Secret Service who traveled with her again waited patiently. The traveling press holed up in a conference room at the airport.

When Jill met them there after her speaking engagement, she remained fired up by the events of the day and was excited by Sauk Valley's efforts to make community college accessible to all. "I've been working on making community college free for so many years," she said. "I always love when I can go to a community college. I guess you have to be on that wavelength."

In remarks earlier in 2021 at Tidewater Community College in Virginia, Joe joked that while deeply committed, education advocacy was also crucial for his marital happiness. "I have to admit if I didn't have these positions I'd be sleeping in the Lincoln bedroom," he teased.

Jill and Joe both advocated for teachers, highlighting their challenges in the pandemic.

"You spoke out for safely reopening schools and more student support," Jill told educators at the annual meeting of the nation's largest teachers' union, the National Education Association, of which she is a member. "You carried families through the darkest year in modern history with patience, compassion, and care. And you did it all while you worried about your own families' health and education and safety."

In early July, Jill surprised contestants at the Scripps National Spelling Bee with an in-person visit. She met with finalists and their families before the event began, and then stayed and watched the competition.

Because of the pandemic, all preliminary rounds of the bee had been held virtually. Only the eleven finalists competed in person, at an ESPN campus near Walt Disney World in Florida.

Jill had previously attended the bee in 2009, when it was held in Washington. She told the contestants she had her own history with competitive spelling.

"In sixth grade I was my school's spelling bee champion," Jill said, adding that she had a chance to advance to the next round. "But on the day of the regional competition, I told my mother that I was sick. The truth was that I was too nervous to go, so I have incredible admiration for each and every one of you."

Unlike her recent predecessors, including Hillary Clinton, Laura Bush, and Michelle Obama, Jill has largely refrained from lobbying Congress or otherwise actively campaigning for the administration's policies outside of free community college.

Progressives and advocates of free college criticized Jill in fall 2021 for not reaching out to lawmakers to advocate for a $111 billion plan that would increase Pell Grant funding, create a federal–state partnership to make community college free, subsidize two years of tuition at HBCUs, tribal universities, and other minority-serving institutions, and fund programs to improve retention rates.

With negotiations over Biden's massive social spending and climate bill continuing as Halloween 2021 approached, it became clear that free community college would be cut from the package. West Virginia senator Joe Manchin, a Democrat whose vote Biden needed to pass his overall agenda in a Senate split 50-50 between the parties, objected to the college plan and other programs and revenue sources Biden had promised as a candidate.

Faced with the reality, Jill pledged to keep fighting for her life's goal.

"We're not giving up. We are not giving up," she told *Good Morning America* in October 2021. "This is round one. This is year one. I'm going to keep going."

Conclusion

"Your life will never change."

Joe Biden made that promise to Jill Jacobs in 1977 after she agreed to marry him after five proposals. But it was a promise the US senator would never be able to keep.

Across our interviews with Jill, the self-described introvert revealed her personality through sly asides and a mischievous sense of humor. She was relaxed and spoke freely, but was clearly aware when an answer made her staff flinch or hold their breath—and often joked about it. She urged us to take the White House cookies she had the staff lay out for us, scolded us about not eating enough on reporting trips to Delaware, and delighted in the cuteness of foreign leaders' children.

In our interviews, we found her something of a contradiction—she's open, but guarded. Remarkably candid, but careful to retell many of the same finely crafted stories she has shared in her memoir or elsewhere. Despite her years as a public figure, Jill repeatedly wondered why anyone would want to read about her life. She remains fiercely protective of the people and things that matter to her, whether it's Joe and their kids and grandkids, her friends, or her career.

But Jill has evolved in major ways across her private and public lives. As a young woman, she approached teaching as a fallback plan and wound up with three advanced degrees and acclaim as the most famous community college professor in America. She went from politically disengaged private citizen to an activist wielding a global platform. At a young age, she both ended a marriage and became a mother. Later in life, she lost a child while occupying one of the most visible positions in the world, grieving a loss no parent ever expects in the public eye.

Since she married Joe, the touchstone events of Jill's personal life—her marriage, her doctorate, the death of her mother, the death of her son, and Hunter's struggles—have nearly always come accompanied by a press release and a round of interviews, or the expectation that they would be chronicled and rehashed in her and her husband's memoirs.

Unlike many past first ladies, who met and married their husbands before politics became part of their lives, Joe was a US senator, a "public man," as he calls himself, when they went on their first date in March 1975. Her insistence, from the beginning, that she continue to live her life, pursue her professional goals, and maintain an identity separate from his paved the way for her to reimagine the role she now occupies.

"We aren't elected," Jill said in an October 2021 speech. "We have to define this role for ourselves."

And the role was ripe for reinvention. American families have evolved and gender roles have changed. It seems only right that the first family, as well as other prominent political families, would evolve, too. The first year of the Biden administration saw not only a first lady working outside the White House for the first time, but the first man to serve as second gentleman and a gay Cabinet secretary—Transportation Secretary Pete Buttigieg—adopt children with his husband.

"We simply couldn't ask for a better first lady for this moment," Michelle Obama said. "We are all better off with her in the White House."

Still, Jill's legacy as first lady will be inextricably linked to her husband's presidency. Will he seek a second term—and if he does, will he win? Will the pandemic ease or will Americans simply grow accustomed to living with the new virus? Will any of the significant promises Biden made to voters on the campaign trail be passed by Congress, where Democrats cling to the narrowest of majorities?

Jill herself would never have predicted a life of presidential campaigns, the death of her son, or a final reentry into politics during a period of cultural strife on a scale the country hasn't seen since she was a sheltered college student. Contrary to Joe's impulsive promise decades ago, change has been the one constant in Jill's life.

"I can say it's changed in a good way," Jill said. "But of course, it's been a journey."

Acknowledgments

Julie Pace

This book was the ultimate team effort, and I'm grateful to everyone who helped us bring Jill's story to life. In particular, my longtime colleague Darlene Superville—we've worked together at The Associated Press for more than a decade and she is among the most diligent, hardworking, and committed journalists I know. It was a pleasure to tackle this new challenge alongside her.

Evelyn M. Duffy is a first-rate collaborator. In addition to her many talents as a writer and editor, she is savvy, encouraging, and completely unflappable. She rolled with every challenge that came our way and always seemed to have a solution. She also brought to the project Sam Corden, whose insights truly made the book better.

Thank you also to researchers Ben Gambuzza and Tyler Loveless, and AP colleagues Josh Housing, who assisted with key interviews, Randall Chase, our longtime Delaware correspondent, and Peter Costanzo, who helped bring the project to life. Bridget Matzie saw the book's potential before anyone else. We also had an instant connection with Vanessa Mobley, our sharp and empathetic editor. Our thanks to editorial assistant Louisa McCullough, copyeditor Scott Wilson, production editor Betsy Uhrig, and production coordinators Erin Cain and Xian Lee at Little, Brown.

So much of this book tracks my years covering the White House and politics for the AP. I'm so appreciative of the colleagues who gave me those opportunities, the ones who helped cover for me while I was working on the book, and the many sources who have seen the value in helping a fact-based news organization like the AP get the story right.

Finally, the biggest thanks to my family: my endlessly supportive parents,

Diane and Jim, sister, Jill, and brother-in-law, Tyler. My husband, Michael, makes everything possible, and my son, Will, makes everything even better.

Darlene Superville

I've thought off and on about writing a book, encouraged by friends and colleagues. I wasn't sure I could do it, so I never did, until *Jill* showed me that I could.

I'm grateful to The Associated Press and especially to Julie Pace for inviting me to be part of the project. I've worked with and for Julie for more than a decade—we shared a claustrophobic booth in the White House press room before her promotions—and she is one of the most impressive journalists and news leaders of her generation. Committed, hardworking, and truly an amazing human being.

I'm also grateful for the collaboration with Evelyn M. Duffy, a talented writer, editor, and cheerleader who has been through this process many times and helped keep our spirits high throughout.

Additional thanks to Sam Corden, for his sharp insights; Ben Gambuzza and Tyler Loveless, for their research skills; and AP colleagues Josh Housing, for help with interviews and transcripts; longtime Delaware correspondent Randall Chase, for his invaluable knowledge of the Bidens; and Peter Costanzo, for shepherding the book from start to finish. Book agent Bridget Matzie brought the idea to the AP, and Vanessa Mobley, vice president and executive editor at Little, Brown, used her sharp eye and red pen to make our manuscript even better.

We would have pursued the project without her, but I do want to give special thanks to Jill Biden, for spending several hours with us, and her team—Anthony Bernal, Elizabeth Alexander, and Michael LaRosa—for their cooperation.

I am grateful to my AP White House colleagues for picking up the slack when I had to step away from daily coverage to work on the book.

I am most thankful for my mom, Vidda, and my brothers and sister, for supporting me as I became the first college graduate, first journalist, and first White House correspondent in our immigrant family. My one regret is that my dad, Leslie, who came to the US from Trinidad in the 1960s, isn't here to see his family name on the cover of a book.

Evelyn M. Duffy

Deep and heartfelt thanks to Sam Corden, who was instrumental at every stage of this book. Sam is a spirited writer, an insightful editor, and a determined researcher. He works both hard and smart, and is adept at wearing a multitude of hats. He has been a sounding board and a friend across the miles and time zones, and he has my lasting gratitude.

Ben Gambuzza and Tyler Loveless are two of the most gifted and tireless researchers I've had the privilege to work alongside. They lent their research and editing talents to this project in dozens of ways, and the story is richer for their efforts.

Love and gratitude to my wife, Jennifer Young, and my mom, Eileen Duffy, for their steadfast support and encouragement. Thanks also to Bridget Matzie, Craig Batchelor, David Wolf, Matt Duffy, Chris Haugh, Wesley Cook, Katie Ruppert, Heather Toye, Madison Gregory, Mary DiPalma, Marie Rudolph, and Tom Bowen. Many thanks to Bob Woodward and Elsa Walsh for their enduring friendship. My last thoughts are with my dad, Edward F. Duffy. I wish he could have seen this book; it would have made him very happy.

Source Notes

In addition to the various memoirs written by members of the Biden family, *Joe Biden: A Life of Trial and Redemption* by Jules Witcover and *What It Takes* by Richard Ben Cramer were invaluable resources.

Introduction

4 *"Life just felt different," she said:* Interview with Dr. Jill Biden by Julie Pace, September 29, 2021.

5 *"I saw this whole world":* Ibid.

6 *"The first lady, at least in my research":* Interview with Myra Gutin by Darlene Superville, September 23, 2021.

Chapter 1

7 *"When we were growing up":* Interview with Dr. Jill Biden by Darlene Superville, September 10, 2021.

8 *"It was never a fancy place":* Julia Lawlor, "Weekender | Ocean City, N.J.," *New York Times,* May 7, 2004.

8 *"Then we'd waitress":* Interview with Dr. Jill Biden by Darlene Superville, September 10, 2021.

8 *"We dated the lifeguards":* Ibid.

8 *"I have always had that vivid picture":* Interview with Barbara Jacobs Hopkins by Julie Pace, August 25, 2021.

Chapter 2

9 *"You'd wake up, you'd eat":* Interview with Dr. Jill Biden by Darlene Superville, September 10, 2021.

9 *Her childhood was "really":* Ibid.

9 *Jill played Spring in the kindergarten play:* "60 Graduate at Hatboro Kindergarten," *Doylestown Daily Intelligencer,* June 3, 1957.

9 *"One of the things that my parents created":* Ibid.

9 *"There were lots of houses":* Ibid.

10 *"There was just something":* Ibid.

10 *Her father grew up:* Interview with Dr. Jill Biden by Darlene Superville, September 10, 2021.

11 *"They weren't quite the Montagues":* Dr. Jill Biden, "My Family's Love Story," *Forbes,* December 20, 2018.

11 *But Jill grew up highly aware:* Jill Biden, *Where the Light Enters,* Macmillan, 2019, p. 9.

11 *"My mother's mother realized":* Interview with Dr. Jill Biden by Darlene Superville, September 10, 2021.

11 *"Ma wasn't a warm woman"*: Jill Biden, *Where the Light Enters*, Macmillan, 2019, p. 6.

11 *"We all just ended up sidestepping"*: Ibid., p. 17.

12 *"We all knew," Jill recalled*: Interview with Dr. Jill Biden by Darlene Superville, September 10, 2021.

12 *"Give me a love like theirs"*: Jill Biden, *Where the Light Enters*, Macmillan, 2019, p. 18.

12 *"I can maybe remember twice"*: Interview with Dr. Jill Biden by Darlene Superville, September 10, 2021.

12 *"We were all so close to my mother"*: Interview with Dr. Jill Biden by Julie Pace and Darlene Superville, September 22, 2021.

13 *"I have all those really good memories"*: Interview with Dr. Jill Biden by Darlene Superville, September 10, 2021.

13 *"Don't disturb Daddy"*: Ibid.

13 *Donald and his daughters would polish*: See "Dr. Jill Biden on family, teaching, loss and levity," *CBS Sunday Morning*, August 9, 2020.

13 *Later Jill recalled, "It was a small thing"*: "Dr. Jill Biden hosts virtual announcement," ABC News Live. facebook.com/watch/live/?ref=watch_permalink&v=437969910901862.

13 *There was, Jill said, "a lot of patriotism"*: Interview with Dr. Jill Biden by Darlene Superville, September 10, 2021.

13 *"She was kind of my little sidekick"*: Interview with Barbara Jacobs Hopkins by Julie Pace, August 25, 2021.

14 *"We got home and Jill's dad really yelled"*: Ibid.

14 *"That grandmother taught me"*: Interview with Dr. Jill Biden by Darlene Superville, September 10, 2021.

14 *"She would give me a subscription"*: Ibid.

14 *"I loved listening to Ma sing"*: Jill Biden, *Where the Light Enters*, Macmillan, 2019, p. 192.

15 *"You know, Jill, you're not a Godfrey"*: Interview with Dr. Jill Biden by Darlene Superville, September 10, 2021.

Chapter 3

16 *Her grandmother "just was so warm"*: Interview with Dr. Jill Biden by Darlene Superville, September 10, 2021.

16 *"I always took a change of clothes"*: Interview with Barbara Jacobs Hopkins by Julie Pace, August 25, 2021.

16 *"The grandmothers would compete"*: Interview with Dr. Jill Biden by Darlene Superville, September 10, 2021.

17 *"I was treated special"*: Ibid.

17 *"My grandfather would come home"*: Ibid.

17 *"She just had beautiful skin"*: Ibid.

17 *They would go shopping*: See "First Lady Jill Biden's favorite hometown sandwich at Bagliani's Market," My Assignment Photojournalist YouTube account, June 4, 2021, youtu.be/03rEgvvcpos.

17 *Grandma Jacobs's family was Dutch*: Interview with Barbara Jacobs Hopkins by Julie Pace, August 25, 2021.

18 *"We'd be rolling out the dough"*: Interview with Dr. Jill Biden by Darlene Superville, September 10, 2021.

18 *"I could still picture Jill"*: Interview with Barbara Jacobs Hopkins by Julie Pace, August 25, 2021.

Chapter 4

19 *Their exhausted parents:* Interview with Dr. Jill Biden by Darlene Superville, September 10, 2021.

19 *"No matter what else was in it":* Ibid.

19 *"I wasn't political, really":* Ibid.

20 *"I'm pretty sure it was a Friday":* Ibid.

20 *The students sat in shock:* Ibid.

20 *"Transfixed" by the live TV:* Jill Biden, *Where the Light Enters*, Macmillan, 2019, p. 29.

20 *"I can just remember watching":* Interview with Dr. Jill Biden by Darlene Superville, September 10, 2021.

20 *"When she got on a subject":* Interview with Barbara Jacobs Hopkins by Julie Pace, August 25, 2021.

20 *"Wrestling would break out":* Jill Biden, *Where the Light Enters*, Macmillan, 2019, p. 15.

21 *"She took care of me":* Julia Terruso, "Jill Biden's Philly Grit," *Philadelphia Inquirer*, October 14, 2021.

21 *In 1964, a boy named Drew:* Jill Biden, *Where the Light Enters*, Macmillan, 2019, p. 20.

21 *"Yo, yo," she once began:* Interview with Barbara Jacobs Hopkins by Julie Pace, August 25, 2021.

21 *Barbara recalled, "I can remember":* Ibid.

21 *Jill's parents, both from Protestant families:* Jill Biden, *Where the Light Enters*, Macmillan, 2019, p. 140.

22 *"Sitting in the candlelight, listening":* Ibid., p. 192.

22 *"I cut school once in a while":* Interview with Dr. Jill Biden by Darlene Superville, September 10, 2021.

22 *"Even now, I can't believe we did this":* Jill Biden, *Where the Light Enters*, Macmillan, 2019, p. 21.

22 *"You're going to smoke these":* Ibid., p. 23.

22 *Jill kept smoking for years:* Ibid., p. 24.

22 *I can picture her so clearly:* Ibid., p. 86.

22 *"My sisters and I always felt":* Ibid., p. 28.

23 *"And of course, we were always late":* Interview with Dr. Jill Biden by Darlene Superville, September 10, 2021.

23 *"I would say I usually had a boyfriend":* Ibid.

23 *"It's like, 'C'mon, guys'":* Ibid.

23 *"She was so tough":* Ibid.

23 *"I would go home, put on my bikini":* Ibid.

23 *That summer, she met and started:* Jonathan Van Meter, "Jill Biden: All the Vice President's Women," *Vogue*, November 2008.

Chapter 5

24 *Rather than questioning her decision:* Jill Biden, *Where the Light Enters*, Macmillan, 2019, p. 22.

24 *"I said to my parents after a month":* Interview with Dr. Jill Biden by Darlene Superville, September 10, 2021.

25 *"They said, let's see how you do":* Ibid.

25 *"I suddenly saw the cracks":* Jill Biden, *Where the Light Enters*, Macmillan, 2019, p. 34.

26 *"I can remember so clearly":* Ibid.

26 *"I had been raised to believe":* Ibid., p. 35.

26 *"My parents were Republicans":* Interview with Dr. Jill Biden by Darlene Superville, September 10, 2021.

26 *"My parents didn't object":* Jill Biden, *Where the Light Enters*, Macmillan, 2019, p. 33.

27 *"Students and local residents":* Jessie Markovetz, "Behind the Stone Balloon: Part 1 of 2 Part Series: The Balloon Rises," *The Review,* 1980.

27 *"I loved the classes I took":* Interview with Dr. Jill Biden by Darlene Superville, September 10, 2021.

Chapter 6

28 *One ad run by Biden read:* Jim Newell, "When Joe Biden Was the Candidate of the Young," *Slate,* June 11, 2019.

28 *Rather than a nasty campaign:* Ibid.

29 *"I didn't decide to become involved":* Interview with Dr. Jill Biden by Darlene Superville, September 10, 2021.

29 *"I remember I was in college":* Ibid.

30 *"She had an easy, natural beauty":* Jill Biden, *Where the Light Enters,* Macmillan, 2019, p. 34.

30 *"I didn't know much about her":* Ibid.

30 Jesus! Joe's going to find out: Richard Ben Cramer, *What It Takes,* Open Road Media (Kindle edition), 2011, p. 1093.

31 *"They flew us to Wilmington":* Joe Biden, *Promises to Keep,* Random House, 2007, p. 105.

31 *"Beau, Hunt, and Naomi":* Ibid.

31 *President Nixon called Joe:* Luke A. Nichter, "When Nixon Taped Joe Biden," *Wall Street Journal,* November 15, 2020. The transcript is available at nixontapes.org/jrb.html.

31 *"I can remember the night":* Interview with Dr. Jill Biden by Darlene Superville, September 10, 2021.

31 *"It's sort of odd":* Ibid.

32 *"We had a number of plans, Neilia and I":* "Biden Boys Witness Swear-In," Associated Press, January 6, 1973.

32 *Neilia's father held the bible:* Details of the swearing-in were drawn from: "New Senator to Take Oath in Hospital," Associated Press, January 3, 1973 and "Watching His Dad," Associated Press wirephoto, January 7, 1973 and accompanying January 5, 1973 text by Associated Press writer Irene E. Shadoan.

32 *"I hope to be a good senator":* Various versions of Biden's speech were quoted in news sources from the day. This is sourced from "Biden Boys Witness Swear-In," Associated Press, January 6, 1973 and "Watching His Dad," Associated Press wirephoto, January 7, 1973 and accompanying January 5, 1973 text by Associated Press writer Irene E. Shadoan.

32 *"Christmas passed with the boys":* Joe Biden, *Promises to Keep,* Random House, 2007, p. 107.

Chapter 7

The dialogue in this chapter is drawn primarily from *Where the Light Enters* by Jill Biden (Macmillan, 2019) and *Promises to Keep* by Joe Biden (Random House, 2007).

33 *"I tried to make the relationship work":* Jill Biden, *Where the Light Enters,* Macmillan, 2019, p. 35.

33 *"Things were a little too rough":* Jonathan Van Meter, "Jill Biden: All the Vice President's Women," *Vogue,* November 2008.

33 *Their divorce would be finalized:* "Civil Divorce Decrees Granted (effective immediately)," *Morning News,* May 13, 1975.

33 *Later,* The Review *reported:* Jessie Markovetz, "Behind the Stone Balloon: Part 1 of 2 Part Series: The Balloon Rises," *The Review,* 1980.

33 *Years afterward, the* Wilmington: Melissa Jacobs, "Action at Newark's State Theater moves from screen to stage," *News Journal,* February 14, 1987.

34 *"It was then that I knew that I'd found":* Kayla Keegan, "Dr. Jill Biden Shares the Most Rewarding Part About Being a Teacher for Over Three Decades," *Good Housekeeping,* August 12, 2021.

34 *Jill, wearing a tank top:* The photo of Jill Biden may be viewed on Tom Stiltz's Instagram account (@tstiltz) at instagram.com/p/CEIa3Prnwvy/.

34 *"She was blond and gorgeous":* Joe Biden, *Promises to Keep,* Random House, 2007, p. 126.

34 *"People aren't going to look at a picture":* Interview with Dr. Jill Biden by Darlene Superville, September 10, 2021.

34 *"Look, Frankie," Joe said:* Jill Biden, *Where the Light Enters,* Macmillan, 2019, p. 38.

35 *"I never expected to be attracted":* Interview with Dr. Jill Biden by Darlene Superville, September 10, 2021.

35 *pondering "what one might wear":* Jill Biden, *Where the Light Enters,* Macmillan, 2019, p. 39.

35 My god, what have I gotten myself into?: Ibid.

35 *"Despite his appearance and dress":* Ibid., p. 40.

36 *"Jill showed no interest in politics":* Joe Biden, *Promises to Keep,* Random House, 2007, p. 126.

36 *"I was so stunned," she recalled:* Interview with Dr. Jill Biden by Darlene Superville, September 10, 2021.

36 *"That sort of sealed the deal":* Ibid.

36 *"She'd married young, was separated":* Joe Biden, *Promises to Keep,* Random House, 2007, p. 127.

36 *Jill later said she thought:* Jules Witcover, *Joe Biden: A Life of Trial and Redemption,* William Morrow Paperbacks revised edition, 2019, p. 128.

36 *As a senator, or a father—or both:* Ibid.

36 *"Three dates, three nights in a row?":* Jill Biden, *Where the Light Enters,* Macmillan, 2019, p. 40.

Chapter 8

37 *Dating her had given him:* Joe Biden, *Promises to Keep,* Random House, 2007, p. 139.

38 *"They were like puppies":* Jill Biden, *Where the Light Enters,* Macmillan, 2019, p. 43.

38 *"I've been wanting to talk to you":* Ibid., p. 45.

39 *"Is it serious?" Barbara asked:* Interview with Barbara Jacobs Hopkins by Julie Pace, August 25, 2021.

39 *Barbara recalled, "My mom":* Ibid.

39 *"It felt like home," Joe wrote:* Joe Biden, *Promises to Keep,* Random House, 2007, p. 140.

39 *"And Joe ate a lot":* Interview with Barbara Jacobs Hopkins by Julie Pace, August 25, 2021.

39 *"Her father was a reliable man":* Joe Biden, *Promises to Keep,* Random House, 2007, p. 140.

39 *"My family seemed to adore him":* Jill Biden, *Where the Light Enters,* Macmillan, 2019, p. 47.

40 *Don't get your hopes up, Jill warned:* Joe Biden, *Promises to Keep,* Random House, 2007, p. 140.

40 *Jill became their "moral support":* Interview with Barbara Jacobs Hopkins by Julie Pace, August 25, 2021.

40 *"When I say that I fell in love":* Interview with Dr. Jill Biden by Darlene Superville, September 10, 2021.

40 *"I saw my mother cry only one time":* Jill Biden, *Where the Light Enters,* Macmillan, 2019, p. 49.

41 *"She could talk with anyone":* Richard Ben Cramer, *What It Takes,* Open Road Media (Kindle edition), 2011, p. 1205.

41 *"After the disappointment of my divorce":* Jill Biden, *Where the Light Enters,* Macmillan, 2019, p. 50.

41 *"Over the years, I've been asked":* Ibid., p. 54.

42 *Joe, in the driver's seat, saw Jill:* Joe Biden, *Promise Me, Dad,* Flatiron Books, 2017, p. 12.

Chapter 9

43 *"I want us to get married," he said:* Jill Biden, *Where the Light Enters,* Macmillan, 2019, p. 49.

43 *The Senate then was like a family:* Interview with Marcelle Leahy by Darlene Superville, September 23, 2021.

44 *"They were so easy to love," she said:* Jules Witcover, *Joe Biden: A Life of Trial and Redemption*, William Morrow Paperbacks revised edition, 2019, p. 129.

44 *"They had endured the loss":* Jill Biden, *Where the Light Enters*, Macmillan, 2019, p. 52.

44 *"One of the things I loved most about Jill":* Joe Biden, *Promises to Keep*, Random House, 2007, p. 139.

44 *"Even in this committee post":* Jules Witcover, *Joe Biden: A Life of Trial and Redemption*, William Morrow Paperbacks revised edition, 2019, p. 132.

45 *Joe was likewise "occupied":* Ibid., 133.

45 *She later recalled that Jimmy:* Ibid., p. 134.

45 *"I heard all the discussions":* Interview with Dr. Jill Biden by Julie Pace and Darlene Superville, September 22, 2021.

45 *"Look," Jill remembers him saying:* Jill Biden, *Where the Light Enters*, Macmillan, 2019, p. 54.

45 *"I could see that he didn't want to lose me":* Ibid., p. 55.

45 *"This is it," Joe said:* Jules Witcover, *Joe Biden: A Life of Trial and Redemption*, William Morrow Paperbacks revised edition, 2019, p. 133.

46 *There was a brief dial tone:* Joe Biden, *Promises to Keep*, Random House, 2007, p. 142.

46 *"If I denied your dream":* Ibid.

46 *"Oh, Jill, don't worry," she later recalled:* Interview with Dr. Jill Biden by Julie Pace and Darlene Superville, September 22, 2021.

46 *"He did say that," she marveled:* Ibid.

Chapter 10

47 *"I remember Joe being so excited":* Interview with Marcelle Leahy by Darlene Superville, September 23, 2021.

47 *"To my relief, no one seemed":* Jill Biden, *Where the Light Enters*, Macmillan, 2019, p. 60.

48 *"They just instinctively understood":* Jill Biden, *Where the Light Enters*, Macmillan, 2019, p. 56.

48 *"Sen. Joseph R. Biden Jr. has married":* "Biden Is Wed in Private Ceremony," Associated Press, June 20, 1977.

48 *Joe's father called the wedding:* "Sen. Biden Married in Private Rite," Associated Press, June 18, 1977.

48 *"We took the honeymoon suite":* Jules Witcover, *Joe Biden: A Life of Trial and Redemption*, William Morrow Paperbacks revised edition, 2019, p. 134.

48 *"That night my life felt back together":* Joe Biden, *Promises to Keep*, Random House, 2007, p. 143.

48 *"I don't want to get her into the political":* Al Cartwright, "Son Told Joe to Marry Jill," *News Journal*, July 17, 1977.

48 *But a week later the paper ran:* Al Cartwright, "Delaware," *Morning News*, July 24, 1977.

48 *"I really felt it was important":* Interview with Dr. Jill Biden by Julie Pace and Darlene Superville, September 22, 2021.

49 *Beau and Hunter did "every sport":* Ibid.

49 *A week or two after they got married:* Ibid.

49 *With Joe away all day working:* Ibid.

49 *Jill found Beau to be:* Ibid.

49 *And with Joe often home late:* Ibid.

49 *"I didn't say a word," Jill recalled:* Ibid.

Chapter 11

50 *"It was a little overwhelming":* Interview with Dr. Jill Biden by Julie Pace and Darlene Superville, September 22, 2021.

50 *"I felt like I was being pulled":* Ibid.

50 *"I can remember going home":* Ibid.

50 *"I would go to every senior center"*: Ibid.

50 *"They loved Joe"*: Interview with Dr. Jill Biden by Julie Pace, September 29, 2021.

51 *"These were done to foster good"*: Interview with Marcelle Leahy by Darlene Superville, September 23, 2021.

51 *Joe's electoral chances in the upcoming*: See Jane Harriman, "Step Right Up and Meet the President," *Morning News*, February 19, 1978; Pat Ordovensky, "Whirlwind Visit Buoys Sen. Biden," *Morning News*, February 21, 1978; and Jules Witcover, *Joe Biden: A Life of Trial and Redemption*, William Morrow Paperbacks revised edition, 2019.

51 *"They got to Washington"*: Jules Witcover, *Joe Biden: A Life of Trial and Redemption*, William Morrow Paperbacks revised edition, 2019, p. 142.

52 *Baxter attacked Biden*: Hugh Cutler, "Wives Enter Campaign Fray in Defense of Politicking Mates," *Morning News*, October 10, 1978.

52 *"I just cannot let this go by"*: Ibid.

52 *She headed up Operation Reindeer*: "Operation Reindeer Needs Donated Gifts," *News Journal*, November 16, 1978.

52 *And she signed autographs*: Scott Hubbard, "Wilmington Hadassah Publishes Favorite Recipes," *Evening Journal*, March 28, 1978.

52 *Once the local papers*: Richard Sandza, "Mrs. Biden's Party Line's Tied Up," *News Journal*, October 24, 1978.

53 *"It was out of that evening"*: Interview with Mark Gitenstein by Julie Pace, July 30, 2021.

53 *Joe would later tell a story*: Katelyn Fossett, "Five Stories That Show Why People Love John McCain," *Politico*, July 20, 2017.

54 *McCain danced*: Robert Timberg, *The Nightingale's Song*, Simon & Schuster, 1996, p. 266.

54 *"They needed reading specialists"*: Interview with Dr. Jill Biden by Julie Pace and Darlene Superville, September 22, 2021.

54 *"They wanted reading specialists"*: Ibid.

54 *Ironically, Claymont had been*: Andrea Miller and Antonio Prado, "Remembering Claymont High: first white public school in Delaware to admit black students," *Hockessin Community News*, October 21, 2008.

55 *"They were desperate" for specialists*: Interview with Dr. Jill Biden by Julie Pace and Darlene Superville, September 22, 2021.

55 *"The country didn't know her"*: Interview with Ted Kaufman by Darlene Superville, August 7, 2021.

Chapter 12

56 *Biden was quoted saying*: Jules Witcover, *Joe Biden: A Life of Trial and Redemption*, William Morrow Paperbacks revised edition, 2019, p. 151.

57 *"Tell Patrick not to tell Joe"*: Interview with Marcelle Leahy by Darlene Superville, September 23, 2021.

57 *"There were so many reasons"*: Jill Biden, *Where the Light Enters*, Macmillan, 2019, p. 68.

57 *"I think I might be pregnant"*: Ibid., p. 69.

57 *In what Jill described*: Ibid.

58 *"Dad! We're having a baby!"*: Ibid.

58 *"Go back to sleep"*: Ibid.

58 *"What can I say? It was the '80s"*: Ibid.

58 *"I remembered how traumatic"*: Ibid., p. 70.

58 *"We brought her home together"*: Ibid.

58 *Ashley "lit up my dad's life"*: Jules Witcover, *Joe Biden: A Life of Trial and Redemption*, William Morrow Paperbacks revised edition, 2019, p. 135.

59 *"Jill and I had a serious talk"*: Joe Biden, *Promises to Keep*, Random House, 2007, p.168.
59 *"Members of the group were all wives"*: "Senate Spouses," Senate Historical Office. See senate
  .gov/artandhistory/history/common/generic/SenateSpouses.htm.
59 *"It's a good way for the spouses"*: Interview with Marcelle Leahy by Darlene Superville, September 23, 2021.
59 *"She greets everybody with equal"*: Ibid.
60 *The press at the time described:* Jan Harriman, "Rockford Center revamps program for adolescents," *News Journal*, November 6, 1984.
60 *She recalled her time there:* Jill Biden, *Where the Light Enters*, Macmillan, 2019, p. 82.

Chapter 13

61 *"I'm taking my family out"*: Jules Witcover, *Joe Biden: A Life of Trial and Redemption*, William Morrow Paperbacks revised edition, 2019, p. 165.
61 *"Can we do this without Jill"*: Nathan Gorenstein, "Biden Stokes Presidential Express," *News Journal*, April 29, 1986.
61 *Joe wove family issues:* Jules Witcover, *Joe Biden: A Life of Trial and Redemption*, William Morrow Paperbacks revised edition, 2019, p. 154.
61 *Now Joe "had to ask himself"*: Ibid., p. 169.
61 *"I think I can do both"*: Ibid., p. 170.
62 *Ashley later told biographer Jules Witcover:* Ibid., p. 165.
62 *"I got off the train. My wife, Jill"*: Darlene Superville, "Biden Helps His Amtrak Family Celebrate Its 50th Anniversary," Associated Press, April 30, 2021.
62 *He "reasoned with" Jill:* Jules Witcover, *Joe Biden: A Life of Trial and Redemption*, William Morrow Paperbacks revised edition, 2019, p. 170.
62 *She sighed—the sound of "concentrated sadness"*: Richard Ben Cramer, *What It Takes*, Open Road Media (Kindle edition), 2011, p. 170.
62 *"This was the big leagues"*: Ibid., p. 466.
63 *Joe's campaign staff "took Jill for a political infant"*: Ibid., p. 556.
63 *After a ski trip that was meant to include:* Ibid., p. 618.
63 *Anything you choose to do:* Ibid.
63 *"That's when Joe woke up"*: Ibid., p. 619.
64 *Cramer wrote that "later, in the bathroom"*: Ibid.
64 *One day in their bedroom, after a meeting:* Joe Biden, *Promises to Keep*, Random House, 2007, p. 187.
64 *"He decided to run, or we decided"*: Interview with Dr. Jill Biden by Julie Pace and Darlene Superville, September 22, 2021.

Chapter 14

65 *After his speech, everyone—Joe, Jill, their kids:* Jules Witcover, *Joe Biden: A Life of Trial and Redemption*, William Morrow Paperbacks revised edition, 2019, p. 173.
66 *"She was more responsible for it"*: Interview with Anita McBride by Darlene Superville, September 23, 2021.
66 *Lady Bird was also the first presidential spouse:* See the Miller Center website: millercenter.org/president/lbjohnson/essays/johnson-1963-firstlady.
66 *Although Lady Bird considered campaigning:* Ibid.
66 *"Before it was over, she would make"*: Meredith Hindley, "Lady Bird Special," *Humanities*, May/June 2013.
67 *"First lady followers and historians"*: Interview with Anita McBride by Darlene Superville, September 23, 2021.

67 *"The American public does still get":* Ibid.

67 *Jill, in contrast, was a schoolteacher:* A report on the Bidens' income may be found in Celia Cohen, "Politicians' finances disclosed," *Morning News*, October 28, 1982, p. A7.

67 *In a column headlined "New Breed":* David Broder, "New Breed of Political Wives Poses Challenges for the Press—and Voters," *Spokesman-Review*, April 19, 1987.

68 *Justice Powell had been nominated:* Jules Witcover, *Joe Biden: A Life of Trial and Redemption*, William Morrow Paperbacks revised edition, 2019, p. 175.

69 *"The more I knew about the judge":* Joe Biden, *Promises to Keep*, Random House, 2007, p. 201.

69 *Joe "responded to concerns":* Jules Witcover, *Joe Biden: A Life of Trial and Redemption*, William Morrow Paperbacks revised edition, 2019, p. 181.

69 *"Up to now, Jill was going along":* Ibid., p. 206.

70 *"I think I found somebody":* Interview with Christine Vilsack by Julie Pace, September 3, 2021.

70 *"My first impression of her was":* Interview with Cathy Russell by Darlene Superville, August 23, 2021.

71 *"Just talk to them," Russell urged:* Ibid.

71 *"I can remember that summer":* Interview with Dr. Jill Biden by Julie Pace and Darlene Superville, September 22, 2021.

71 *"I saw the response in Iowa":* Ibid.

Chapter 15

72 *She told a German film crew:* Roger Simon, "Jill Biden and her husband campaign as a team," *The Herald* (Jasper, Indiana), August 13, 1987.

72 *"As a mother, my children are my first priority":* Ibid.

72 *"I want a school system that does not":* Alan Sverdlik, "Candidates' wives tell what they'd do as first lady," *Atlanta Constitution*, July 27, 1987.

72 *"It's my profession," she said:* "Real running mates: Wives of presidential candidates hitting the trail," *Los Angeles Times Special*, July 29, 1987.

72 *But times were changing:* Mireille Grangenois Gates, "Poll Finds Most Voters Want Career First Ladies," Gannett News Service, June 14, 1987.

73 *"Hey, where she comes is where I go":* Roger Simon, "Jill Biden and her husband campaign as a team," *The Herald* (Jasper, Indiana), August 13, 1987.

73 *"I've supported him for ten years":* Ibid.

73 *"Hey! You were great!" Joe said:* Ibid.

73 *Columnist Roger Simon concluded:* Ibid.

73 *"I thought it was you," Donilon said:* Interview with Cathy Russell by Darlene Superville, August 23, 2021.

74 *"That was the beginning of the relationship":* Interview with Christine Vilsack by Julie Pace, September 3, 2021.

75 *"Traveling with her was kind of an adventure":* Interview with Cathy Russell by Darlene Superville, August 23, 2021.

75 Oh, for the love of God, Jill: Ibid.

Chapter 16

76 *Kinnock's speech resonated with Joe:* Neil Kinnock, Speech to Welsh Labor Party Conference in Llandudno, May 15, 1987. speech.almeida.co.uk/neil-kinnock.

77 *"The debate went fine, and when I got":* Joe Biden, *Promises to Keep*, Random House, 2007, p. 192.

77 *"All I had to say was, 'Like Kinnock'":* Jules Witcover, *Joe Biden: A Life of Trial and Redemption*, William Morrow Paperbacks revised edition, 2019, p. 193.

77 *"I followed him for three days":* Ibid.

77 *Jill was angry. She "wanted to take some starch"*: Joe Biden, *Promises to Keep*, Random House, 2007, p. 234.

77 *"I just really felt that he was going to do this"*: Interview with Dr. Jill Biden by Julie Pace and Darlene Superville, September 22, 2021.

78 *"Our basic game plan went like this"*: Jeff Wilser, *The Book of Joe*, Crown, 2017, p. 71.

78 *The next bombshell fell*: James R. Dickinson, "Biden Academic Claims 'Inaccurate,'" *Washington Post*, September 22, 1987, and E. J. Dionne Jr., "Biden Was Accused of Plagiarism in Law School," *New York Times*, September 17, 1987.

78 *"I've done some dumb things"*: "Biden News Conference," C-SPAN, September 17, 1987, c-span.org/video/?3686-1.

78 *"The floodgate had opened"*: Jules Witcover, *Joe Biden: A Life of Trial and Redemption*, William Morrow Paperbacks revised edition, 2019, p. 199.

79 *"It was tough. I mean, it was really tough"*: Interview with Dr. Jill Biden by Julie Pace and Darlene Superville, September 22, 2021.

79 *"They had had such hopes for their dad"*: Ibid.

80 *"There's only one way to stop the sharks"*: Joe Biden, *Promises to Keep*, Random House, 2007, p. 230.

80 *"I think it's time to get out," she said*: Ibid., p. 231.

80 *"If I let the story drag on so long"*: Ibid., p. 229.

80 *"You've got to quit" and beat Bork*: Interview with Dr. Jill Biden by Julie Pace and Darlene Superville, September 22, 2021.

80 *"I felt that with everything I had"*: Ibid.

Chapter 17

81 *"Hello, everybody. You know my wife"*: Joe Biden, *Promises to Keep*, Random House, 2007, p. 231.

81 *"I thought he was strong"*: Interview with Dr. Jill Biden by Julie Pace and Darlene Superville, September 22, 2021.

81 *As Joe remembered, she uttered*: Joe Biden, *Promises to Keep*, Random House, 2007, p. 232.

82 *"Nothing else matters, man"*: Ibid.

82 *"I called Mom-Mom"*: Interview with Dr. Jill Biden by Julie Pace and Darlene Superville, September 22, 2021.

82 *The day after the announcement*: "Biden, in Iowa for Farewell, Expresses 'No Rancor,'" Associated Press, September 25, 1987.

82 *"We had established Teachers"*: Interview with Christine Vilsack by Julie Pace, September 3, 2021.

83 *"It just felt so prickly," she said*: Interview with Dr. Jill Biden by Julie Pace and Darlene Superville, September 22, 2021.

83 *"He needed to be vindicated"*: Jules Witcover, *Joe Biden: A Life of Trial and Redemption*, William Morrow Paperbacks revised edition, 2019, p. 231.

83 *"We got a whole generation of decent jurisprudence"*: Ibid., p. 235.

83 *"After being such a rock"*: Joe Biden, *Promises to Keep*, Random House, 2007, p. 239.

83 *"It's hard to smile," Jill said*: Ibid., p. 240.

Chapter 18

84 *"It was getting back to normal"*: Interview with Dr. Jill Biden by Julie Pace and Darlene Superville, September 22, 2021.

84 *"I just kept thinking it was pressure"*: Ibid.

85 *"Hey! You think we can still"*: Richard Ben Cramer, *What It Takes*, Open Road Media (Kindle edition), 2011, p. 1507.

85 *"Bullshit," his brother Jimmy:* Ibid., p. 1509.

85 *"You've got to go home":* Interview with Dr. Jill Biden by Julie Pace and Darlene Superville, September 22, 2021.

85 *"His color was just—he was gray":* Ibid.

86 *"I had Joe's staff calling":* Ibid.

86 *"Wait, wait, wait":* Ibid.

86 *In her memoir she wrote, "I yell so rarely":* Jill Biden, *Where the Light Enters*, Macmillan, 2019, p. 91.

86 *The priest "got up and out he went":* Interview with Dr. Jill Biden by Julie Pace and Darlene Superville, September 22, 2021.

86 *"That just changed life in an instant":* Ibid.

87 *"Well, you've really ruined Valentine's Day":* Jill Biden, *Where the Light Enters*, Macmillan, 2019, p. 92.

87 *"Why are we stopped?" Jill asked:* Joe Biden, *Promises to Keep*, Random House, 2007, p. 246.

87 *"Wait a minute, this is my husband":* Interview with Dr. Jill Biden by Julie Pace and Darlene Superville, September 22, 2021.

87 *Later Jill wrote, "In that moment":* Jill Biden, *Where the Light Enters*, Macmillan, 2019, p. 95.

87 *"It wasn't like the movies—there wasn't big stuff":* Richard Ben Cramer, *What It Takes*, Open Road Media (Kindle edition), 2011, p. 1512.

88 *"I guarantee you," Joe told the boys:* Ibid.

88 *"Jill was so strong," Joe wrote later:* Joe Biden, *Promises to Keep*, Random House, 2007, p. 248.

88 *It was "like an Irish wake":* Richard Ben Cramer, *What It Takes*, Open Road Media (Kindle edition), 2011, p. 1513.

Chapter 19

89 *"Jilly, is that you?" he asked:* Joe Biden, *Promises to Keep*, Random House, 2007, p. 250.

89 *"Those moments stick with you":* Interview with Dr. Jill Biden by Julie Pace and Darlene Superville, September 22, 2021.

89 *"Sorry, it's just emotional moments":* Ibid.

89 *"I had two little boys":* Ibid.

90 *"Honestly, I believe this":* Ibid.

90 *"It was my contract":* Ibid.

90 *"Everybody pitched in and took days":* Ibid.

90 *"I could walk into that classroom":* Ibid.

91 *"I've asked you all to come today":* Joe Biden, *Promises to Keep*, Random House, 2007, p. 255.

91 *"The world kept spinning":* Ibid.

91 *"They knew what they were doing":* Interview with Dr. Jill Biden by Julie Pace and Darlene Superville, September 22, 2021.

91 *"The biggest thing it changed," Joe said:* Jules Witcover, *Joe Biden: A Life of Trial and Redemption*, William Morrow Paperbacks revised edition, 2019, p. 244.

91 *"When you almost die," Val said:* Ibid., p. 243.

Chapter 20

92 *"I leave school, go sit":* Interview with Dr. Jill Biden by Julie Pace and Darlene Superville, September 22, 2021.

92 *"It was a full life":* Ibid.

93 *"It's something you live," she said:* Ibid.

93 *"We knew the highs were so high":* Ibid.

93 *"I guess that's the hardest part":* Ibid.

93 *"I would come prepared"*: Dawn E. Warden, "Ashley Biden Takes on the World," *Delaware Today*, August 22, 2018.
93 *"Ashley was an activist to save"*: Interview with Barbara Boxer by Julie Pace, September 22, 2021.
93 *The 1990 Dolphin Protection Consumer*: See Denise Cabrera, "Two Canners Won't Buy Tuna from Nets That Kill Dolphins," Associated Press, April 12, 1990.
93 *"I loved it and never forgot it"*: Interview with Barbara Boxer by Julie Pace, September 22, 2021.
94 *Around the same time, Ashley wrote*: Jules Witcover, *Joe Biden: A Life of Trial and Redemption*, William Morrow Paperbacks revised edition, 2019, p. 313.
94 *The Violence Against Women Act*: Joseph R. Biden Jr., "Crime bill helps to take back our neighborhoods," *Daily Times*, January 20, 1995.
94 *"The first discussion I had with Jill"*: Joe Biden, *Promises to Keep*, Random House, 2007, p. 269.
94 *"There's no parking there"*: Ibid.
95 *"There was a vote," she remembered*: Interview with Dr. Jill Biden by Julie Pace and Darlene Superville, September 22, 2021.
95 *"At that time, I could have called anybody"*: Ibid.
95 *"We all knew that, and we all knew"*: Interview with Barbara Boxer by Julie Pace, September 22, 2021.
95 *"Girls are a little bit, you know"*: Interview with Dr. Jill Biden by Julie Pace and Darlene Superville, September 22, 2021.
95 *Ashley was strong-willed — "which is a good thing"*: Ibid.
95 *"With Ashley, I also saw the relationship"*: Jill Biden, *Where the Light Enters*, Macmillan, 2019, p. 73.
95 *"That's how I became a runner"*: Interview with Dr. Jill Biden by Julie Pace and Darlene Superville, September 22, 2021.
96 *"After sounding the horn"*: Rebecca Rothbaum, "I'm a Runner: Dr. Jill Biden," *Runner's World*, August 2, 2010.
96 *She started with short races*: Ibid.

Chapter 21

Much of this chapter is drawn from the following Associated Press accounts: James Rowley, "Hill accuses Thomas in vivid detail; he denies wrongdoing," October 11, 1991; Jocelyn Noveck, "Nearly 3 decades later, Anita Hill sees the needle moving," October 14, 2017; Thomas Beaumont, "As he considers 2020, Biden airs regrets of Thomas hearings," September 21, 2018; Mark Sherman, "Senate hearing shaped by lessons learned from Thomas process," September 26, 2018; Lindsay Whithurst, "Anita Hill says #MeToo movement can create lasting change," September 27, 2018; "Biden says he didn't treat Hill badly," April 26, 2019; Steve Peoples, "Biden criticizes 'white man's culture,' role in Hill hearing," March 27, 2019; Jessica Gresko, "Justice Clarence Thomas' moment may finally have arrived," May 4, 2019.
97 *"What disturbs me as much"*: Marjorie Williams, "From Women, an Outpouring of Anger," *Washington Post*, October 9, 1991.
97 *"This isn't pleasant, and it isn't happy"*: "Thomas confirmation debate," C-SPAN, October 8, 1991, c-span.org/video/?21887-1/.
98 *"Everybody was glued to their TV"*: Interview with Dr. Jill Biden by Julie Pace and Darlene Superville, September 22, 2021.
98 *On September 27, 1991, a motion*: See the Committee on the Judiciary, "Judiciary Committee Votes on Recent Supreme Court Nominees."
99 *"There were so many people calling"*: Interview with Dr. Jill Biden by Julie Pace and Darlene Superville, September 22, 2021.

99 *"It felt like a swirl"*: Ibid.

99 *"I didn't pepper him with questions"*: Ibid.

99 *In a larger sense, she said:* Ibid.

99 *"He has more of a calm to him"*: Ibid.

99 *"He's pretty even keeled"*: Ibid.

Chapter 22

100 *"You've got to come by," the coworker said:* Jill Biden, *Where the Light Enters*, Macmillan, 2019, p. 84.

100 *"I wasn't sure," Jill wrote:* Ibid.

100 *"Working with community college"*: Ibid., p. 85.

101 *"Everybody knew she was Senator Biden's wife"*: Interview with Mary Doody by Darlene Superville, August 24, 2021.

102 *"As an educator, my first thought"*: See the Essential Estrogen interview quoted in Max Follmer, "Meet Jill Biden," *Huffington Post*, September 23, 2008.

103 *"I was seventeen when I had my first"*: Interview with Sherry Dorsey Walker by Julie Pace, August 11, 2021.

103 *"The best part of it was going"*: Ibid.

104 *"I was ecstatic. I have to say it was"*: Rebecca Rothbaum, "I'm a Runner: Dr. Jill Biden," *Runner's World*, August 2, 2010.

Chapter 23

Much of this chapter is drawn from Alexandra Jaffe, "How the Sept. 11 attacks would shape Biden's presidency," Associated Press, September 9, 2021.

105 *"Welcome home," she said:* Joe Biden, *Promises to Keep*, Random House, 2007, p. 312.

106 *"Nothing has fundamentally altered"*: Andrew Throdahl, "9/11 Flashback: Biden Called for Resilience as Country Braced for Attacks," ABC News Radio, September 11, 2011.

106 *Back in Delaware, Jill ended class:* See Gabrielle Chung, "Jill Biden Remembers the Moment That 'Changed Us All in Some Way' on 20th Anniversary of 9/11," *People*, September 11, 2021.

Chapter 24

107 *"There were always so many people"*: Interview with Dr. Jill Biden by Julie Pace and Darlene Superville, September 22, 2021.

107 *"He knew that I wasn't in favor"*: Ibid.

107 *His press secretary, Larry Rasky:* Jules Witcover, *Joe Biden: A Life of Trial and Redemption*, William Morrow Paperbacks revised edition, 2019, p. 359.

108 *While the meeting unfolded, Jill decided:* Jill Biden, *Where the Light Enters*, Macmillan, 2019, p. 112.

108 *"All these men—and they were mostly men"*: Interview with Dr. Jill Biden by Julie Pace and Darlene Superville, September 22, 2021.

108 *"As I walked through the kitchen"*: Jill Biden, *Where the Light Enters*, Macmillan, 2019, p. 112.

108 *On a Sunday in August 2004:* The material about the fire is largely drawn from Jill Biden, *Where the Light Enters*, Macmillan, 2019, chapter 11.

110 *Joe later joked to a group:* Donovan Slack, "Biden honors firefighters, jokes they saved his Corvette," *Politico44* blog, May 9, 2013.

Chapter 25

111 *"I felt terrible for John"*: Joe Biden, *Promises to Keep*, Random House, 2007, p. 380.

111 *Joe felt he "didn't dare"*: Ibid., p. 382.

111 *"I looked at Jill and remembered"*: Ibid.

111–12 *Beau had joined the Delaware:* "National Guard Headquarters to be named for Beau Biden," 166th Airlift Wing press release, May 25, 2016.

112 *"Look what Bush is doing to this country"*: Jules Witcover, *Joe Biden: A Life of Trial and Redemption*, William Morrow Paperbacks revised edition, 2019, p. 374.

112 *"I was so against the war"*: Interview with Dr. Jill Biden by Julie Pace and Darlene Superville, September 22, 2021.

112 *"I went in more eyes wide open"*: Ibid.

112 *"Things sort of evolve"*: Ibid.

112 *"We're having a family meeting"*: Joe Biden, *Promises to Keep*, Random House, 2007, p. 384.

113 *Later she said, "I feel like"*: Jules Witcover, *Joe Biden: A Life of Trial and Redemption*, William Morrow Paperbacks revised edition, 2019, p. 374.

113 *"Jill was aboard," Rasky said:* Ibid.

113 *"We were inexorably moving"*: Ibid., p. 366.

113 *"I know I'm supposed to be more coy"*: Ibid., p. 367.

Chapter 26

Much of this chapter is drawn from *Student Retention at the Community College: Meeting Students' Needs*, by Jill Jacobs-Biden through the University of Delaware, Fall 2006. The full text is online at s3.documentcloud.org/documents/20407226/bidens-dissertation.pdf.

114 *She dedicated her dissertation:* Jill Jacobs-Biden, *Student Retention at the Community College: Meeting Students' Needs*, University of Delaware, Fall 2006, p. iv.

115 *"The holistic approach—academic, social"*: Ibid., p. 37.

115 *When Jill got home she saw Joe:* Libby Copeland, "Jill Biden sticks to a mostly quiet life," *Washington Post*, October 26, 2008.

115 *"I'll never forget when she got"*: Interview with Marcelle Leahy by Darlene Superville, September 23, 2021.

115 *"The role I have always felt most"*: Jill Biden, *Where the Light Enters*, Macmillan, 2019, p. 26.

Chapter 27

116 *"You've got to believe, or else"*: Interview with Dr. Jill Biden by Julie Pace and Darlene Superville, September 22, 2021.

117 *On the day Biden was scheduled:* Jeremy Pelofsky, "Biden starts White House run with controversy," Reuters, January 31, 2007.

117 *"When somebody says something"*: Interview with Dr. Jill Biden by Julie Pace, September 29, 2021.

117 *"Jill's authenticity at once disarms"*: Statement provided by former first lady Michelle Obama on October 24, 2021.

118 *Christine Vilsack remembered seeing:* Interview with Christine Vilsack by Julie Pace, September 3, 2021.

118 *"Education is something that people"*: Ibid.

118 *"There's just so much that you"*: Interview with Dr. Jill Biden by Julie Pace and Darlene Superville, September 22, 2021.

119 *"That didn't sting the way"*: Ibid.

119 *On the way back to Delaware:* Ibid.

119 *"I want to be part of this organization"*: Interview with Dr. Jill Biden by Julie Pace and Darlene Superville, September 22, 2021.

119 *"Defending our nation should not"*: Jill Biden, "Remember our neighbors who serve," *News Journal*, June 28, 2008.

119 *"When she came to us initially"*: Ibid.
119 *The* Philadelphia Inquirer *reported*: Ibid.

Chapter 28

120 *"If you win, I'll do anything"*: Jules Witcover, *Joe Biden: A Life of Trial and Redemption*, William Morrow Paperbacks revised edition, 2019, p. 409.
120 *People frequently mentioned*: Interview with Dr. Jill Biden by Julie Pace and Darlene Superville, September 22, 2021.
120 *"But it wasn't in the forefront"*: Ibid.
121 *"He'd call not so much to ask for advice"*: Jules Witcover, *Joe Biden: A Life of Trial and Redemption*, William Morrow Paperbacks revised edition, 2019, p. 409.
121 *"Barack called me," Joe's voice boomed*: Interview with Dr. Jill Biden by Julie Pace, September 29, 2021.
121 *"I obviously didn't say this lightly"*: Joe Biden, *Promise Me, Dad*, Flatiron Books, 2017, p. 62.
122 *"My ninety-year-old mother"*: Ibid., p. 63.
122 *"You've got to push him"*: Interview with Dr. Jill Biden by Julie Pace, September 29, 2021.
122 *"I kept pushing, but it ultimately had to be his decision"*: Ibid.
122 *"I must have said it to her a good deal"*: Joe Biden, *Promises to Keep*, Random House, 2007, p. 65.
122 *"'C'mon, Joe,'" Jill finally said*: Ibid.
123 *"We had the equity in our home"*: Ibid.
123 *"We got to Valerie Biden's house"*: Interview with David Axelrod by Darlene Superville, July 28, 2021.
124 *"My God, we can't even go to the driveway"*: Interview with Dr. Jill Biden by Julie Pace, September 29, 2021.
124 *Jill turned to Joe one night*: Ibid.
124 *Mary Doody remembered this time*: Interview with Mary Doody by Darlene Superville, August 24, 2021.

Chapter 29

125 *"Barack called and asked me to be VP"*: Interview with Dr. Jill Biden by Julie Pace, September 29, 2021.
125 *"It felt good to say yes"*: Joe Biden, *Promise Me, Dad*, Flatiron Books, 2017, p. 67.
125 *"Joe, I'm happy for you"*: Interview with Dr. Jill Biden by Julie Pace, September 29, 2021.
125 *"Oh great," Joe joked*: Joe Biden, *Promise Me, Dad*, Flatiron Books, 2017, p. 68.
126 *"My God, I just met you"*: Interview with Dr. Jill Biden by Julie Pace, September 29, 2021.
126 *Michelle had a "practical yet effortlessly"*: Jill Biden, *Where the Light Enters*, Macmillan, 2019, p. 129.
126 *"Jill, have you given any thought"*: Ibid.
127 *"The way she talked me into"*: Interview with Cathy Russell by Darlene Superville, August 23, 2021.
128 *"These guys have been my family"*: Ben Feller, "Biden stops at hometown train station," Associated Press, August 26, 2008.

Chapter 30

129 *"I began shaking"*: Jill Biden, *Where the Light Enters*, Macmillan, 2019, p. 118.
129 *"Caught between two realities"*: Ibid., p. 100.
130 *"The worst part of watching"*: Ibid., p. 99.

130 *"At the end of that week"*: Rachel Kipp, "Life in the Shadows But Ready for the Spotlight," *News Journal*, October 26, 2008.

130 *"I could not be more grateful"*: Statement provided by former first lady Michelle Obama on October 24, 2021.

130 *"Suddenly, Beau, Hunter, Ashley"*: Jill Biden, *Where the Light Enters*, Macmillan, 2019, p. 80.

131 *"It's just like being a teacher"*: Interview with Cathy Russell by Darlene Superville, August 23, 2021.

131 *"There were always different parts"*: Interview with Dr. Jill Biden by Julie Pace, September 29, 2021.

131 *In addition to his wicked sense*: "Jimmie Rex McClellan," Living Legends of Alexandria, 2012, alexandrialegends.org/jimmie-rex-mcclellan/.

132 *"There were different pieces"*: Interview with Dr. Jill Biden by Julie Pace, September 29, 2021.

132 *"God bless her," Palin said*: "Transcript: The Vice-Presidential Debate," *New York Times*, October 2, 2008.

132 *"My heart is full of love and pride," Joe said*: Mike Allen, "Biden son headed to Iraq," *Politico*, November 13, 2008.

132 *Jill later recalled feeling*: "Remarks by the President, the Vice President, the First Lady, and Dr. Biden at Launch of 'Joining Forces' Initiative," The White House, April 12, 2011.

132 *"We've made no special considerations"*: Jeff Brown, "Delaware's citizen soldiers, including Biden, prepare to head to Iraq," *Review Atlas*, October 8, 2008.

132 *"I could see she was ready"*: Aaron Nathans, "Joe Biden's mother-in-law dies at 78," *News Journal*, October 6, 2008.

133 *"Your mother has taken a turn"*: Jill Biden, *Where the Light Enters*, Macmillan, 2019, p. 100.

133 *"In one emotionally racked week"*: Ibid.

133 *She called everyone in her eight thirty a.m.*: Libby Copeland, "Jill Biden sticks to a mostly quiet life," *Washington Post*, October 26, 2008.

133 *In her mother's absence*: Interview with Dr. Jill Biden by Darlene Superville, September 10, 2021.

Chapter 31

134 *"Morning," Jill said chipperly*: "Joe Biden Votes in Wilmington, Delaware on Election Day 2008," YouTube account BarackObamadotcom, November 4, 2008, youtu.be/dYJfNy DF83Y.

134 *"How about your girl?"*: Interview with Mary Doody by Darlene Superville, August 24, 2021.

135 *"I absolutely cannot do that, Jill"*: Interview with Cathy Russell by Darlene Superville, August 23, 2021.

135 *"Don't worry," Jill said.*: Ibid.

135 *"It wasn't her chosen path"*: Ibid.

136 *"Teaching is my internal compass"*: Jill Biden, *Where the Light Enters*, Macmillan, 2019, p. 86.

136 *"I did think it was crazy"*: Interview with Cathy Russell by Darlene Superville, August 23, 2021.

136 *"She'd sit there for hours"*: Ibid.

136 *"This was a way that she's always"*: Ibid.

136 *And Jill juggled her obligations*: Interview with Valerie Jarrett by Darlene Superville, July 21, 2021.

137 *"The vast majority of my students"*: Jill Biden, *Where the Light Enters*, Macmillan, 2019, p. 86.

137 *"Teachers have been sometimes maligned"*: Interview with Christine Vilsack by Julie Pace, September 3, 2021.

Chapter 32

138 *"She was very involved and very thoughtful"*: Interview with Cathy Russell by Darlene Superville, August 23, 2021.

138 *"Okay, these are the things I'm interested in"*: Ibid.

138 *Jamie Lawrence, one of the second lady's policy directors*: Interview with Jamie Lawrence by Darlene Superville, September 2, 2021.

138 *"She wanted to engage, she wanted to be with people"*: Interview with Kirsten White by Darlene Superville, September 3, 2021.

139 *"Hoping that car never drove up"*: "Remarks by President Biden to U.S. Air Force Personnel and Families Stationed at Royal Air Force Mildenhall," The White House, June 9, 2021.

139 *"She was having an impact"*: Interview with Cathy Russell by Darlene Superville, August 23, 2021.

139 *The* Washington Post *reported*: Jada Yuan and Annie Linskey, "Jill Biden is finally ready to be first lady. Can she help her husband beat Trump?" *Washington Post*, August 17, 2020.

139 *"I would say I ask them to write a lot"*: Janae McKenzie, "Dr. Jill Biden in Conversation with *Glamour*'s Editor in Chief on the Value of Community College," *Glamour*, July 13, 2021.

140 *"In a global economy where the most valuable skill"*: Kevin Hechtkopf, "Obama on Education," CBS News, February 24, 2009.

140 *"By 2020, America will once again have"*: Ibid.

140 *Instead, by 2021*: Tom Fish, "The 12 Most Educated Countries in the World," *Newsweek*, June 20, 2021.

140 *Although the costs of attending college*: See Table 346, "Average undergraduate tuition and fees and room and board rates charged for full-time students in degree-granting institutions, by type and control of institution and state or jurisdiction: 2008-09 and 2009-10," in the *Digest of Education Statistics*, nces.ed.gov/programs/digest/d10/tables/dt10_346.asp.

140 *The administration's push "led to the enrollment"*: Josh Mitchell, *The Debt Trap*, Simon & Schuster, 2021, p. 139.

141 *"When there was a break, she was diligent"*: Interview with Marcelle Leahy by Darlene Superville, September 23, 2021.

Chapter 33

142 *Barbara Bush once famously noted*: Laurie Kellman, "Jill Biden, Joe's chief protector, stepping up as first lady," Associated Press, November 29, 2020.

142 *"Oh, my gosh, those guys"*: Interview with Mary Doody by Darlene Superville, August 24, 2021.

143 *He had long said it was her unrelenting*: "Vice President Biden's mother dies at 92," Associated Press, January 7, 2010.

143 *"Jill came upstairs and said he was downstairs"*: Interview with Mark Gitenstein by Julie Pace, July 30, 2021.

Chapter 34

144 *He'd been taken to the Christiana Medical Center*: Ginger Gibson, "Beau Biden taken to Phila. hospital," *News Journal*, May 12, 2010.

144 *The vice president's office released*: Kendra Marr, "Beau Biden suffers 'mild stroke,'" *Politico*, May 12, 2010.

145 *Beau was "doing great, thank God"*: Patrick Walters, "Beau Biden's on the Mend," NBC10 Philadelphia, May 13, 2010.

145 *First Lady Michelle Obama told the group*: Michelle Obama, Remarks by the First Lady at the National Military Family Association Summit at Georgetown University Online by Gerhard Peters and John T. Woolley, The American Presidency Project.

145 *"I need to pretend you're not here"*: Rebecca Rothbaum, "I'm a Runner: Dr. Jill Biden," *Runner's World*, August 2, 2010.

Chapter 35

146 *"At just twenty or twenty-two"*: Jill Biden, *Where the Light Enters*, Macmillan, 2019, p. 130.

147 *As they worked on ways to make the visits*: Interview with Kirsten White by Darlene Superville, September 3, 2021.

147 *"Somehow it felt like we were at her house"*: Interview with Sam Kass by Darlene Superville, August 9, 2021.

148 *"Humor was clearly a real coping mechanism"*: Ibid.

149 *"It was like the wind got knocked"*: Interview with Sunny Anderson by Darlene Superville, August 24, 2021.

Chapter 36

150 *Joe had gone alone the previous year*: Kim Gamel, "Biden spends July 4 with son, other troops in Iraq," Associated Press, July 4, 2009.

150 *"I couldn't know that Joe was here"*: Interview with Kirsten White by Darlene Superville, September 3, 2021.

150 *"We then spent two full days"*: Ibid.

151 *Jill announced the event in an op-ed*: Jill Biden, "Community Colleges: Our Work Has Just Begun," *Chronicle of Higher Education*, April 14, 2010.

151 *The community college summit*: Interview with Kirsten White by Darlene Superville, September 3, 2021.

151 *Ojeda hadn't initially considered college*: "Presidential Remarks on Community Colleges," C-SPAN, October 5, 2010, c-span.org/video/?295820-1/.

152 *"For more and more people"*: Ibid.

152 *"I'm so grateful for Jill being willing"*: Ibid.

152 *"I want it on the record"*: Ibid.

Chapter 37

153 *"We owe them a lot," he said*: "Remarks by the President, the Vice President, the First Lady, and Dr. Biden at Launch of 'Joining Forces' Initiative," The White House, April 12, 2011.

154 *Neither Michelle nor Jill had*: Interview with Tina Tchen by Darlene Superville, August 30, 2021.

155 *Less than one percent*: See Mona Chalabi, "What Percentage of Americans Have Served in the Military," FiveThirtyEight, March 19, 2015, and "Demographics of the U.S. military," Council on Foreign Relations, July 13, 2020.

155 *"The next day I saw her"*: Interview with Jeremy Bernard by Darlene Superville, August 25, 2021.

156 *"We went out for martinis and french fries"*: Interview with Kirsten White by Darlene Superville, September 3, 2021.

156 *"She called me the morning of the test"*: Ibid.

Chapter 38

157 *"What can we do?" Jill asked*: Interview with Cathy Russell by Darlene Superville, August 23, 2021.

157 *"I just couldn't imagine, being a mother"*: Jill Biden's appearance on *Anderson Cooper 360*, August 9, 2011.

158 *"I think for Jill it was a devastating moment"*: Ibid.

Chapter 39

159 *During an event in New Hampshire:* Donovan Slack, "Jill Biden tiptoes into 2012 election," *Politico*, October 1, 2012.

159 *In June 2012, Ashley Biden married:* "Ashley Biden and Howard Krein," *New York Times*, June 2, 2012.

160 *She held leadership roles:* Leah Bourne, "Ashley Biden's New Sweatshirt Line Is Equal Parts Style and Social Conscience," *Glamour*, February 21, 2017.

160 *The centerpiece of Jill's role:* "US Democratic National Convention, Jill Biden Speech," AP Archive, September 6, 2012.

162 *The two couples spent a few private minutes:* KUNC Staff, "Live Blog Recap & Results: Election Night 2012," November 6, 2012.

162 *"She was without question an inspiration":* Email exchange between Kirsten White and Darlene Superville, October 14, 2021.

163 *After Joe's remarks of sympathy:* "Jill Biden at Boston Bombing Memorial," CNN YouTube channel, July 21, 2016, youtube.com/watch?v=60Pimsn79K0.

Chapter 40

164 *"He had all the best of me":* Joe Biden, *Promise Me, Dad*, Flatiron Books, 2017, p. 19.

164 *Joe was thinking of "shifting":* Ibid.

164 *After what White House officials said:* Jeff Black, "Beau Biden undergoes medical tests in Houston after 'disorientation and weakness,'" NBC, August 19, 2013. See also "Beau Biden at cancer center," Associated Press, August 20, 2013.

164 *In Joe's book,* Promise Me, Dad, *he described:* Joe Biden, *Promise Me, Dad*, Flatiron Books, 2017, p. 33.

165 *"I knew, deep down in my gut":* Jill Biden, *Where the Light Enters*, Macmillan, 2019, p. 139.

Chapter 41

166 *"Unfortunately, I've lived":* Joe Biden, *Promise Me, Dad*, Flatiron Books, 2017, p. 86.

166 *"Joe's working too hard," she said:* Ibid.

166 *"You've got to stop, Joe":* Ibid.

166 *During Jill's spring 2014 semester:* "Remarks for Dr. Jill Biden at Villanova University Commencement," The White House, May 27, 2014, and "Dr. Jill Biden Stressed 'The Urgency of Now,'" Ninth Annual Navigation and Survivorship Conference, Academy of Oncology Nurse & Patient Navigators, March 1, 2019.

166 *Jill told her students she would miss:* "Remarks for Dr. Jill Biden at Villanova University Commencement," The White House, May 27, 2014.

166 *"I brought out my reassuring smile":* Jill Biden, *Where the Light Enters*, Macmillan, 2019, p. 84.

167 *The stem cell treatments were successful:* "Dr. Jill Biden Stressed 'The Urgency of Now,'" Ninth Annual Navigation and Survivorship Conference, Academy of Oncology Nurse & Patient Navigators, March 1, 2019.

167 *"So as bad as it would get," Jill recalled:* Interview with Dr. Jill Biden by Julie Pace, September 29, 2021.

167 *"You've got to run," Beau said:* Jill Biden, *Where the Light Enters*, Macmillan, 2019, p. 27.

167 *Joe remembered the February 2015:* Joe Biden, *Promise Me, Dad*, Flatiron Books, 2017, p. 112.

168 *"For more than twenty years, at any meeting":* Ibid., p. 115.

168 *"We all understood how much Beau wanted":* Ibid.

169 *"He was reading all he could":* Ibid., p. 161.

169 *"In my own head, the race":* Ibid., p. 162.

170 *"We really may have something":* Ibid., p. 163.

Chapter 42

171 *"I used to exercise a lot"*: Interview with Dr. Jill Biden by Julie Pace, September 29, 2021.

171 *"People would see Beau in public"*: Interview with Mary Doody by Darlene Superville, August 24, 2021.

172 *"I'll give you the money"*: Joe Biden, *Promise Me, Dad*, Flatiron Books, 2017, p. 78.

172 *"Mary, I just have to keep"*: Interview with Mary Doody by Darlene Superville, August 24, 2021.

172 *"She didn't want Beau to get"*: Joe Biden, *Promise Me, Dad*, Flatiron Books, 2017, p. 78.

172 *"There's just so many ironic"*: Interview with Dr. Jill Biden by Julie Pace and Darlene Superville, September 22, 2021.

172 *"And then what happened"*: Ibid.

173 *"It was the same thing"*: Ibid.

173 *"She just never, never"*: Interview with Cathy Russell by Darlene Superville, August 23, 2021.

173 *"I really believe he's going"*: Interview with Valerie Jarrett by Darlene Superville, July 21, 2021.

Chapter 43

174 *"You have to tell them"*: Joe Biden, *Promise Me, Dad*, Flatiron Books, 2017, p. 185.

174 *Hunter recalled in his memoir*: Hunter Biden, *Beautiful Things*, Gallery Books, 2021, p. 21.

174 *After Beau's tracheostomy*: Ibid.

174 *"Go to a happy place, Beau"*: Joe Biden, *Promise Me, Dad*, Flatiron Books, 2017, p. 187.

174 *"Go to the dock"*: Ibid.

174 *"It's a sign from God," Jill said*: Ibid.

Chapter 44

175 *The first of two viewings*: See Jonathan Starkey, Esteban Parra, and Jon Offredo, "For mourners, public wake a chance to honor Beau Biden," *Delaware Online*, June 5, 2015.

175 *"All of Delaware went through"*: Interview with Sherry Dorsey Walker by Julie Pace, August 11, 2021.

176 *He called Beau*: "Remarks by the president in eulogy in honor of Beau Biden," The White House, June 6, 2015.

176 *"We were raw from those final weeks"*: Jill Biden, *Where the Light Enters*, Macmillan, 2019, p. 139.

177 *The Bidens joined President Obama*: See Peter Baker, "Obama and Biden to Attend Funeral for Clementa Pinckney," *New York Times*, June 22, 2015.

177 *"Their collective faith seemed"*: Jill Biden, *Where the Light Enters*, Macmillan, 2019, p. 140.

177 *"Everything we talked about"*: Joe Biden, *Promise Me, Dad*, Flatiron Books, 2017, p. 218.

178 *"Understand, if you lose"*: Ibid., p. 220.

Chapter 45

179 *"I stayed home that summer"*: Interview with Dr. Jill Biden by Julie Pace, September 29, 2021.

179 *"I felt honored they invited me"*: Interview with Christine Vilsack by Julie Pace, September 3, 2021.

179 *"My son Beau also served"*: Matthew M. Burke, "Vice president's wife caps Asian trip with Kadena block party," *Stars and Stripes*, July 23, 2015. See also "Jill Biden to promote education, military families in Asia," Associated Press, July 9, 2015.

179 *"I had no idea"*: Interview with Jamie Lawrence by Darlene Superville, September 2, 2021.

180 *"Joe, this is your decision," she told him*: Interview with Dr. Jill Biden by Julie Pace, September 29, 2021.

180 *"You can't just lose a child"*: Ibid.

181 *"Certainly, he's got something at stake here":* Julie Pace, "Family feud? Obama caught between Clinton, Biden ambitions," Associated Press, August 25, 2015.

Chapter 46

182 *Earlier in 2015:* Nancy Benac, "Obama renews push for free community college," Associated Press, September 10, 2015.

182 *On September 9, 2015, Jill and President Obama:* Nancy Benac, "Jill Biden under klieg lights as she fronts for Obama," Associated Press, September 9, 2015, and "Obama renews push for free community college," Associated Press, September 10, 2015.

183 *"If you didn't know she was the wife":* Nancy Benac, "Jill Biden under klieg lights as she fronts for Obama," Associated Press, September 9, 2015.

183 *"Look, I don't think any man or woman":* Joe Biden, *Promise Me, Dad,* Flatiron Books, 2017, p. 234.

Chapter 47

185 *"By the end of the meeting it was clear":* Joe Biden, *Promise Me, Dad,* Flatiron Books, 2017, p. 239.

185 *The next day,* Politico *ran a story:* See Edward-Isaac Dovere, "Exclusive: Biden himself leaked word of his son's dying wish," *Politico,* October 6, 2015.

185 *"I didn't think anybody would believe":* Joe Biden, *Promise Me, Dad,* Flatiron Books, 2017, p. 240.

186 *"Come to the Rose Garden":* Josh Lederman and Julie Pace, "Out of time: How Biden decided against running in 2016," Associated Press, October 22, 2015.

186 *"Unfortunately, I believe":* "Full text: Biden's announcement that he won't run for president," *Washington Post,* October 21, 2015.

186 *"We intend—the whole family":* Ibid.

Chapter 48

187 *Kass, by then a senior food analyst:* Maison Van Den Boer, "World Economic Forum" post, January 22, 2016, maisonvandenboer.com/en/catering/events/wef-davos.aspx.

187 *"And in the middle of it," Kass recalled:* Interview with Sam Kass by Darlene Superville, August 9, 2021.

187 *"Everything there is intense":* Ibid.

188 *In his final State of the Union address:* Ben Mathis-Lilley, "Obama Appears to Have Surprised Joe Biden with an Assignment to Cure Cancer," *Slate,* January 12, 2016.

188 *"He remains today, even after all":* CNN Live Event transcript, July 27, 2016, cnn.com/TRANSCRIPTS/1607/27/se.03.html.

Chapter 49

189 *"I truly believed Hillary was":* Interview with Dr. Jill Biden by Julie Pace, September 29, 2021.

189 *"I went to bed thinking Hillary":* Ibid.

190 *"What happened? Why didn't you wake me":* Ibid.

190 *"I hope they enjoy this home":* "Vice President Joe Biden Lunch with Vice President-Elect Mike Pence," C-SPAN, November 16, 2016, c-span.org/video/?418616-1.

190 *"I said, 'Joe, for gosh sakes,'":* Emily Heil, "Jill Biden reveals her husband's oversharing during a visit with the Pences," *Washington Post,* November 17, 2016.

191 *"Fast company here," he joked:* "Biden signs desk drawer in ceremonial office," Associated Press, January 6, 2017.

192 *When asked about it in an interview:* Tierney McAfee, "The Bromance Is Real: Barack Obama and Joe Biden 'Really Love One Another,' Their Wives Say," *People,* December 9, 2016.

192 *"Oh, they'll find each other":* Ibid.

Chapter 50

193 *"Jill, I want to give Joe the Medal of Freedom"*: "Joe Biden and Dr. Jill Biden Chat About the Medal of Freedom from President Barack Obama," Joe Biden YouTube channel, October 4, 2020, youtu.be/PokI0XiHIlA.
193 What in the hell is going on?: Ibid.
193 I don't know why the hell: Ibid.
193 *"I just wanted to get some folks"*: Melissa Chan, "Read the full transcript of President Obama surprising Joe Biden with the Medal of Freedom," *Time*, January 12, 2017.
194 *"I was so excited for him," Jill said*: "Joe Biden and Dr. Jill Biden Chat About the Medal of Freedom from President Barack Obama," Joe Biden YouTube channel, October 4, 2020, youtu.be/PokI0XiHIlA.

Chapter 51

195 *Going forward, they occasionally saw*: Interview with Dr. Jill Biden by Julie Pace, September 29, 2021.
196 *"There was no difference between"*: Interview with Nazila Jamshidi by Julie Pace, July 21, 2021.
196 *The result was a summit for Afghan students*: Lauren Lumpkin, "Most people know her as Jill Biden. But to some she is Dr. B, the compassionate and challenging educator who went the extra mile," *Washington Post*, January 12, 2021.
198 *"I wanted it to be the kind of place"*: Jonathan Van Meter, "Jill Biden on the Campaign of a Lifetime," *Vogue*, March 17, 2020.
198 *The Bidens put up two signs*: Will Weissert, "Biden's beach hideaway has political sun shining on Rehoboth," Associated Press, November 15, 2020.

Chapter 52

199 *"I think I could have won"*: Martin Pengelly, "Joe Biden: I regret not running for president— because I could have won," *The Guardian*, March 27, 2017.
199 *"The louder the roar"*: Interview with Dr. Jill Biden by Julie Pace, September 29, 2021.
200 *"After Donald Trump praised"*: "Jill Biden talks about life on campaign trail, why Joe Biden decided to run for president," 3TV/CBS5, October 29, 2020.
200 *At an Axios event in Philadelphia*: Jovan Alford, "Biden: Political climate Trump has created 'is eating at the fabric of this country,'" Associated Press, November 9, 2017.
200 *"I haven't decided to run," Joe said*: Ibid.

Chapter 53

201 *"If you and Joe want this, go for it"*: Interview with Dr. Jill Biden by Julie Pace, September 29, 2021.
202 *"I had never experienced"*: Lucy Flores, "An Awkward Kiss Changed How I Saw Joe Biden," *New York*, March 29, 2019.
202 *Joe said in a statement*: Valerie Richardson, "Joe Biden addresses Lucy Flores' accusations of unwanted touching," Associated Press, March 31, 2019.
202 *Jill defended her husband, addressing the matter*: "Dr. Jill Biden on family, teaching, loss and levity," *CBS Sunday Morning*, August 9, 2020, and Jill Biden appearance on *CBS Sunday Morning*, CBS, May 7, 2019.
202 *She was careful to note the courage*: Ibid.
202 *"Now they speak up. Now they have the courage"*: Ibid.
203 *"If we give Donald Trump eight years"*: Steve Peoples, "Biden enters Democratic race with strong anti-Trump theme," Associated Press, April 26, 2019.

203 *"I cannot be satisfied"*: Sheryl Gay Stolberg and Carl Hulse, "Joe Biden Expresses Regret to Anita Hill, but She Says 'I'm Sorry' Is Not Enough," *New York Times*, April 25, 2019.

203 *"We believed Anita Hill"*: Danielle Kurtzleben, "Jill Biden Says 'It's Time To Move On' from Anita Hill Controversy," NPR, May 7, 2019.

203 *"He apologized for the way"*: Ibid.

204 *"This book was a little dreamlike"*: "Jill Biden, 'Where the Light Enters,'" Politics and Prose YouTube account, May 14, 2019, youtube.com/watch?v=rQt9BnZwbeo.

204 *"My life changed, and changed"*: Ibid.

204 *The book received favorable reviews*: Connie Schultz, "Jill Biden's memoir—like Michelle Obama's—is not meant to be political," *Washington Post*, May 10, 2019, and Maddie Dolan, "Jill Biden memoir establishes how love makes a family," *Military Families Magazine*, May 23, 2019.

204 *Joe leaned over to the pastor's wife*: Emily Wakeman, "First Lady Jill Biden's prayer partner in the Midlands to pray at 59th Inaugural Prayer Service," WIS News, January 21, 2021.

204 *"And I thought, 'Prayer partner?'"*: "First Lady Jill Biden on Keeping Faith After Son Beau's Death," *The Kelly Clarkson Show*, February 25, 2021.

205 *Later Jill would say, "I thought maybe"*: Ibid.

205 *In 2021, Jill returned to Brookland Baptist*: Darlene Superville, "Jill Biden says SC 'prayer partner' helped change her life," Associated Press, October 18, 2021.

Chapter 54

206 *"Sometimes in between events"*: Interview with Christine Vilsack by Julie Pace, September 3, 2021.

207 *"Joe really is the perfect person"*: Mary Pieper, "Iowa Caucus—'Joe really is the perfect person': Jill Biden stumps for husband in Mason City," *Globe Gazette*, September 7, 2019.

207 Wow, *Christine recalled thinking*: Interview with Christine Vilsack by Julie Pace, September 3, 2021.

207 *Joe, she said, would "lift up the profession of teaching"*: Mary Pieper, "Iowa Caucus—'Joe really is the perfect person': Jill Biden stumps for husband in Mason City," *Globe Gazette*, September 7, 2019.

207 *"One thing I've tried to say"*: Elizabeth Meyer, "Jill Biden Talks Faith, Family as She Tours Across Iowa," *Iowa Starting Line*, October 6, 2019.

208 *"It's that empathy that made them"*: Interview with Christine Vilsack by Julie Pace, September 3, 2021.

208 *In a sign of how critical Jill was to the campaign*: Katie Glueck and Steve Eder, "Why Jill Biden Is Taking Time Off to Help Her Husband Get a Job," *New York Times*, February 1, 2020.

208 *"Iowa was a hard one," Christine Vilsack conceded*: Interview with Christine Vilsack by Julie Pace, September 3, 2021.

209 *"I've been disappointed by Iowa"*: Interview with Dr. Jill Biden by Julie Pace, September 29, 2021.

209 *"There was a discussion about asking"*: Jonathan Allen and Amie Parnes, *Lucky*, Crown, 2021.

Chapter 55

210 *"We weren't going to drop out"*: Interview with Dr. Jill Biden by Julie Pace, September 29, 2021.

210 *"Hold on 'til South Carolina"*: Ibid.

210 Okay, we're on track: Ibid.

211 *In a deeply personal endorsement*: Steve Peoples, Meg Kinnard, and Bill Barrow, "Biden claims momentum as Sanders marches past debate fray," Associated Press, February 26, 2020.

211 *As he left church to meet up*: Jonathan Allen and Amie Parnes, *Lucky*, Crown, 2021.

211 *By the end of the night:* Meg Kinnard and Bill Barrow, "Biden nabs Clyburn endorsement before South Carolina primary," Associated Press, February 26, 2020.

212 *While Joe refrained from mentioning:* "Joe Biden Victory Speech Transcript: Biden Wins South Carolina Democratic Primary," Rev.com, February 29, 2020.

212 *"It was incredible, it was so reaffirming":* Interview with Dr. Jill Biden by Julie Pace, September 29, 2021.

212 *"I'm a marathon runner," she told CNN:* Veronica Rocha and Mike Hayes, "The 2020 South Carolina primary," CNN, February 29, 2020.

Chapter 56

213 *"It felt like a whirlwind":* Interview with Dr. Jill Biden by Julie Pace, September 29, 2021.

214 *"He didn't know that I was going to fly in":* Ibid.

214 *"People called me up and said":* Interview with Barbara Jacobs Hopkins by Julie Pace, August 25, 2021.

214 *Interviewed about it by the* Philadelphia Inquirer: Rob Tornoe, "Jill Biden confronts heckler during her husband's New Hampshire rally: 'I'm a good Philly girl,'" *Philadelphia Inquirer*, February 11, 2020.

Chapter 57

215 *"We were doing Zoom after Zoom":* Interview with Dr. Jill Biden by Julie Pace, September 29, 2021.

215 *"Mr. Biden is mired in his basement":* David Axelrod and David Plouffe, "What Joe Biden Needs to Do to Beat Trump," *New York Times*, May 4, 2020.

215 *The Trump campaign released an ad:* Arijeta Lajka, "Trump campaign ad used altered photos to make Biden appear to be 'alone' when he wasn't," Associated Press, August 5, 2020.

216 *"The idea that somehow we are being hurt":* Bill Barrow and Steve Peoples, "Basement-bound Biden campaign worries some Democrats," Associated Press, May 13, 2020.

216 *In May, Joe began easing back into campaign travel:* Will Weissert, "Planes, pizza and Cher: Biden resumes campaign travel," Associated Press, August 31, 2020.

216 *"There was a little girl in California":* Senator Kamala Harris in the Democratic presidential debate on June 27, 2019.

217 *"With what he cares about, what he fights for":* Edward-Isaac Dovere, *Battle for the Soul*, Viking, 2021. See also Alex Thompson and Theodoric Meyer, "'Red Row' returns: the Bedingfield-Psaki story," *Politico*, May 20, 2021.

217 *In her memoir, Jill wrote that* "I end up being": Jill Biden, *Where the Light Enters*, Macmillan, 2019, p. 24.

217 *"The gist was like, 'You're Bidens now'":* Interview with Doug Emhoff by Darlene Superville, October 7, 2021.

Chapter 58

218 *From beginning to end:* See Bill Barrow and Nicholas Riccardi, "Key takeaways from night 2 of the Democratic convention," Associated Press, August 18, 2020.

218 *"My dad was a healthy sixty-five-year-old":* Rashaan Ayesh, "DNC speaker: My dad's 'only pre-existing condition was trusting Donald Trump,'" Axios, August 18, 2020.

219 *She juggled several jobs at once:* See Bill Barrow and Nicholas Riccardi, "Key takeaways from night 2 of the Democratic convention," Associated Press, August 18, 2020.

219 *"I am heartbroken by the magnitude":* "Jill Biden's full speech at the 2020 Democratic National Convention | 2020 DNC Night 2," *PBS NewsHour* YouTube channel, August 18, 2020.

Chapter 59

221 *The 2020 presidential debate:* Jill Colvin and Aamer Madhani, "Debate veers from 'How you doing?' to 'Will you shut up?'" Associated Press, September 30, 2020. See also "Donald Trump & Joe Biden 1st Presidential Debate Transcript 2020," Rev.com, September 29, 2020.

221 *He rebuked Trump for reportedly calling:* "Donald Trump & Joe Biden 1st Presidential Debate Transcript 2020," Rev.com, September 29, 2020.

222 *Being arrested "scared me":* Hunter Biden, *Beautiful Things*, Gallery Books, 2021, p. 88.

222 *"I knew I'd let down Dad":* Ibid.

222 *In 2013, when Hunter was forty-two, he joined:* Colleen McCain Nelson and Julian E. Barnes, "Biden's Son Hunter Discharged from Navy Reserve After Failing Cocaine Test," *Wall Street Journal*, October 16, 2014.

222 *After serving in the role for just over:* "VP's son, Hunter Biden, discharged from Navy Reserve after drug test," Associated Press, October 17, 2014.

222 *At the time, the vice president's office:* Javier E. David, "Ukraine gas producer appoints Biden's son to board," CNBC, May 13, 2014.

222 *"In the last five years alone":* Hunter Biden, *Beautiful Things*, Gallery Books, 2021, p. 17.

223 *"One day out of the blue":* Ibid., p. 226.

223 *"I lashed out at my mother":* Ibid., p. 228.

223 *"I don't think I knew the extent":* Interview with Dr. Jill Biden by Julie Pace, September 29, 2021.

223 *"If ever there was a star-crossed coupling":* Hunter Biden, *Beautiful Things*, Gallery Books, 2021, p. 189.

223 *When the* New York Post *reported on the relationship:* Emily Smith, "Beau Biden's widow having affair with his married brother," *Page Six*, March 1, 2017.

223 *"We are all lucky that Hunter and Hallie":* Hunter Biden, *Beautiful Things*, Gallery Books, 2021, p. 194.

224 *After the article ran, Hunter wrote:* Ibid.

224 *On his first dinner date:* Ibid., p. 245.

224 *Joe thanked Melissa for:* Ibid., p. 254.

224 *"I would like you to do us a favor":* Michael D. Shear and Maggie Haberman, "'Do Us a Favor': Call Shows Trump's Interest in Using U.S. Power for His Gain," *New York Times*, September 25, 2019.

224 *"It was unbelievable to me that he focused":* Interview with Dr. Jill Biden by Julie Pace, September 29, 2021.

224 *"I told Dad not to duck":* Hunter Biden, *Beautiful Things*, Gallery Books, 2021, p. 262.

225 *In the debate, Trump launched:* "Donald Trump & Joe Biden 1st Presidential Debate Transcript 2020," Rev.com, September 29, 2020.

Chapter 60

226 *"Our next first lady":* Alex Gangitano, "Jill Biden visits NC polling site: 'We feel confident, we feel excited,'" *The Hill*, November 3, 2020.

226 *"We've been on this campaign trail":* Ibid.

226 *It was "heartbreaking," Jill said:* Interview with Dr. Jill Biden by Julie Pace, September 29, 2021.

228 *"I swear, I felt like I was going to kill":* Ibid.

228 *The khaki-clad MSNBC election analyst:* Samantha Kubota, "Gap reports spike in khaki sales after 'map guy' Steve Kornacki rocked them," *Today*, November 11, 2020.

228 *"We all ran to the porch and screamed":* Hunter Biden, *Beautiful Things*, Gallery Books, 2021, p. 260.

228 *"It was just incredible," Jill recalled:* Interview with Dr. Jill Biden by Julie Pace, September 29, 2021.

228 *"We just did the best we could," Jill later said:* Ibid.

228 *Jill stepped on stage:* Isabel Jones, "Jill Biden's Election Night Outfit Included a Secret Message," *InStyle*, November 4, 2020.

Chapter 61

229 *On December 11, 2020:* Joseph Epstein, "Is there a doctor in the White House? Not if you need an M.D.," *Wall Street Journal*, December 11, 2020.

229 *Doug Emhoff, Kamala Harris's husband:* @DouglasEmhoff, "Dr. Biden earned her degree through hard work and pure grit. She is an inspiration to me, to her students, and to Americans across this country. This story would never have been written about a man." December 12, 2020, Twitter.

229 *Reflecting on the attack on Jill:* Interview with Doug Emhoff by Darlene Superville, October 7, 2021.

229 *"Here's a woman who went out there":* Ibid.

230 *"Her name is Dr. Jill Biden":* @HillaryClinton, "Her name is Dr. Jill Biden. Get used to it." December 13, 2020, Twitter.

230 *And on Instagram, Michelle Obama wrote:* Michelle Obama's post may be viewed on her official Instagram account (@michelleobama) at instagram.com/p/CIx4Zsdr7XX/.

230 *"All of us in these positions":* Interview with Barbara Boxer by Julie Pace, September 22, 2021.

230 *"Together, we will build a world":* @DrBiden, "Together, we will build a world where the accomplishments of our daughters will be celebrated, rather than diminished." December 13, 2020, Twitter.

230 *"I hope it's helped make me stronger":* Interview with Dr. Jill Biden by Julie Pace and Darlene Superville, September 22, 2021.

230 *Jill's fellow faculty at NOVA surprised:* Bo Erickson, "Jill Biden's return to the classroom: 'I want students to see me as their English teacher,'" CBS News, March 31, 2021.

231 *"The American public does still get a little uncomfortable":* Interview with Anita McBride by Darlene Superville, September 23, 2021.

231 *"Things are qualitatively different with Hillary":* Interview with Myra Gutin by Darlene Superville, September 23, 2021.

231 *During the Obama administration:* Jada Yuan and Annie Linskey, "Jill Biden is finally ready to be first lady. Can she help her husband beat Trump?" *Washington Post*, August 17, 2020.

Chapter 62

Much of this chapter is drawn from the following Associated Press accounts from January 21, 2021: Julie Pace, "Analysis: Biden issues call to unity that comes with urgency"; Jocelyn Noveck, "Hollywood on the Potomac: A-list turns out for Biden-Harris"; and Jonathan Lemire, Zeke Miller, and Alexandra Jaffe, "Biden takes the helm, appeals for unity to take on crises."

233 *On January 6, the day Congress was slated:* Ted Anthony, "A fight or a 'fight'? In impeachment, a clash about context," Associated Press, February 12, 2021.

234 *Responding to the events from Wilmington:* Alexandra Jaffe, "Biden blames Trump for violence at Capitol that's shaken US," Associated Press, January 8, 2021.

234 *"We have much to do in this winter of peril":* President Joe Biden, Inaugural Address, January 20, 2021.

234 *Joe never mentioned his predecessor by name:* Ibid.

234 *Biden would only tell reporters:* Reuters staff, "President Biden says Trump wrote him a very generous letter," Reuters, January 20, 2021.

235 *Two days after the inauguration, Jill visited:* Darlene Superville, "Jill Biden thanks Guard members with chocolate chip cookies," Associated Press, January 22, 2021.

235 *"I just want to say thank you":* Ibid.

235 *"The White House baked you some":* Ibid.

235 *"I'm a National Guard mom":* Ibid.

235 *"I truly appreciate all that you do":* Ibid.

Chapter 63

236 *"I just wanted some joy":* "Bidens view Valentine's Day decorations on White House lawn," Associated Press, February 12, 2021.

236 *"I was kind of, 'Oh my God' ":* Darlene Superville, "Jill Biden sees teachable moment in the depths of the pandemic," Associated Press, March 8, 2021.

236 *The first lady's official Twitter account:* Emily Tannenbaum, "First Lady Jill Biden Wore a Scrunchie While Shopping and People Felt So Seen," *Glamour*, February 13, 2021.

237 *"It's kind of surprising":* Jonathan Van Meter, "A First Lady for All of Us: On the Road with Dr. Jill Biden," *Vogue*, June 29, 2021.

237 *"They weren't fishnets":* Ibid.

238 *The matching cashmere coat included a Ben Franklin quote:* "Dr. Jill Biden's Inaugural Evening Dress," Gabriela Hearst, gabrielahearst.com/blogs/stories/dr-jill-biden-inaugural-evening-dress.

238 *Both dresses were embroidered with flowers:* Ibid.

238 *Samantha Barry, the editor in chief of* Glamour: Alaina Demopoulos, "Jill Biden Likes Fashion, but Don't Bother Asking Her About It," *Daily Beast*, July 3, 2021.

238 *"By rewearing her clothes":* Vanessa Friedman, "Jill Biden, Changing the Fashion Game," *New York Times*, July 26, 2021.

238 *In October 2021, Jill spoke reflectively:* Alexandra Jaffe, "Jill Biden speaks candidly about challenges of her role," Associated Press, October 20, 2021.

Chapter 64

239 *"Until Dr. Biden, everybody else":* Interview with Anita McBride by Darlene Superville, September 23, 2021.

239 *Valerie Jarrett observed:* Interview with Valerie Jarrett by Darlene Superville, July 21, 2021.

239 *"I am an English teacher at NOVA—not First Lady":* Bo Erickson, "Jill Biden's return to the classroom: 'I want students to see me as their English teacher,'" CBS News, March 31, 2021.

239 *She had initially asked to be allowed:* Ibid.

240 *"One thing she never loved was computers":* Interview with Mary Doody by Darlene Superville, August 24, 2021.

240 *Joe joked in a speech:* "Remarks by President Biden Celebrating the Significant Progress Virginia Has Made in the Fight Against COVID-19," The White House, May 28, 2021. See also Darlene Superville and Aamer Madhani, "Jill Biden gets Delaware beach day for her 70th birthday," Associated Press, June 2, 2021.

240 *He said she'd spent:* Ibid.

240 *"They really depended":* Samantha Barry and Janae McKenzie, "Dr. Jill Biden in Conversation with *Glamour*'s Editor in Chief on the Value of Community College," *Glamour*, July 13, 2021.

240 *"April Fools!":* FLOTUS press pool report, April 2, 2021.

240 *The reporters were:* Ibid.

240 *The mischievous first lady:* Ibid.

240 *"It brings her joy":* Interview with Valerie Jarrett by Darlene Superville, July 21, 2021.

241 *"Historians will study this time"*: Jill Biden, 2021 commencement address at George Mason University, May 14, 2021.

241 *"It was fascinating to me"*: Interview with Dr. Jill Biden by Julie Pace, September 29, 2021.

241 *"And of course as"*: Ibid.

242 *Jill had "seen firsthand"*: Interview with Nazila Jamshidi by Julie Pace, July 21, 2021.

242 *"And then they just sort of soar"*: Interview with Dr. Jill Biden by Julie Pace, September 29, 2021.

242 *After months of teaching English and writing*: Darlene Superville, "Jill Biden heads back to classroom as a working first lady," Associated Press, September 7, 2021.

242 *The* Washington Post *noted*: Jada Yuan, "Jill Biden returns to the classroom, live and in person," *Washington Post*, September 3, 2021.

242 *The* New York Times *reported that students*: Katie Rogers, "Jill Biden Is Chasing the President's Most Elusive Campaign Promise: Unity," *New York Times*, September 19, 2021.

242 *"It's going great"*: Interview with Dr. Jill Biden by Julie Pace and Darlene Superville, September 22, 2021.

242 *Reflecting on Jill's devotion*: Interview with Mary Doody by Darlene Superville, August 24, 2021.

Chapter 65

243 *By mid-October 2021, Jill had taken nearly*: See Darlene Superville, "Jill Biden's travels show range of missions and emotions," Associated Press, July 3, 2021; subsequent reporting brought the total to nearly thirty trips.

243 *"She's really trying to do her part"*: Interview with Cathy Russell by Darlene Superville, August 23, 2021.

243 *"What I try to tell my students is"*: FLOTUS press pool report, March 3, 2021.

243 *"We have to remember what this time"*: Ibid.

244 *Valerie Jarrett thought*: Interview with Valerie Jarrett by Darlene Superville, July 21, 2021.

244 *Jill noted that about half*: Felicia Fonseca, "Jill Biden hears from Navajo women on needs, priorities," Associated Press, April 23, 2021.

244 *"It's on all of us together"*: Ibid.

245 *"That sort of breaks my heart"*: Ibid.

245 *"Everybody on the Navajo Nation"*: Ibid.

246 *Yet school board members said*: Felicia Fonseca, "Navajo students describe pandemic struggles to Jill Biden," Associated Press, April 23, 2021.

246 *"If you could write"*: Ibid.

246 *"I'm here today to ask"*: FLOTUS press pool report, June 22, 2021.

246 *"The vaccines might feel like"*: Ricardo Alonso-Zaldivar, "As variant rises, vaccine plan targets 'movable middle,'" Associated Press, June 27, 2021.

246 *She told a reporter that Biden's*: Ibid.

247 *"Vaccine, vaccine, vaccine"*: Cole Johnson, "First Lady Jill Biden tours pop-up vaccine clinics in Nashville," Video—2:35 mark, News Channel 5 Nashville, June 22, 2021.

247 *"Well, you're booing yourselves"*: Leah Willingham, "Jill Biden touts vaccine in poorly inoculated Mississippi," Associated Press, June 22, 2021, and FLOTUS press pool report, June 22, 2021.

247 *"I couldn't be doing what I'm doing"*: Interview with Doug Emhoff by Darlene Superville, October 7, 2021.

247 *Later in Savannah, Georgia, promoting vaccinations*: "Jill Biden makes surprise stop for pies at Savannah eatery," Associated Press, July 13, 2021.

248 *To support the restaurant, Jill ordered*: FLOTUS press pool report, July 9, 2021.

Chapter 66

249 *Until the modern era:* See "A Role Without a Rulebook," by Natalie Gonnella-Platts and Katherine Fritz, George W. Bush Presidential Center.

249 *Rather than play the role:* Allida M. Black, "The Modern First Lady and Public Policy: From Edith Wilson through Hillary Rodham Clinton," *OAH Magazine of History,* Spring 2001, Vol. 15, No. 3, p. 17.

249 *Pat Nixon became the first first lady:* Carl Sferrazza Anthony, *First Ladies: The Saga of the Presidents' Wives and Their Power,* William Morrow, 1990, p. 186.

249 *Rosalynn Carter undertook a controversial:* See Kathy B. Smith, "The First Lady Represents America: Rosalynn Carter in South America," *Presidential Studies Quarterly,* Vol. 27, No. 3, The Presidency in the World (Summer, 1997), p. 540–48, and Robert P. Watson, *The Presidents' Wives: Reassessing the Office of First Lady,* Lynne Rienner, 2000.

249 *The trip garnered mixed reactions:* Robert P. Watson, *The Presidents' Wives: Reassessing the Office of First Lady,* Lynee Rienner, 2000, p. 162.

249 *Jill later said Joe:* Alexandra Jaffe and Aamer Madhani, "Message in a jacket: Jill Biden offers 'love' during UK trip," Associated Press, June 10, 2021.

249 *"Joe loves foreign policy":* Ibid.

249 *She joked:* Ibid.

250 *"Prepping for the G7":* Libby Cathy and Molly Nagle, "Jill Biden wears 'LOVE' jacket to global summit: 'We're bringing love from America,'" ABC News, June 10, 2021.

250 *There was an uncomfortable history:* Jonathan Lemire, Aamer Madhani, Jill Lawless, "Biden, Johnson strike warm tone in first meeting," Associated Press, June 10, 2021.

250 *"We're bringing love":* Alexandra Jaffe and Aamer Madhani, "Message in a jacket: Jill Biden offers 'love' during UK trip," Associated Press, June 10, 2021.

250 *"This is a global conference":* Ibid.

250 *"I told the prime minister":* Jonathan Lemire, Aamer Madhani, Jill Lawless, "Biden, Johnson strike warm tone in first meeting," Associated Press, June 10, 2021.

250 *Johnson laughed:* Ibid.

250 *"I'm not going to disagree":* Ibid.

250 *She visited a preschool for children:* FLOTUS press pool report, June 11, 2021.

251 *"They're scared to death":* Liam James, "Kate Middleton and Jill Biden join class reading Greta Thunberg-inspired book on tour of Cornwall primary school," *Independent,* June 11, 2021.

251 *"It's the quietest class":* Ibid.

251 *Jill thanked the news media:* "Jill Biden, Duchess of Cambridge learn bunny care on tour," Associated Press, June 11, 2021.

251 *"I just don't know where to begin":* Justin Gomez, "Jill Biden, Kate Middleton visit school to focus on early childhood education," ABC News, June 11, 2021.

251 *"but as an educator myself":* Simon Perry, "Kate Middleton Shares Her Passion for Empowering the Next Generation with First Lady Dr. Jill Biden," *People,* June 11, 2021.

251 *"For the longest time":* Ibid.

251 *"But I think one of the positive parts":* Ibid.

252 *"I'm committed to this":* Ibid.

252 *Later in the week, Jill and Kate:* First Lady Jill Biden and HRH The Duchess of Cambridge, "Jill Biden and the Duchess of Cambridge: This is what our kids deserve," CNN, June 12, 2021.

252 *"No, I didn't":* "Jill Biden, Duchess of Cambridge learn bunny care on tour," Associated Press, June 11, 2021.

252 *During the trip, Jill managed to weave in:* "Jill Biden tells English surf therapy group about her board," Associated Press, June 12, 2021.

252 *She arrived in Tokyo in late July:* Mark Thiessen and Darlene Superville, "Jill Biden in Tokyo for Olympic Games, meets prime minister," Associated Press, July 22, 2021.

253 *"She sees it as an act of patriotism":* Interview with Valerie Jarrett by Darlene Superville, July 21, 2021.

253 *"They're putting themselves at risk":* Ibid.

Chapter 67

Much of this chapter is drawn from the following Associated Press accounts: Alexandra Jaffe and Zeke Miller, "Biden visits wounded soldiers at Walter Reed, where son died," January 29, 2021; Aamer Madhani, "Biden pays respects to US troops killed in Afghanistan," August 29, 2021; "The Latest: Bidens visit wounded troops at Walter Reed," September 3, 2021; Brian Melley and Amy Beth Hanson, "Slain Marine who cradled baby at Kabul airport loved her job," August 28, 2021.

254 *"We know what we have to face":* Lily Rothman, "This Is What Eleanor Roosevelt Said to America's Women on the Day of Pearl Harbor," *Time*, December 6, 2018.

254 *In the late 1980s:* "NASA Honors Former First Lady Nancy Reagan," NASA, June 27, 2018.

254 *During the memorial service:* Bernard Weinraub, "Reagan Pays Tribute to 'Our Challenger Heroes,'" *New York Times*, February 1, 1986.

254 *"She appeared on multiple networks":* Erika Cornelius Smith, "Speaking From the 'Velvet Pulpit,'" *Media Relations and the Modern First Lady*, Lexington Books, 2020.

255 *"My husband needed me":* Michelle Obama, *Becoming*, Crown, 2018.

255 *There was no shortage of tragedy:* "Biden inauguration to feature memorial for COVID victims," Associated Press, December 31, 2020.

255 *In the melancholy moments just before:* Interview with Doug Emhoff by Darlene Superville, October 7, 2021.

255 *"There was no way she could have explained":* Ibid.

255 *On the twentieth anniversary of September 11:* Zeke Miller and Darlene Superville, "Biden to mark 20th anniversary of 9/11 at 3 memorial sites," Associated Press, September 4, 2021.

256 *"That was a campaign promise he made":* Interview with Dr. Jill Biden by Julie Pace, September 29, 2021.

256 *At a memorial in Midway Park:* Claire Curry, "Makeshift memorial for 13 service members killed in Afghanistan continues to grow, businesses paying tribute," ABC8 News, August 30, 2021, and Cheyenne Pagan, "First lady Jill Biden visits Camp Lejeune, meets with military families," WNCT9, September 1, 2021.

257 *"We are a military family":* Interview with Dr. Jill Biden by Julie Pace, September 29, 2021.

Chapter 68

258 *Alex Acevedo, owner of an art gallery:* Nicholas Conca, Jessica Sonkin, and Kate Sheehy, "Hunter Biden's artwork is actually good and will be worth a lot, experts say," *New York Post*, June 15, 2021.

258 *In his memoir, Hunter wrote:* Hunter Biden, *Beautiful Things*, Gallery Books, 2021, p. 264.

259 *"minimal compared with Trump":* Alexandra Jaffe, "Hunter Biden paintings pose ethical challenge for president," Associated Press, July 9, 2021.

259 *"The clause is specific to the President":* Bo Erickson, "Jill Biden's return to the classroom: 'I want students to see me as their English teacher,'" CBS News, March 31, 2021.

259 *The issue was resolved:* Ibid.

Chapter 69

260 *"She was never afraid to show up"*: Statement provided by former first lady Michelle Obama on October 24, 2021.

260 *Even before the election:* Samantha Barry and Janae McKenzie, "Dr. Jill Biden in Conversation with *Glamour*'s Editor in Chief on the Value of Community College," *Glamour*, July 13, 2021.

260 *"Community colleges meet students where"*: "First Lady Jill Biden Visits Community College in Dixon," NBC Chicago, April 19, 2021.

260 *"We can't continue to exclude"*: "Jill Biden promotes community colleges during Illinois visit," Associated Press, April 19, 2020.

261 *"I've been working on making community college"*: FLOTUS press pool report, April 19, 2021.

261 *In remarks earlier in 2021 at Tidewater Community College:* Josh Boak and Alexandra Jaffe, "Biden promotes education spending at stops in Virginia," Associated Press, May 3, 2021.

261 *"I have to admit if I didn't have"*: Ibid.

261 *"You spoke out for safely"*: Collin Binkley, "Biden says teachers deserve 'a raise, not just praise,' " Associated Press, July 2, 2021.

261 *In early July, Jill surprised contestants:* Ben Nuckols, "First lady congratulates National Spelling Bee finalists," Associated Press, July 8, 2021.

261 *"In sixth grade I was my"*: Ibid.

Conclusion

263 *"Your life will never change"*: Interview with Dr. Jill Biden by Julie Pace and Darlene Superville, September 22, 2021.

264 *Unlike many past first ladies:* Joe Biden, *Promise Me, Dad*, Flatiron Books, 2017, p. 188.

264 *"We aren't elected," Jill said:* Alexandra Jaffe, "Jill Biden speaks candidly about challenges of her role," Associated Press, October 20, 2021.

264 *"We simply couldn't ask for a better"*: Statement provided by former first lady Michelle Obama on October 24, 2021.

264 *"I can say it's changed in a good way"*: Interview with Dr. Jill Biden by Julie Pace and Darlene Superville, September 22, 2021.

Index

St. Mark's High School (New Castle Co.), 43
St. Petersburg, Fla., 226
Sanders, Bernie, 180–181, 184, 206, 208, 209, 211–214
Sanders, Symone, 214
Sandy Hook, 162, 254–255
Saturday Night Massacre, 69
Sauer, Joachim, 155
Sauk Valley Community College, 260–261
Savannah, Ga., 247–248
school desegregation, 54–55
Scobee, June, 254
Scranton, Pa., 84
Scripps National Spelling Bee, 261
second spouses, 191, 264
Secret Service, 4, 126, 129, 132–133, 136, 140, 142, 143, 145, 214, 240, 260
Senate Foreign Relations Committee, 44, 56, 84, 107, 116, 120, 121
Senate Historical Office, 59
Senate Judiciary Committee, 44, 56, 61, 68, 79, 97–99, 120, 127
Senate Ladies Red Cross Unit. *see* Senate Spouses
Senate NATO Observer Group, 116
Senate Spouses, 59, 94–95, 141
September 11, 2001 terrorist attacks, 105–107, 254, 255–256
Sierra Leone, 158
Sign of the Dove (New York City), 48
Simon, Jeanne, 67
Simon, Roger, 73
Simpson, Alan, 82
60 Minutes, 254
Smith, Erika Cornelius, 254
Somali refugees, 157
The Soul of America (Meacham), 200
South Africa, 45
South America, 249
South Carolina, 177, 208–211, 213
South Korea, 179
Soviet Union, 20
Space Shuttle Challenger, 254
Springfield, Ill., 126
State of the Union address (2013), 162
stem cell replacement, 166–167
Stevens, Catherine, 95
Stevens, Ted, 95
Stevenson, Bill, 23, 25–30, 33–34, 63
Stiltz, Tom, 34
student busing, 54, 216

Suga, Makiko, 253
Suga, Yoshihide, 253
Super Tuesday primaries, 211, 212–214
Surfside condo collapse, 255
Susan G. Komen Race for the Cure, 96

Talese, Gay, 8
Taliban, 231, 256
Tampa, Fla., 226
Taylor, James, 155
Tchen, Tina, 154
Teachers for Biden, 74, 82
Team USA, 253
Temple University, 25
Tennessee, 213, 247
Texas, 131, 132, 227, 237
Thatcher, Margaret, 76
Thomas, Clarence, 97–99, 203
Thomas Jefferson University Hospital (Philadelphia), 144
Thunberg, Greta, 251
Tidewater Community College, 261
"Till Kingdom Come" (song), 176
Timberg, Robert, 54
Today show, 152
Tokyo, Japan, 252–253
tribal universities, 262
Truman Balcony, 155
Trump, Barron, 231–232
Trump, Donald, and administration
    accusations against Hunter, 221, 224–225
    impeachment, 224
    and Inauguration Day (2020), 234
    and January 6 attack on US Capitol, 233
    and Middle East wars, 256
    presidential campaign (2016), 3–4, 188–191, 199–200
    presidential campaign (2020), 5, 203, 213, 215, 218, 226–228, 233–234
    presidential debate (2020), 221, 224–225
    presidential election (2020), 211, 233
Trump, Ivanka, 259
Trump, Melania, 231–232, 236–237
Tsarnaev brothers, 162
Tuba City, Ariz., 245
Tulane University, 160
Turkey Trot (Nantucket), 141
24th Marine Expeditionary Unit, 256
Twitter, 236–237